YOU'LL SEE IT WHEN YOU BELIEVE IT

Dr. Wayne Dyer is the author of *Your Erroneous Zones*, a record-breaking bestseller in the field of psychology. Following his own advice and through his enjoyment of working in the media, he has become a national television and press celebrity. He is a practising therapist and a former associate professor in the Graduate School at St. John's University in New York. He is the author or co-author of seven other books and has written many professional and popular magazine articles.

Also in Arrow by Wayne W. Dyer

PULLING YOUR OWN STRINGS

WHAT DO YOU REALLY WANT
FOR YOUR CHILDREN?

YOU'LL SEE IT WHEN YOU BELIEVE IT

Dr. Wayne W. Dyer

ARROW

First published in Arrow 1990

13 15 17 19 20 18 16 14

Arrow Books
The Random House Group Limited, 20 Vauxhall Bridge Road, London, SW1V 2SA

Random House Australia (Pty) Limited
20 Alfred Street, Milsons Point, Sydney, New South Wales 2061, Australia

Random House New Zealand Limited
18 Poland Road, Glenfield, Auckland 10, New Zealand

Random House (Pty) Limited
Endulini, 5a Jubilee Road, Parktown 2193, South Africa

The Random House Group Limited Reg. No. 954009

www.randomhouse.co.uk

A CIP catalogue record for this book is available from the British Library

Papers used by Random House are natural, recyclable products made from wood
grown in sustainable forests. The manufacturing processes conform to the
environmental regulations of the country of origin

Printed and bound in Great Britain by
Bookmarque Ltd, Croydon, Surrey

ISBN 0 09 974130 X

Contents

Introduction   15

1 TRANSFORMATION   25
Why you may be resisting this principle 39. Some
suggestions for personal transformation 41

2 THOUGHT   47
The how and why of visualization 56. You are the
dreamer of dreams 64. Why we resist 75 Your way out
of the cage 79

3 ONENESS   88
A new perspective on our place in this onesong 89. My first
contact with oneness 92. Getting a clear reference to
the whole 100. A very brief look at the history of the
human being 104. Cultivating a reference to the whole
107. Oneness and the dream 110. Why you may resist
the principle of oneness 113. Some suggestions for
applying the universal principal of oneness in your own
life 116.

4 ABUNDANCE   122
Transcending a scarcity consciousness 123. Whatever you
focus your thoughts on expands 124. You are it all
already 127. You cannot own anything! 129. Tuning in
to abundance 132. Freedom and abundance 134. How
I made the major decisions in my life 135. Abundance
and doing what you love 141. Putting it into practice
145. Why you may be resisting the principle of
abundance 151. Some ideas for bringing abundance
into your life 153.

5 DETACHMENT 158

Understanding what detachment means 160. Flowing as a means to detachment 162. How your form functions in the universe 163. How I learned to apply this principle 166. Our most common attachments 177. Networking: a helpful means to detachment 188. Why you may resist detachment 190. Implementing detachment in your life 192.

6 SYNCHRONICITY 200

Synchronicity in all our lives 201. The easiest connectors to believe in 204. More difficult connections: form to hidden form 205. Even more difficult connections: form to invisible form 205. Invisible connections: human form to human form 206. Our own connections: our thought to our form 207. Incomprehensible connections: human thought to another human form 208. Your own connections: thought to thought 209. Synchronicity: human thought to other human thought 210. The formless connections between human beings 211. What are these connectors made of? 213. The awakening process 215. Miracles? 223. Everything that has happened had to happen; everything that must happen cannot be stopped 234. Why you may find it difficult to embrace synchronicity 236. Some ideas for putting synchronicity to work 238.

7 FORGIVENESS 247

The universe does not forgive because it does not blame 248. Ridding yourself of blame, revenge, judgment 250. Forgiveness 259. My own voyage of forgiveness 261. Putting forgiveness into action 265. Giving is the key to forgiving 266. Forgiving yourself: and why not? 272. Surrendering: the ultimate act 274.

Index 281

Introduction

You cannot drink the word 'water.' The formula H_2O cannot float a ship. The word 'rain' cannot get you wet. You must experience water or rain to truly know what the words mean. Words themselves keep you several steps removed from the experience.

And so it is with everything that I write about in this book. These are words that are meant to lead to the direct experience. If the words that I write ring true, it is very likely that you will take the ideas presented here and create your experience of them. I believe these principles and see them working all the time and want to share my experience of how they have worked for me.

You too see, in your own life, essentially what you believe. If, for example, you believe strongly in scarcity, think about it regularly, and make it the focus of your conversations, I am quite certain that you see a great deal of it in your life. On the other hand, if you believe in happiness and abundance, think only about them, talk about them with others, and act on your belief in them, it is a very good bet that you are seeing what you believe.

Oliver Wendell Holmes once said, 'Man's mind, stretched to a new idea, never goes back to its original dimension.' The principles that I write about in this book may require you to stretch to new ideas. Should you take these words and apply them to your life, you will feel the stretch marks in your mind, and you will never again return to the being that you were before.

The word 'it' appears twice in the title of this book

and refers both times to what could be called personal transformation. That transformation comes with knowing deep within you that each and every human being is far more than a physical body, and that the essence of being human includes the ability to think and feel, to possess a higher consciousness, and to know that there is an intelligence suffusing all form in the universe. You are able to tap into that invisible part of you, to use your mind in any way that you choose, and to recognize that this is your essential humanity. Your humanness is not a form or a body at all, but something much more divine, guided by forces that are always at work in the universe.

The principles in this book start with the premise that you are a soul with a body, rather than a body with a soul. That you are not a human being having a spiritual experience, but rather a spiritual being having a human experience. I have illustrated these principles with many experiences that are a part of my own personal transformational journey to bring the essential messages home to you. I know that these principles are working in the universe even as you sit and read these words. They are working independent of your opinion about them, very much like the principles of digestion and pulmonary circulation are working within your body right now without your help. Whether you believe in these universal principles or not, they are going to work. But should you decide to tune in to them, you may find yourself living at an entirely new level and enjoying a higher kind of awareness – an awakening, if you will.

As long as you resist, you will not see the benefits. By this I mean you will stay with your old ways, live the 'I'll believe it when I see it' mentality. Hoard your toys and work even harder to accumulate more money. Continue to make appearances more important than quality. Live by rules rather than ethics. If you are only slightly wavering, then stay with what you are familiar with, until you can no longer resist. Because once you start to make the transformational awakening journey, there is no going back. You develop a knowledge that is so powerful that you will wonder how you could have lived any other way. The awakened life begins to own you, and then you simply know within that you are on the right path, and you don't even hear the protestations of those who have chosen something quite different for themselves.

I never imagined myself needing to change. I did not have a plan to change my old ways, or a set of goals to improve anything in my life. I felt confident that I had my life running the way I wanted it to. I was extremely successful professionally, and nothing seemed to me to be missing. Yet I have undergone a major transformation that has added a luster to each of my days that I never even contemplated a few years ago.

I was born in 1940, the youngest of three boys, all under the age of four. My father, whom I have never seen, abandoned this family when I was two. From all accounts, he was a troubled man who avoided honest work, drank excessively, physically abused my mother, and had run-ins with the law and spent some time in prison. My mother worked as a candy girl at a dime store on the east side of Detroit, and her weekly wages of seventeen dollars barely covered her streetcar and baby-sitting expenses. There was no aid to dependent children or welfare then.

I spent many of my early years in foster homes, where my mother visited me whenever possible. All I knew of my father was what I heard from others, particularly my two brothers. I pictured an abusive, noncaring person who wanted nothing to do with me or my brothers. The more I heard, the more I hated. The more I hated, the angrier I became. My anger turned to curiosity, and I dreamed constantly about meeting my father and confronting him directly. I became fixated on my hatred and on my desire to meet this man and get the answers firsthand.

By 1949 my mother had remarried and reunited our family. Neither of my brothers ever voluntarily mentioned my father, and my inquiries were met with a look that implied, 'He's no damn good. Why do you want to know any more about him?' But my curiosity and my bad dreams persisted. Often I would wake up sweating and crying after a particularly intense dreaming sequence about him.

As I grew into adulthood my determination to meet this man became even fiercer. I became obsessed with finding him. His side of the family protected him, because they felt that my mother would have him arrested for years of nonsupport. Yet I still asked questions, made phone calls to relatives I didn't even know, and made trips to meet his ex-wives in distant cities to discover what this man was like. Always, my search ended in frustration. I would run out of funds to chase down a lead, or I would have to return to my own personal responsibilities of being on active duty in the military, or going to college, or raising my family.

In 1970 I received a call from a cousin I had never met, who had heard a rumor that my father had died in New Orleans. But I was in no position to investigate it. At the time I was completing my doctoral studies, moving to New York to become an associate professor at St. John's University, going through a painful divorce, and 'stuck in place' when it came to my writing. In the next few years I co-authored several texts on counseling and psychotherapy. I knew that I did not want to continue writing for strictly professional audiences, and yet nothing else would come to me. I was stuck, personally (divorce), physically (overweight and out of shape), and spiritually (a pure pragmatist with no thoughts about metaphysics). My dreams about my father intensified. I would awaken in a fit of anger, having been dreaming about beating my father while he smiled back at me. Then came the turning point in my life.

In 1974 a colleague of mine at the university invited me to take an assignment in the South. She was the coordinator of a federally financed program that was looking into the compliance rate of Southern colleges to the civil rights legislation of the 1960s. She wanted me to make a visit to the Mississippi State College for Women in Columbus, Mississippi. When I decided to go, I telephoned the infirmary in New Orleans where my cousin had reported my father to have been, and I learned that Melvin Lyle Dyer had died there ten years earlier of cirrhosis of the liver and other complications, and that his body had been shipped to Biloxi, Mississippi. Columbus, Mississippi, is about two hundred miles from Biloxi. I decided that this was it – when I finished my visit at the college, I was going to complete my journey and do whatever it took to close out this chapter in my life.

I contemplated bringing this unresolved relationship to some kind of resolution. I was curious to know if my father had told the hospital officials that he had three sons and if our names would be on the death certificate. I wanted to talk to his friends in Biloxi to see if he had ever mentioned us. Did he ever secretly try to find out how his ex-wife and children were doing? Did he care? Did he have a capacity for love that perhaps he had hidden from everyone? Mostly I wanted to know how he could have turned his back on his family for a lifetime. I always looked for a loving reason that he might have left, and yet my anger at his behavior in those years still haunted me. At thirty-four years of age I was controlled by a man who had been dead for almost a decade.

I rented a brand-new car in Columbus to make the drive to Biloxi. I mean *brand*-new! The odometer read 00000.8 miles. As I settled in behind the wheel I reached for the lap belt and discovered that the right-hand belt was missing. I got out of the car, took out the entire bench seat, and there was the belt, attached to the floorboard of the car with masking tape, the buckle encased in plastic wrapping, and a rubber band around the plastic wrapping. When I ripped off the tape and the plastic, I found a business card tucked inside the buckle. It read: 'Candlelight Inn . . . Biloxi, Mississippi.' and had a series of arrows leading to the inn. I thought it was odd, since the car had not been used before I rented it, but I stuck the card in my shirt pocket.

I arrived at the outskirts of Biloxi at 4:50 P.M. on Friday and pulled into the first gas station I saw to call the cemeteries in Biloxi. There were three listed, and after a busy signal at the first and no answer at the second, I dialed the third and least impressive listing. In response to my inquiry, an elderly-sounding male voice said he would check to see if my father was buried there. He was gone for a full ten minutes, and just as I was about to give up and wait for Monday morning to do more research, he came back with the words to end a lifetime journey. 'Yes,' he said, 'your father is buried here,' and he gave me the date of his interment.

My heart pounded with the emotion of this powerful moment. I asked him if it would be all right if I visited the grave right away.

'Certainly, if you will just put the chain up across the driveway when you leave, you are welcome to come now,' he said. Before I could ask for directions, he continued, 'Your father is buried adjacent to the grounds of the Candlelight Inn. Just ask someone at the station how to get there.'

Shivering, I reached into my shirt pocket and looked at the business card and the arrows on it. I was three blocks from the cemetery.

When I finally stood looking at the marker on the grass, MELVIN LYLE DYER, I was transfixed. During the next two and a half hours I conversed with my father for the very first time. I cried out loud, oblivious to my surroundings. And I talked out loud, demanding answers from a grave. As the hours passed, I began to feel a deep sense of relief, and I became very quiet. The calmness was overwhelming. I was almost certain that my father was right there with me. I was no longer talking to a gravestone, but was somehow in the presence of something which I could not, and still cannot, explain.

When I resumed my one-way conversation, I said, 'I somehow feel as if I were sent here today and that you had something to do with it. I don't know what your role is, or even if you have one, but I am certain that the time has come to abandon this anger and hatred that I have carried around so painfully for so long. I want you to know that as of this moment, right now, all of that is gone. I forgive you. I don't know what motivated you to run your life as you did. I am sure that you must have felt many forlorn moments knowing that you had three children you would never see. Whatever it was that was going on inside of you, I want you to know that I can no longer think hateful thoughts about you. When I think of you it will be with compassion and love. I am letting go of all this disorder that is inside me. I know in my heart that you were simply doing what you knew how to do given the conditions of your life at the time. Even though I have no memory of ever having seen you, and even though it was my fondest dream to someday meet you face to face and hear your side, I will not let those thoughts ever hold me back from also feeling the love I have for you.' As I stood at that lonely grave marker in southern Mississippi I said words I've never forgotten, because they signified how I would be conducting my life from then on: 'I send you love . . . I send you love . . . Honestly, I send you love.'

In one pure honest moment I experienced feeling forgiveness for the man who was my father and for the child I had been who wanted to know and love him. I felt a kind of peace and cleansing that was entirely new for me. Though I was unaware of it at the time, that simple act of forgiveness was the beginning of an entirely new level of experiencing life for me. I was on the threshold of a stage of my life that was to encompass worlds I could not even imagine in those days.

When I went back to New York, miracles began to

appear everywhere. I wrote *Your Erroneous Zones* with ease. An agent arrived in my life through a series of 'strange' circumstances at exactly the right moment. I had a meeting with an executive of T. Y. Crowell Publishers, and a few days later he called to tell me that Crowell was going to publish my book.

Every step along the way of the *Your Erroneous Zones* story was another miracle waiting to happen. Strange and wonderful events occurred with delightful frequency. The exactly 'right' person would be there when needed. The perfect contact would materialize out of the strangest coincidences. My speaking schedule increased, and my performances in front of audiences became effortless. I abandoned my notes, though often talking for six and eight hours at seminars. Later, these seminars became a series of successful tapes. My personal family life improved almost immediately, and I made decisions that I previously had pondered over for years. In what seemed fast-forward, I had achieved what most authors dream about. I had the top-selling book in the United States and was having the time of my life appearing on the talk shows. In the years that followed, my writing seemed to be taking me in new directions. I went from writing about 'How to' utilize specific strategies in self-understanding to 'How to' become a more assertive human being. I went from telling people how to do something to writing about the importance of being at transcendent levels as a human being.

Today, I am convinced that my experience of forgiveness, while emotionally draining at the moment it was occurring, was the beginning of my transformation. It was my first encounter with the power of my own mind to go beyond what I previously considered the constraints of the physical world and my physical body.

Pablo Picasso said, 'While I work I leave my body outside the door, the way Moslems take off their shoes before entering the mosque.' I did the same thing as I wrote this book. I left my body outside the room. By that I mean that I left outside the world of aches and intrusions which are experienced in form, and allowed only my mind to enter my writing domain. In this world of pure thought there are no limits. What is the limit to your imagination? This part of me that is my thoughts is pure energy allowing the ideas to coalesce into words in my mind, and then into form on my typewriter. No excuses, no fatigue, no fears, no anguish, simply energy that is somehow flowing through me to you without any limitations. As I create I know that these words and ideas are not mine to own. That I am the conduit through which they flow, and that when I am open and unattached, when I leave my body at the door as Picasso said, I am a part of the creative process that is related to being awakened. This awakening process and the rewards that go with being bitten by the transformational bug are precisely what this book is about.

To begin the awakening process you must become very comfortable with the concept of paradox. Why? Because you are one big walking, talking, breathing paradox at all moments of your life. It is simply the way of things. The Bhagavad Gita, one of the most ancient spiritual books on our planet, sums up paradox as follows:

> By passion for the 'pairs of opposites,'
> By those twin snares of Like and Dislike, Prince,
> All creatures live bewildered, save some few
> Who, quit of sins, holy in act, informed,
> Freed from the 'opposites' and fixed in faith
> Cleave unto Me.

And bewildered you will continue to be until you can get very comfortable with opposites like the following. You are simultaneously in form, with all of the rules and laws that apply to form, and in nonform, with a completely opposite set of rules and laws. You are both shy and aggressive within the same body. You are lazy and hardworking. You get the most approval when you care the least about it. The tighter you squeeze the water, the less you have. The things that upset us in others are the lessons we have to learn ourselves. You cannot exclusively examine the north pole of a magnet. No matter how thin you slice it, there is always a south pole to consider. The dualism is always there. Rather than dismissing this concept with your left-brain linear side, remember that you have, at the same time, a right-brain intuitive side that can allow opposites to live comfortably with each other. I delight in Ram Dass's description of paradox in *Be Here Now:*

The most exquisite paradox . . . as soon as you give it all up, you can have it all . . . As long as you want power, *you* can't have it. The minute you don't want power, you'll have more than you ever dreamed possible.

Until you are blissfully comfortable with this concept, and until you come to grips with your own predicament of being in form and formless simultaneously, you will be struggling with this paradox.

After listening to my tapes on transformation, a woman wrote to me, 'Wow, this stuff really works when you truly let it in.' I couldn't say it any better than that. But William James, writing back in 1926, put it this way:

The further limits of our being plunge, it seems to me, into an altogether other dimension of existence from the visible world. Name it the mystical region, or the supernatural region, whichever you choose . . . we belong to it in a more visible world. When we commune with it, work is actually done upon our finite personality, for we are turned into new men.

One thing I know for certain: by communing with all of these universal principles, by writing about them, by living them every day, I have been transformed into a new man, a happier, more purposeful, more fully alive man than I ever dreamed possible for myself. Now I hope that my efforts and energy are visible in this book and will help to make a positive, loving difference in your life as well.

In love and light,
Wayne W. Dyer
1989

1
Transformation

*Transformation is the ability and willingness
to live beyond your form*

I feel as if I have gone through a gate which will not
allow me to go back to the place where I used to live.
To me, going through the gate symbolizes transformation.
But what do I mean by that?

Start with the word 'form,' the centre of transformation.
It is a term that describes the physical you. It includes all of
the physiological properties that you have come to associate
with the human being that is you. Form includes the total
weight of your bones, arteries, blood vessels, skin, eyeballs,
toenails, heart, lungs, kidneys, and anything else that you
can name in your physiology. Yet certainly you are much
more than a pile of bones, skin, and component parts.
Everything that you would see in that pile of form you will
also find in a pig or a horse. The real you, the unique you, is
99 percent invisible, untouchable, unsmellable, and impervious to the physical senses, which know only form. The
largest chunk of who you really are is something beyond
form. It has been called your mind, or your feelings, or
your thoughts, or your higher consciousness, but whatever
it is, it certainly is not form. All of your thought and your
spiritual awareness are in this other formless dimension.

Now consider the prefix 'trans,' which means 'beyond,'
'above,' or in literal terms, 'over.' When we place that
prefix in front of 'form,' we get 'transform.' We now add
the suffix 'ation,' which means 'action' or 'result,' and we
have the word 'transformation.' To me this word means
the result or action of *going beyond one's form*. And it is
literally the challenge of this book: to help you to see

18

yourself as someone much more advanced and divine than a mere form.

Your form must follow the rules of form. It will change many times during your lifetime. In fact, every single cell of your entire form will change every seven years or so, and yet *you* will still exist. You were already in a tiny little baby body, a preadolescent, a teenager body, and depending on the current age of your form, in other bodies as well. The form has completely changed many times, and yet the real you has remained constant. Once you understand this concept you will be on your way to going through the gate.

Every man-made creation starts with a thought, an idea, a vision, a mental image. The thought is then applied in some way to form a new product. At this moment I am taking my thoughts, applying them to a typewriter, and creating a new product called a book. We all go through this process thousands of times every day. The ultimate in becoming a transformed person is seeing ourselves as unlimited by our form.

When you live exclusively in form, you live in a world of limitations. Think about all of the limits that are placed on your form. Limits are boundaries that dictate things. You can only lift so much weight. You can only run so fast. You can only work so hard. But limits are all in the dimension of form.

Now consider the part of you without physical limits, the dimension of thought. There are no limits to your ability to think. You can *imagine* yourself doing anything. You can have a perfect relationship with your mate in pure thought. You can be anything, go anywhere, experience all that you want, in this dimension of thought, exclusive of form.

I am suggesting that you can experience a major portion of your life in this dimension of transcending your form, that is, in transformation. At the same time you will be able to maintain your form and honor its requirements

19

and lovingly understand its signals, while still knowing it is serving you, the *real* you. The emphasis in our culture is on the value of the external, the physical appearance. I am suggesting that the emphasis be shifted to a concern for the formless self, being ever mindful that the form houses the real you. With enough practice in this dimension, you will eliminate virtually all limitations in your life. You will get past your form, and do as Paul suggests in Romans 12:2:

And be not conformed to this world: But be ye *transformed* by the renewing of your mind, that ye may prove what is that good, and acceptable, and perfect, will of God.

This is the place of transformation. This is the place where you can not only live a miracle, but create miracles as well.

You can make higher and higher levels of living a regular part of your daily regimen without going to a guru or mastering courses in metaphysics. How? By believing you are a soul with a body rather than a body with a soul. You will create for yourself a life that is literally without limitations. You will begin to see miracles occurring simply because you believe in them and expect them to materialize for you. In fact, you will become a miracle worker yourself.

You will begin to see the phenomenal miracle that you are when it comes to healing your own body. You will begin to change self-defeating habits such as overeating and avoiding exercise, without having to set goals or work at self-discipline. Your new habits will automatically follow your new sense of appreciation for *all* that you are, even thought you cannot define it in physical terminology. Your belief in your body's ability to heal itself will begin to reflect how you take care of the precious temple that houses you. Fear of death will dissolve as you come closer to an awareness that thought, thinking, your essential self, never dies. Thought cannot die. It is the energy that composes the very existence of the universe, and once you belive this within your being, you will never need to fear death again.

A beautiful woman by the name of Peace Pilgrim walked across this country a few years back, spreading her message of peace and love and personal transformation. She described the characteristics of personal transformation in this short list.

SOME SIGNS AND SYMPTOMS OF INNER PEACE

A tendency to think and act spontaneously rather than on fears based on past experiences
An unmistakable ability to enjoy each moment
A loss of interest in judging other people
A loss of interest in interpreting the actions of others
A loss of interest in conflict
A loss of the ability to worry
Frequent, overwhelming episodes of appreciation
Contented feelings of connectedness with others and nature
Frequent attacks of smiling
An increased susceptibilty to the love extended by others as well as the uncontrollable urge to extend it.

This is what is in it for you. Life will become a fascinating journey, filled with joy and awe. The part of you that resided for so long in the limitations that you imposed on yourself by living exclusively in form will become free to *see* a whole new panorama . . . if and when you *believe* it.

You will find yourself slowing down and living in that quiet inner space where you can appreciate what comes your way. You will know in your heart that you need not be threatened by the views or actions of anyone else. You will receive more joy and ease in your life, because that is what you will be sending out. You will find it easier to accept contrary views, knowing that you are not defined by anything or anyone external to yourself. You will find great joy in the ease that replaces rancor and pain. You will eliminate conflict and confrontation as you find it unnecessary to prove yourself to anyone. In effect, you will begin to tap the enormous power of your mind. You will peacefully meditate though others about you may be in a frenzy. You will *be* the power of a quiet mind, and you will choose to go there often. You will discover things about yourself that you perhaps never considered before. You will be in that perfect intelligence that is within all form, in that miraculous inner space where everything that you can visualize is possible.

I have come to know that there is an invisible, untouchable, odorless, and yet very real intelligence in back of, or supporting, all form. This intelligence has been labeled many things. Some call it God, others the life force, higher consciousness, the divine spirit. The label is unimportant. The living of it matters immensely. It is a feeling similar to what Carl Jung was expressing when an interviewer asked him if he believed in God. His startling answer was, 'No.' After a thoughtful pause, he continued, 'I *know* there is a God.'

Observe a tree and contemplate the intelligence within or behind that tree that allows it to function perfectly in form. The leaves come and go, the sap drips out, it flowers when it is supposed to. It is much more than simple form. It contains a life force that makes it alive. We cannot see that life force, but it is very real.

I look at the skin on the back of my hand quite often these days. When I pinch it, it no longer snaps back as it once did; it sort of meanders back to its original position. There are wrinkles about my eyes that were never there. I have taken to growing ear hairs, and losing head hairs. I see my form changing all the time. If I thought that was all that I am, I would feel distressed over my physical changes. But I know that I am much more than this form that I occupy. I know that I am a soul with a body, rather than a body with a soul. This thing that some call a soul and I call my being or my self is the very essence of what we are. It is the intelligence behind the form, and the biggest difference between me today and me several years ago is that I now love the fact that I am not exclusively my form.

Buckminster Fuller once said that 99 percent of who you are is invisible and untouchable. It is your ability to think and go beyond your form that determines the quality of your life. Being able to express and experience the statement, 'I am my ability to think and feel, I am not only form' is the major transformational difference in my life today.

I see myself having chosen a variety of roles in this lifetime. I used to believe that those roles were the real me, and that everything that I did determined my essence. I experience my form doing what I have chosen to do, and at the same time I can get mentally in back of that form and observe myself going through the doing motions of my humanity. Thus, I work and sweat, and play tennis, and write, and speak to large audiences, and make love to my wife, and walk along the beach, and pay my bills, and strive to save some money, and talk on the telephone about my investments, and hug my children, and do all of the other actions that I choose for myself. Those actions, those roles, have a magically enhanced quality to them when my being is in the doing. When I involve that invisible, untouchable part of myself, or my Self, then do I recognize that my physical self, my form, is not all that I am. When I bring my thoughts and feelings to my physical actions I experience a balance, a wholeness, a me-ness. My ability to *be* thought itself is the real miracle than I am a part of.

No one can get behind my eyeballs and experience my inner reality, and likewise, I cannot enter anyone else's form and become the process that is that person's. But I can and do allow myself to become my mind rather than my form. I now live each day as if that intelligence that is in all living things, including myself, is the real essence of life. I no longer fear death, since I know that we are never formed, but are always in a state of transition, and that though form may ultimately look as if it has died, you simply cannot kill thought.

The major difference that I note in myself is the phenomenal new compassion that seems to have swept into my being in recent years. Where I previously was able to ignore others or to live in my own world, so to speak, now I find myself more emotionally connected to the inner energy of all life forms. For instance, I do a lot of traveling for speaking engagements, and in the past I have proceeded single-mindedly through a crowded airplane to get to my seat. I now find myself helping someone stow hand luggage in the overhead compartment, when I would have squeezed by that person a few years back. I love this new compassion. It empowers me to greater things, and of course it helps to create a more loving experience in others as well.

I also have found that I am developing a new-to-me style of intelligence, without a conscious effort. I find that I have a sensitivity to and understanding of concepts that at one time seemed fuzzy or bizarre. I enjoy reading about quantum reality, relativity, metaphysics, and all measure of Eastern thought, find it fascinating, where I previously found it unfathomable and even dull. In bookstores I find myself in the sections on philosophy, the New Age, metaphysics, and the like, regretting that I do not have the time to read everything that is out there. I have a new fascination with these subjects, but, more significant, they seem to fit into my personal readiness level now. I have become more open-minded about everything in the universe. My vision allows me to explore without the judgment that previously clouded it.

Even more intriguing is that it now makes perfect sense to me. I understand what was previously muddled. This is quite an extraordinary awakening experience for me, and I am, quite frankly, in awe of it. I often find myself reading books or listening to tapes that 'blow me away' with internal excitement. I am not sure if it is my openness to these new ideas, or if I have simply developed a greater intelligence through my studies, but in any case, I love it, and even more, I love sharing it with you and others. It is as if in one swift instant I have begun to understand and live the teachings of spiritual masters. Not by prolonged study programs, not by trying to improve my spiritual consciousness, simply by changing to a new me that is filled with wonder at the miraculousness of it all.

I also have a decreased sense of attachment to acquisitions and possessions. I no longer identify myself with my accomplishments and my résumé. It is as if now that I am a me without boundaries, I have less rigidity about defining myself. I feel as if I can stand in back of myself (of my form) and allow my Self to be anything I want to be, without having to define myself by my deeds. I am defined by some internal knowingness or beingness that defies external descriptors. It no longer matters as much *what* I accomplish as that I am in tune with my own sense of belonging to the human race. Self labels are no longer necessary.

It is not that the deeds have ceased, but that they are expressed in the process of my own self-definition. The less importance I have attached to these externals, the fewer restrictions I find in my life. I feel capable of anything at all, as long as I follow the inner voice which only I can hear.

I sense a strong shift in my personal ethics. Anyone in my life who attempts to be controlling or judgmental will not engage my emotional energy. I have lost my need to prove myself or justify my beliefs. I have no attachment to convincing anyone of the rightness of my position or to be on a confrontational receiving end of their viewpoint. A peaceful sense of who I am radiates and intermingles with respect for otherness.

I have found that some of my personal relationships have grown deeper and more profound, particularly with my wife and immediate family, while others have become less important. I still enjoy myself immensely in the company of others at a social gathering, but I no longer define myself as needing to be a part of these activities, whereas they played a much larger role in earlier years. I prefer spending time alone or in the rich close personal relationships I enjoy with my family and a few associates.

Virtually all dependency relationships, except for those with my small children, are nonexistent in my life. I am uninterested in having others dependent on me for their emotional or any other kind of sustenance. Paradoxically, I have become more generous in giving myself to others. I enjoy more than anything else in my life helping others. It is both strange and wonderful to function exclusively on what I know to be my truth and at the same time to welcome without judgment those who are operating at a different frequency. Similarly, I find it easier to radiate at my own frequency, and to ignore the pleadings of others to live my life their way. What has happened is that the boundary between my Self and others has dissolved. I see others on their own paths and I can now love them for being precisely where they are.

When others attempt to impose their self-serving values and attitudes on me, as I once did on others, I know that this can alter my balance and harmony. But now I simply shift into being a peaceful observer of what they are expressing about themselves and their truth. The authentic me, the thoughts and inner feelings that I live, are no longer engaged in defense, and I can watch without a need to prove them wrong. My path remains crystal-clear. This is a new kind of vision that allows me to live in formlessness and form at the same time without being threatened or controlled by anyone. It is a gloriously peaceful place.

I have lost my ability to blame others for the circumstances of my life. I no longer view the world in terms of unfortunate accidents or misfortunes. I know in my being that I influence it all, and now find myself considering why I created a situation, rather than saying 'Why me?'

This heightened awareness directs me to look inside of myself for answers. I take responsibility for all of it, and the interesting puzzle become a fascinating challenge when I decide to influence areas of my life in which I previously believed I was not in control. I now feel that I control it all.

I know that I create what I have and what I need, and that I am capable of performing miracles when I am balanced inwardly and using my thinking dimension to create the world that I want for myself. I know now that my circumstances do not make me what I am, but that they reveal who I have chosen to be. The quieter I can make my mind, the more I can perceive the link between my thoughts and how I feel. The quieter my mind, the less judgmental and negative I tend to be. Having a quiet mind gives me a peaceful life, and helps others around me to choose peaceful, serene, effective lives for themselves. Consequently, how I think can directly affect those around me. It was said of Jesus and Buddha and other highly spiritual beings that their presence in a village could raise the consciousness of everyone in the village. I can now value and appreciate that idea. I have found that when I am totally at peace within, and radiate that serenity outward, the consciousness of those in the same room with me can become peaceful.

Recently I gave a speech to a large audience in Chicago, and in the room were some five hundred children, many of them toddlers and infants. The noise level was quite high, but after a while I became accustomed to it and it was not bothersome. At one particularly poignant moment in the speech, as I was about to recite a gentle poem that is very meaningful to me, the entire room, including the infants and toddlers, became silent. A kind of magic communication was transmitted to everyone, through the dimension of thought.

The changes in myself and my life patterns have all happened without goals or any life plan. Yet these inner changes are as much a part of me as are my lungs and my heart.

Similarly, there have been many changes in my physical way of being in the world. I run a minimum of eight miles daily, and have not missed a day since I began at age thirty-six. Not once! I tell people that running is not something that I do, it is something I am. It is a part of my being. It fits as regularly into my health regimen as does being scrupulous about dental care. Simply what I am as a healthy human being.

My 'old me' was well aware of the benefits to my form. Those benefits remain and continue while I now experience a new level of benefit involving my inner Self, a loss of myself, an unawareness of my physicality as I run. I now have higher levels of energy than I ever experienced, and I attribute it and my involvement in being healthy and fit to my higher-consciousness approach to life.

I find it interesting that I eat no red meat, which I once thrived on; that I eat my food without adding salt, where I used to use the salt shaker before I even tasted my food; that sugar, caffeine, and other nutritionally empty foods are seldom part of my diet. I find all that *interesting*, but what is *astonishing* to me is that this tendency toward wholesome eating habits has flowed from a more loving approach to myself and to all of life, not from a desire to enhance my physical attractiveness or strength or to achieve physical longevity.

I seem to be trusting some sort of inner perfect consultant rather than relying on cultural norms, old habits, or what I was taught as I grew up. The part of me that wants to be in balance is choosing my food intake. I feel balanced inside, and somehow this almost magically translates to a salubrious approach to nutrition and exercise.

I seldom wear a watch, yet a few years ago I would not be caught without one. Time has lost its importance in the linear sense, and I do not feel compelled to keep track of when and where and how fast I live my life. This happened without any goals or objectives. I simply stopped wearing a watch and referring to time and scheduling my life, and I have found that I am more efficient as a result.

I am intrigued with the paradox of letting go of a need or desire for time limits and feeling I have discovered unlimited time for things I want to do. More than that even. Without physical time constraints, my life not only flows more efficiently but has increased richness and texture.

I experience the paradox of letting go of time limits quite often in places like checkout lines in stores. I am sure you too know the feelings that the 'old me' had when someone ahead of me in line was taking too long to complete a trans-action – I was impatient, agitated, critical; I even crowded closer to try to prod the slow person on. The 'new me' does not feel trapped in time and therefore does not need to worry about getting out of the store in a prescribed number of minutes. Instead I often experience a new level of being with time. I discover my Self in thought a part of the person checking out. My thoughts are of kindness and gentleness toward *my* slowness or awkwardness, a loving message of relaxation and nonpressure to the me that has been there, is there. The permission of unconditional love which I would choose for myself in that situation seems to transmit itself to the other person and help him or her find the right coin or whatever else is needed. And often this thought process creates a smile, an understanding energy between that person and my Self, a richness and texture.

One of the most beautiful and at the same time hardest-to-describe interactions is the experience of physical and emotional intimacy with another person. The physical orgasmic sensations are truly wonderful aspects of our sexuality. But the soaring inner emotional loving feelings are a beautiful part of this experience. Sex to me is now perfect love, rather than the obligatory function of a married man. Making love is an expression of the inner love which we can reach, when we are both balanced and fulfilled, and it is our mutual expression of that love.

I have lost the desire to organize myself in strictly
linear ways, and in the process my life has become
richer, more fluid and flowing and perfectly balanced.
My new perspective allows me to tackle any project with
a sense of inner excitement and the awareness that I do
not have to prove myself or be judged by the results. I
simply am who I am, doing what I choose to do, with a
sense of acceptance about the outcome or lack of outcome.
Interestingly, I accomplish more and acquire more (which
I give away in large measure). I achieve more than I ever
dreamed possible in my old linear days.

My diminished motivation to achieve and acquire is particularly noticeable when it comes to competition. Earlier
in my life I was always having to beat the other guy in
order to prove myself. In recent years my inclination is
away from competition. I still play tennis, but I send my
opponent good wishes right in the middle of a tough match,
and somehow, paradoxically, I raise my own level of play.
I feel this is a natural result of radiating out from my
Self the feelings and thoughts of unconditional love and
nonjudgment.

Cooperation has replaced competition in all facets of
my life, and the results are amazing for myself and all
the others whom I touch in one way or another. I feel
strongly attracted to the message in the statement 'In
a world of individuals, comparison makes no sense at
all.' External events are irrelevant to me except to the
extent they produce order or disorder in the world. I
assess whatever I do. If an act produces some kind of
harmony for myself and others, it is a positive act. If it
creates turbulence or disorder, I will work to reverse the
impact.

I see my mission as helping others to shift their consciousness, so that all of their waking thoughts and actions
are in the direction of order and harmony. It means living
as if the intelligence behind all form really matters, and
not doing anything that destroys or harms life. Tapping

into the inner energy that is our Self with an accepting attitude contributes to a personal sense of balance and harmony. As more and more of us evolve to this personally balanced level, we will create the outer form in our world. In this way, we will all participate in the transformation of our universe. I revel in the love of life and learning of my six beautiful children. I teach only love and I see them treating one another and people outside the family in the same way.

My wife and I have grown to love and respect ourselves and our own uniqueness, so that we are able to radiate that inner glow outward toward each other. We have a wonderful absence of judgment and negativity toward each other, because we have both learned to be that way within ourselves. Disagreements, yes! Disagreeableness, never!

I want to emphasize that this new me is still assertive and firm about my own life. I am not making the case for gushing sugar and honey at the evils of the world, in the hope that they will disappear. On the contrary, what I am experiencing is a much deeper involvement with life, wherein I know precisely what I am about, and I cannot be deterred from that path. I am able to stay on my path, doing what I love and loving what I do, precisely because I have transformed myself from a person who had absolute judgments which required fixed and rigid responses to a person who sees and knows that any human experience is an opportunity to reflect on where I am or am not. It comes down to surrendering some old, deeply entrenched patterns. It means catching myself right in the middle of acting in a nonharmonious way, and seeing that this is where I am and also where I am not right now! Then it means using my mind to be where I want to be inside of myself, and slowly but surely moving more in the direction of that inner harmony.

Recently I had an experience that illustrates how this works. My wife told me that one of the children had done something wonderful in her first-grade class, and she concluded by saying, 'I am so glad that I worked with her on this project and taught her how to perform in front of the class without any anxiety or self-doubt.' At an earlier time in my life I would have said, 'Wait a minute. I am the one who taught her that behavior, and you want to take all of the credit. You do that all the time.' My reaction now is: 'Great! I am so happy that she is gaining confidence, and you are a great help to her in this regard.' Inside, I feel I also contributed to her success, and I can appreciate my internal feeling without demanding external acknowledgment. I know that our daughter's confidence is the result of numerous inputs from both of us, from her own inner self, and from many others as well. My happiness is for her; it is not based on needing some credit, or on taking some credit away from my wife. Competition and turbulence inside me have been replaced by inner peace and harmony. It is unconditional love, beginning with Self.

When you retreat to your peaceful inner solitude, you enter that fourth dimension that opens up an entirely new world. But, before you can get there, you may need to examine your resistance to this powerful new idea of self-transformation.

Why you may be resisting this principle

Why would anyone choose to resist this state of being? Possibly to remain in the illusion of safety. As long as you are convinced that you are only your form, you needn't consider your own greatness and the risks that go with transformation.

Think about if for a moment. All of the impediments to your success and happiness can be neatly explained away as simply the boundaries of your physical existence. In this frame of mind you can decide that other people are just plain lucky or they were born with advantages you did not get, or they got all the breaks. These are the thoughts of someone who remains stuck in form. To experience transformation requires opening up to the possibility of an entirely new idea. Most of us reject new ideas for the safety of those to which we have become so comfortably accustomed.

It is also quite comfortable and natural to take the opposite position from that in the title of this book. That is, 'I'll believe it when I see it! And not a moment before!' Most people do not like to go beyond their comfort zones. You may know in your heart that life resists purely physical explanations and that science cannot conclusively answer questions such as 'What is life? Where does it go when it dies? How do I think?' Despite this awareness you may prefer to stay with that which you can see – that is, with form and form alone. Perhaps believing in formlessness is just too spooky and weird for you at this time. Yet you know in your heart that you have to be much more than just that body you live in.

It is risky in the beginning to toss out all of the old comforts and take the step that will allow you to interact with your inner beingness. That is where you live, in that inner place. That is where you feel everything. That is where all of your thoughts reside. And you may not be quite ready to explore this place where you have complete responsibility for all that you are experiencing.

You might also resist transformation because you are afraid of change, or of examining something that you do not understand. I call this the head-in-the-sand approach to your own spirituality. 'Let someone in a pulpit preach about what I am supposed to do in the spiritual realm. Me? I'll take care of paying off my mortgage. All of this mystical stuff is for deep thinkers or dedicated religious believers.' We have been conditioned to believe that matters pertaining to higher consciousness are the concern primarily of organized religious leaders. Yet if you consider the teachings of highly spiritual masters, they all say the same thing in different ways. 'The kingdom of heaven is within.' 'Do not ask God to do it for you, but in fact recognize your own great divinity and magnificence.' 'Look within, not without.'

You may feel that an attempt to achieve personal transformation conflicts with your specific religious training. But nothing that I am writing about conflicts with the teachings of the spiritual masters. Nothing! Transformation is about love, peace, personal fulfillment, treating others with respect, and achieving harmony on this planet as one family of man. Nothing I write about is in any way an attempt to criticize or ridicule anyone's religious beliefs. While I find some of the acts that are perpetrated against human beings in the name of God or organized religion anathema, I do not find fault with the essential beliefs of the religion. A transformed being is incapable of behaving in nonspiritual ways toward others.

Finally, you may resist this process of transformation because you feel that you really do not have the capacity to transcend the life that you have created for yourself. You may feel that you have in fact reached the limit of how far you can go, and you do not want the stress and anxiety that goes with soaring above the life to which you have accustomed yourself. You may not want to imagine what you can be, because you are not ready to make that shift, you want to stay with the familiar and within your own zone of comfort.

Most of your resistance to accepting the possibility of transformation come from being willing to carry on pretty much as you always have. Yet, I know that you would not be reading these pages this moment if you were not at least curious about the possibility of soaring beyond that which you have known as your accustomed life-style up until now. And I can assure you that there is very little real work to do. Once you realize that you are much more than a pile of bones, muscle, organs, and blood, you are on your way. Once you begin to ask who this person is that you have come to call yourself, you are on your way. Once you begin to realize that you yourself are divine just by the fact that you have a mind and a universal intelligence that backs up your form, you are already zooming ahead. The rest will happen almost automatically.

Some suggestions for personal transformation

• Practice thinking about yourself and others in formless ways. Take a few moments each day to evaluate yourself not in terms of your performance in the physical world, but in terms of pure thought and feeling. Imagine yourself actually standing in back of your physical self. Watch yourself acting and interacting and feel what you are feeling. Do not criticize or judge, simply note how your form is behaving and what it is feeling. Be an observer as your form is going through its chosen motions.

• Use the observer exercise with other people. Begin to notice how they destroy their potential for happiness and success because they identify exclusively with their forms. As you watch them going through their frustrating motions, know that this is not really the total human being at all, that behind each one of the people you meet every single day is a divine invisible thinking being. In your close relationships, meet your loved ones in a place where there can be no limits, in thought behind the form, and you will see that most of your differences are unimportant, that the real human being behind that form is much more than your physical eyes reveal. Vow to relate to that part.

•Make an effort to go beyond your own comfort zones on a regular basis. Listen to the real you inside who is encouraging you to transcend yourself, rather than the old you who said you were incapable of such a task. Ask yourself, 'What patterns in my life do I continuously repeat because that is where I am most comfortable?' When you have an honest answer, work to begin a new approach to your thought processes. If you have not spent any time in the wilderness because the idea violates one of your comfort zones, make a commitment to do precisely that. By extending yourself to new levels, you will put transformation in your life.

• Make an effort to cease labeling yourself as a means of identifying who you are as a human being. Long ago I stopped identifying myself by any professional title. When people ask me what I do, I usually reply with some silly remark like 'pleasure is my business.' Yet behind that little wisecrack is a lot of truth. I do everything because I am everything. Yes, of course I write, but that is only a small portion of what I am, and essentially my writing is a means of expressing my thoughts. Yes, I do professional speaking, but again that label would only serve to restrict me. My speaking is also an expression of my humanity. Eliminating the titles and labels reduces our inclination to compartmentalize and restrict our lives. Søren Kierkegaard said, 'Once you label me, you negate me.' Almost all of our labels refer somehow to form and what we do with our physical bodies. When you stop identifying yourself exclusively through form, then your profession, age, race, sex, nationality, financial picture, list of accumulations, awards, handicaps, level of fitness, and any other label become meaningless. Discontinuing the labeling process will help you to define who you are in more spiritual and profound terms. If you must label, try this one on: 'I am connected to the perfect intelligence that supports all form, and therefore I am a part and parcel of it all. I have no limitations and no compartments. I am not going to *get* it all, I am it all already.'

• Begin to view your mind, your nonform side, as new and miraculous. Know that your mind is capable of transcending your form, and that your body is in large part controlled by your mind. Imagine yourself with a lemon in your hand. Now imagine bringing the lemon close to your mouth and biting right into it. This exercise will create a rush of saliva into your mouth, as your body's reaction to the imaginary invasion of citric acid. This is transformation in action. Your mind is causing your physical self to respond. That is precisely what hypnosis is about. It is a way of directly contacting the state of mind that allows you to transcend your form, to transcend pain by refusing to register painful signals. This amazing power is always with you.

● Work each day to clear yourself of the two factors that do the most to inhibit your personal transformation: negativity and judgment.

The more negative your thoughts, the more likely you are to look exclusively at the physical side of you, and to behave in such a way as to destroy your body as well. Every negative thought is an inhibitor to personal transformation. It keeps you clogged up just as cholesterol clogs up an artery. When you are filled with negativity, you are kept from attaining higher and more bountiful levels of happiness.

The inclination to judge others also serves as a gigantic inhibitor of your personal transformation. *When you judge another person, you do not define him or her, you define yourself.* Your judgment of another says nothing at all about that person; it only says that you need to judge the person in the way that you are doing. So you are saying more about yourself than about the other.

When you find yourself thinking and behaving in negative or judgmental terms, remind yourself that this is an indication of both where you are at the moment and where you are not; that here may be a signal that you are identifying in some way with the judged person. What bothers us most about others quite often is something we refuse to acknowledge in ourselves, or even something we need more of! Try to be more interested in what is causing you to feel judgmental than in what is 'wrong' with that other person. After a while you will find yourself replacing negativity and judgment with a gentle and loving inward look at why this is 'hooking' you. Higher consciousness or personal transformation involves putting the golden rule into practice, and when you slip, applying that same rule to yourself. You will discover that the world has not changed, but that *you* are now a totally different human being, a transformed human being. It is truly a great feeling to take over your own inner life.

● Examine how you treat the physical or visible you. As you begin the clearing process above, you will find yourself becoming more and more in balance, improving your exercise habits and nutritional intake. As negativity and judgment go, so will habits of self-abuse directed at your form. You will begin to know that the food you eat is maintaining the wondrous temple that houses your being. You will see the old self-defeating habits of form-destruction disappear, and you will honor the form as a manifestation of you. It all works perfectly together, when you allow it.

● Allow yourself time to meditate quietly by yourself. Meditation is a powerful tool, and it is as simple as breathing. You should choose your own style of meditation. Maybe it will help you if I tell you a little bit about mine.

I go to a quiet place, and with eyes closed, I visualize a pastel kind of light. Any thought is pushed away by the power of the light. As I become more and more peaceful I see a white light in the center of the field of pastel and feel I am moving closer and closer to the white. When I finally go through that light, is is very much like going through the gate I described. I feel energized and totally in control of myself and my surroundings. 'Exquisite peace' is the best term I can think of for this place. I feel as rested as if I had slept soundly for eight hours.

When I leave this level I feel totally connected to all of mankind. In fact, I call this meditation my connection to all of eternity, because someplace deep inside of me I am freed from my form completely. After meditating I know that I can accomplish anything! Some of my most profound ideas, my very best speeches, and my most personally satisfying writing emerge after meditating. And my appreciation for my loved ones can only be described as a peak experience.

Try it. Use your own method. But give yourself the time and quiet space to be alone with the invisible you. Miracles are waiting for you in that spectacular space. Go there. It is truly exquisite!

• Above all else, be kind and understanding of yourself. Be especially kind to yourself if you behave in a way that you dislike. Talk kindly to yourself. Be patient with yourself when you find it difficult to be a 'holy' person. It takes a lot of practice, just as it took a lot of practice to develop neurotic and judgmental habits. Forgive yourself, and then when you do not act as you want to, use your actions as a reminder of where you are and where you are not. The more you extend kindness to yourself, the more it will become your automatic response to others.

By way of summary, I offer the broccoli metaphor. Imagine yourself going to your local grocery store and buying a package of frozen broccoli because you are attracted by the beautiful picture on the wrapper. When you get the broccoli home you are still so attracted to the picture that you empty the contents into the garbage and proceed to prepare the wrapper for dinner. As you put the picture of the broccoli on your plate, you suddenly realize that you are going to be very hungry if all you have is the packaging.

Your life may be just like that. You may be paying so much attention to the package that contains the real you that you toss away the most vital ingredients. Your form is the package, and while its beauty and appearance may seem all-important, it primarily serves to contain all the rest of your magnificent humanity. The container cannot give you the pleasure and satisfaction and nourishment that the contents do. Even though you cannot see what is inside that beautiful package, you know that whatever it is provides you with important and irreplacable nourishment. A lifetime of focusing exclusively on the package will result in a spiritually undernourished and quite unhappy you.

2
Thought

You are not a human being having a spiritual experience
You are a spiritual being having a human experience

Thought is much more than something that you do. It is in fact what you, and all the rest of us, *are* as well. Thought constitutes our entire being except for the portion of us that is form, or the packaging that carries around our minds. Try thinking of thought as something that exists not only within you, but outside of you as well. This may be difficult, because you are accustomed to believing that your thoughts are an internal mechanism that guides the part of you that is form. Try instead to consider thought as a universal that you were born into. It is something that you do, as well as something that you are! Once you get used to this new idea, it will become easier and easier for you to view *all* thought as something that is very much a part of you.

Here is a mini-lesson in what thought is. Your *desire* to improve your life is really your thought to improve your life. Your *will* to live is really your thought to live. Your *attitudes* about your entire life are really your thoughts on these matters. Your *entire past* up until this moment is really nothing more than thought. Your *entire future* from this moment onward is nothing but thought. Your *relationships* to everyone in your life are nothing more than thought. Your *determination* to succeed is nothing more than your thought to do so. The idea of success is really the *thought* of success.

Since you can never get behind the eyeballs of another human being and feel as that person does, you are actually one step removed from that person's process and experience him or her also through thought. You relate to everything and everyone on this planet through the mechanism of thought. It is not what is in the world that determines the quality of your life, it is how you choose to process your world in your thoughts.

So many highly respected thinkers in disparate disciplines have concluded that thought, the mind, is the total determiner of how our lives will go. The Dutch philosopher Spinoza said, 'I saw that all things I feared, and which feared me, had nothing good or bad in them save insofar as the mind was affected by them.' Albert Ellis, the founder of Rational Emotive Therapy, stated, 'People and things do not upset us, rather we upset ourselves by believing that they can upset us.' 'We become what we think about all day long,' according to Ralph Waldo Emerson. 'There is nothing either good or bad, but thinking makes it so,' Shakespeare tell us. Abraham Lincoln said, 'People are about as happy as they make up their mind to be.' 'Change your thoughts and you change your world' was how Norman Vincent Peale put it. Jesus tells us, 'As you think, so shall ye be.'

Our futures are formed by the thoughts we hold most often. We literally become what we think about, and we are all given the gift of being able to write our own story. For me this is as close to an absolute truth as anything I know. In my parable *Gifts from Eykis*, Eykis says, 'There is no way to happiness, happiness is the way.'

My thoughts have always created my world.

After my mother successfully reunited her family, we lived on the east side of Detroit. I spent many nights watching *The Tonight Show*, starring Steve Allen, on a tiny black-and-white Admiral television set, while everyone else slept. I loved Allen's zaniness. Sitting in that small living room on Moross Road, I would picture myself on *The Tonight Show* and in my mind I would practice talking with Steve Allen. I would actually work on routines, editing this and that out of my conversation, as I imagined myself being a guest on the show.

But my mind's picture was not me at thirteen; it was me as an adult who was making an appearance and discussing things I knew to be true. Most of these guest appearances centered around my beliefs, held even then, that we are able to choose our own destiny, able to make others laugh. These thoughts were so real to me that I would tell my brothers and friends what I was going to say on *The Tonight Show* when I appeared. They considered me a kid with a wild imagination who was always in another world anyway, and so they would humour me and move on to something more realistic.

But my internal pictures were never damaged by the attitudes of others. For as long as I can remember, I have been able to enter this world of 'pure thought,' and it is as real for me as the world of form is to all of us. Many times as a young boy I would know what was going to happen to me before it actually occurred, because I had experienced it in my mind so often. As a youngster, I never did anything with this ability, and eventually I ceased telling others about it.

As I mentioned in the Introduction, when I returned to New York City in 1974 after my transformational experience at my father's grave, I knew that I had to make some big changes in my life. Though I loved teaching at the university, something inside of me said that I needed to go off on my own, needed to shift gears and go in an entirely new direction.

I struggled for almost a year with the idea that I had to go out on my own and leave the security of a bimonthly pay cheque. I had wonderful pictures in my mind's eye. I saw myself talking to everyone in America about the ideas I had just finished writing about in *Your Erroneous Zones*. I could see in my mind that the book was going to be very successful. And so one day I announced to my advanced doctoral seminar that I would be leaving the university very shortly and going out on my own. After I made the announcement, I was in shock. Here I was only in the talking stages with my family, and yet I was making a public announcement. Apparently my form was following the invisible force of my inner world.

The morning came when the picture was very clear in my mind. I saw myself all alone in my venture, without any guarantees, and yet as peaceful as I had ever been in my lifetime. I knew that this was the day, that within a few hours I would officially be out on my own, no longer able to rely on a paycheque.

When I arrived on campus, I went immediately to the dean's office. I had not told my wife or family members that this was the day. It was the vision I had had that morning that made it clear for me. The entire process of my entering the dean's office was a mental one. All thoughts. All visions that were private to me. All images of myself that I could no longer erase. I could hardly believe it myself. Here I was waiting to announce to the dean that I was resigning, effective within a few weeks at the end of the current semester.

Our conversation was brief. I said I wanted to go out and do something that I genuinely believed in. She asked me to reconsider and discuss it with my family and some of my colleagues, but I told her that it was already accomplished in my mind – my thoughts – and that I was now simply going through the formality of making it real in the physical world as well. She pointed out all of the risks, how unlikely it was that I would be able to make a living writing and speaking, and that jobs such as the one I held were exceedingly difficult to come by in the 1970s because of a glut of professors and very few openings in the academic world. I told her that I was aware of the risk, and that was one of the big reasons why I was taking this turn in my life. I was headed down the path that Robert Frost called 'The Road Less Traveled.'

*

Two roads diverged in a wood, and I—
I took the one less traveled by,
And that has made all the difference.

When I left the dean's office, I walked to my own with
an inner glow. I was free, free to advance confidently in
the direction of my dreams.

I cleaned out my desk, made some announcements to
my students and doctoral advisees, and drove home along
the expressway knowing that I was taking the biggest step
of my lifetime. Here I was, completely unknown to the
media, leaving my secure position to go out and tell the
world about the ideas in my new book. Yet, I was ecstatic,
for I had seen all of it in my mind before experiencing it
in the world of form.

I discussed my new adventure with my wife and
daughter, and they gave me their full support and encouragement. Since I had always been a responsible person,
had always met my financial obligations, I relied on this
history, rather than creating in my mind some kind of
impending disaster concerning my family obligations. We
would use our accumulated savings; I would borrow money
if need be; and we would scale down some of our expenditures if that became a necessity. My family was in complete
agreement with me: money was not going to be the reason
to avoid following my bliss. They seemed to know that this
was something that I had to pursue, and, as is almost always
the case when people love you, they not only encouraged
me, but also seemed to have the same intuitive feeling that
everything was going to work out just fine. They too were
willing to take the risks, in the knowledge that we would
all be happier for the effort.

Every obstacle that came my way became an opportunity.
I was told that there were a minimal number of copies of
my book in print, and that even if I did go out and talk
to people in the media, it would do no good because most
bookstores would not have my book in stock. So I decided

to buy up a large quantity of books and take them out to the people myself. I literally became my own distributor initially.

I left my books on consignment with store owners across America in 1976, and I had the great fortune to have some wonderful people come into my life at just the right time. One such person, Donna Gould, became such an ardent believer after reading my book that she worked on her own time to help me get bookings all across the country. Donna knew I was paying most of my own expenses, and she contributed many many hours of her time and tons of her energy to help me. My publisher became more of a believer as he saw the results of my excitement about this project. Before long I was out in my own car, traveling from small city to smaller city appearing on talk shows and doing local newspaper interviews.

First I went up and down the East Coast, then to the Midwest, and ultimately on a long cross-country tour with my wife and daughter, paying my own expenses, staying in cheap motels, and, most important, enjoying every single minute of this new adventure. I seldom thought about making money. I had published three successful textbooks and many professional articles without financial profit; consequently, I was not motivated now by a desire to make a fortune. I was simply doing something that I loved to do and answering to no one along the way. Since I was using my own savings to finance this trip and to purchase the books, I had total control over every aspect of this promotion.

As the months rolled by, my interview schedule increased to as many as fifteen a day. Bookstores in cities that I had visited began to reorder from the publisher. At the start, I had been able to get bookings only in the smaller cities, but now the media in larger cities were beginning to book me on their shows.

I had been told by an 'expert' in publicity and publishing that the only way to talk to everyone in America in the

1970s was on network television, but that this option was pretty much closed to me because I did not have a national reputation. He suggested I should be happy if I sold a few thousand books in the local New York area, had a couple of printings, and got a publication credit toward a promotion at the university. This was the view of many others who knew the publishing industry inside out. They seemed to me to be unaware of the great truth of Victor Hugo: 'Nothing is more powerful than an idea whose time has come.'

What is an idea but a thought? The experts had their own ideas, and they acted on them. I too had my idea. I agreed that the easiest way to talk with everyone in America was through the network media, but I believed it was not the only way. I could reach everyone in America if I was willing to take the time, spend the energy, and absorb the risks that go with such an approach. I was willing and very eager as well. I would use every barrier as an opportunity to see if I could get past it. And it worked every single time. As much as I was making things happen through my thoughts, I was also letting things happen by not fighting anyone or anything, by doing it all with good cheer and love. It was great fun, every single day, every interview, every new city, every new friend. All very exciting.

The months became a year, and my family and I were still on the road. Somehow the financial stuff took care of itself, and then one day, while I was appearing on radio station KMOX in St. Louis, I received a call from Arthur Pine, my friend and agent, who informed me that my book would appear on the *New York Times* national best-seller list the following week, debuting at position number eight. I had accomplished what almost everyone said was impossible. Without one national television or radio appearance, I had been able to go to the people of this country and have enough of those people buy my book to put it on the national best-seller list. I was in awe and in shock.

But this was only the beginning of how my internal images, my thoughts, began manifesting. I was becoming in form what I had been thinking about each day, and most important, I was opening myself to allowing my purpose to find me. I had begun clearing myself of the negativity and judgment that had previously interfered with the flow of my process.

Other changes started then. I began exercising each day. Slowly at first, but very much an everyday thing. In August of 1976 I ran my first mile without stopping. At the end I was huffing and puffing and in a state of exhaustion, but nevertheless I finished with a wonderful sense of inner satisfaction. The next day I made the effort to accomplish this task again. Then again on the following day, and within one week I was running a mile comfortably. Two months later, I ran eight miles without stopping, and thus began my running streak, which continues today, of eight miles per day, every day without fail, since October 7, 1976. I became more attentive to my eating habits and gradually discontinued many foods which we now recognize as nutritionally unsound.

The clearer I became, the less negative and judgmental, the more I began to treat my physical self in healthier ways. As I allowed my purpose to find me, I began to feel happier and more in harmony with myself. Ultimately it was as if I forgot about myself and tuned in automatically to my strong sense of mission and purpose.

This is how the enlightenment process seems to work. One proceeds through a series of phases of first focusing on oneself and consciously working at improving oneself until the inner tumult disappears. As that inner turmoil fades, you find yourself feeling much more purposeful in sharing yourself with others. When you have an inner authentic sense of love and harmony, that is precisely what you have to give away.

As my book began to appear regularly on best-seller lists across America, the demand for me to make personal and media appearances increased dramatically. Shows that previously had turned Donna down cold were now calling to check on my availability. One by one I started making the circuit stops. And within a few months, the book had catapulted to the top of the list, where it was to stay for almost two years.

Then one day I received the magic phone call that was to lead to the fulfillment of that image I had had as a young boy watching television back on the east side of Detroit.

Howard Papush of *The Tonight Show* staff had been handed a copy of my book by someone at a party on Long Island. He took the book with him on his flight back to Los Angeles. The next week I received a call from a staff person for *The Tonight Show*, asking me if, when I was next in Los Angeles, I would be willing to come into the Burbank studios for a pre-interview for the show!

Within ten days I was sitting in Howard's office talking to him about all of the ideas that I believed in so strongly. By this time I had done hundreds of interviews, and I had learned that the best strategy was simply to be myself. Just me, talking to whoever was interviewing me as if we were in my living room. Howard and I hit it off beautifully, and to this day remain very close friends. Within a week I was to make my very first appearance on *The Tonight Show*. The guest host that Monday evening was Shecky Greene, well-known Las Vegas comedian. As I stood in the hallway next to the green room before the start of the show, I noticed a bank of pay phones. I decided to call my wife and share the excitement I was feeling. As I talked, I noticed someone using the telephone adjacent to me. It was the first guest of the evening, the man I had talked to so many times in my own mind almost nightly nearly a quarter of a century before, Mr. Steve Allen.

The evening's taping was sensational from my point of view. I had almost fifteen minutes on national television to tell about the ideas that were so important to me. It was a dream come true. When I went to the airport to catch an all-night flight back to the East Coast, I was filled with elation. Then over a loudspeaker, I heard a page for my name. It was Howard on the phone to give me the bad news that the show had been preempted for the first time in many years, because of an overrun at the Republican National Convention. It would not be shown until an unspecified future free date.

I flew back home wondering if the show would ever be aired, but the following day I received another call from Howard, asking me to fly out the next day to make an appearance with Johnny Carson which would be aired that week. So I made a third cross-country flight, arrived in Los Angeles, and did the show with Johnny on a Wednesday evening. But we had only six or seven minutes at the end of the show, and because of the shortness of the interview, Johnny asked me on the air if I could stay over two days and reappear on Friday evening!

I stayed over two days and did the show that Friday evening, and it went beautifully. A week from the next Monday, the preempted show aired. So I had gone from an unknown person who was able to get himself booked only on local shows to one with three *Tonight Show* appearances on national television, all airing within an eleven-day period. It seemed clear to me that Thoreau was absolutely right when he wrote, 'If one advances confidently in the direction of his dreams, and endeavors to live the life which he has imagined, he will meet with a success unexpected in common hours.'

Your Erroneous Zones was eventually published in twenty-six languages around the world. Other books have followed, as have tapes, articles, international travel for professional speaking engagements, and an opportunity for me to make a difference in the lives of millions and millions of people. I received more money in the first year I was out on my own without the security of a regular paycheque than I had in the entire thirty-six years of my life before then.

The how and why of visualization

I am firmly convinced that thoughts are things. Thoughts, when properly nourished and internalized, will become a reality in the world of form. You see, we think in pictures, and these pictures become our inner reality. When we learn the how and why of this imaging process, then we are on our way to 'success unexpected in common hours.'

Four principles of effective visualization

Consider the process of producing thoughts as an inner visualization without any of the limitations of the physical realm. You can go forward or backward in thought, and you do not need the five senses to enter the world of thought; you do it in dreams while you are sleeping. Cause and effect is not a prerequisite. You can create with thought any pictures that you choose, and these pictures are the very stuff of your life.

Four basic principles will enable you to make this formless realm work for you in your physical as well as your mental arena.

1 *Your actions come from your images.* All of our behavior results from the thoughts that preceded it. If you visualize yourself as incompetent in a given area, and you continuously reinforce this with a mental picture, eventually you will act out this scenario. Suppose you are about to load up your car and you discover you have six suitcases to put into a trunk that was designed to hold only five. The picture you form in your mind will determine how much luggage you take on this trip! If you think, 'I'm going to have to cut down to five suitcases – this car will not hold six,' then that is what you will do. But if you picture yourself going on your trip with all six suitcases, and hold that image in your mind, you will then act upon the thought 'I know I can get them all in. I'll just shift things around and work

at it until they fit.' I refer to thoughts as *things*, because they have just as much to do with how you drive off on your vacation as do the other things, such as your car, your suitcases, your maps, your supply of gasoline, your money, and everything else in the world of form. Understanding that a thought is the first step in this process of living contributes to your seeing the value of visualization in a positive framework.

Apply the notion of thoughts as things to the acquisition of wealth. If you picture yourself acquiring abundance, if you keep this vision in your mind regardless of the obstacles you encounter, and if you absolutely see it for yourself, then you will act on this image. You will allow this picture to be the dominant image in your mental world. You will make fifteen calls a day instead of three or four. You will find yourself saving a part of your income and thereby paying yourself first, a crucial step in the acquisition of wealth. You will think wealthy thoughts and surround yourself with people who encourage your visions. You will find yourself attending classes on the important subjects which make up your life mission. You will be in a continual state of self-improvement. You will seek out the knowledge and expertise of those who have achieved success in your field. You will spend time reading about people who have succeeded in spite of humble origins. Your entire life experience will revolve around the image of you with abundance in your life, all based upon one single thing, a thought.

The reverse of this picture is also important to examine. If you picture yourself poor, you will act out your daily life based upon this image. You will surround yourself with people who lack abundance, you will read about the failures, you will avoid trying new things or believing in self-improvement because the idea in your head is that you are poor. Your behavior will constantly flow from this visualization. You will consider successful people as lucky or born into the right circumstances. You will go into every encounter that might help you to gain abundance with the thought that it won't work out for you anyway.

Virtually everything that you do is a result of the picture that you place in your mind before you make the attempt. See yourself as unable to stand in front of an audience, and you will not. You will simply stay away from that experience and justify it by labeling yourself a shy person. Shy persons make shy pictures over and over in their minds, and until they can see themselves as unafraid, they will always act on the picture they create.

Regardless of the circumstances of your life, you are the writer, director, and producer of your mental images. You will always act out those pictures. Your circumstances do not determine what your life will be; they reveal what kinds of images you have chosen up until now. From the quality of your physical appearance, to your level of nutritional health, to the state of your financial holdings, to the quality of your relationships and everything else that requires an action by you, you are acting on images. Your mind stores away all of the images that you elect, and you daily carry out the assignments of those thoughts.

You cannot have a feeling without first having a thought. Your behavior is based upon your feelings, which are based upon your thoughts. So the thing to work on is not to change your behavior, but those *things* inside of your consciousness that we call thoughts. Once your thoughts reflect what you genuinely want to be, the appropriate emotions and the consequent behavior will flow automatically. Believe it, and you will see it!

2 *Tell yourself that everything you visualize is already here.* Remember what Einstein taught us about time! Time does not exist in the linear world – it is man's invention because of his limited vision and his need to compartmentalize everything. There really is no such thing as time. Just let these words sink in and be open to the possibility that they are truthful. Now, in a universe in which time does

not exist, everything that you are capable of thinking of is already here. Where else could it be? That thing in your head that we call a thought is really already here in the physical world. It is not in another solar system or another universe. It is here. But you cannot simply visualize something and then sit around and wait for it to materialize in your life. You must understand that the opportunity for bringing the thought to a physical reality is up to you, and that the physical reality is already here, on this plane and available for you to make the connection. Your job as a visualizer is to learn to bring it from the astral world of thought to the physical world of form.

Suppose that you visualize yourself selling five million widgets you have invented. You might say to yourself, 'How can this image already be here if they haven't even been manufactured yet?' Because everything you visualize is already here. But who is going to buy one widget apiece? Where are those five million people? On another planet? In another solar system? Of course not. They are here already. Of course, there are many steps in bringing that to form. You must know how to manufacture, distribute, and advertise your product. The rest of the steps are already in thought. All you have to do is connect your thoughts with their thoughts to purchase a widget, and what you visualized begins to materialize in the world of form.

Suppose you visualize yourself as someone who can run a twenty-six-mile marathon. Where are you going to do that? Right here! Not in another reality system, but right here, now. When the Wright brothers visualized a plane flying, that reality was already here. We did not need to invent a new reality system in order to produce flying possibilities for humans. We needed to connect our thoughts to the reality that was already here. Once those thoughts were tuned in to the frequency of flying as a possibility, that became our reality. The healthy person that you visualize yourself to be is already here, albeit surrounded by the unhealthy earlier thoughts. Understanding that everything that you are capable of seeing within your mind is already here will help you to take responsibility for the entirety of your life.

Every *thing* is energy. Nothing is solid. Everything vibrates at its own level of reality, and while form appears to be solid, a simple examination under a microscope reveals that that solid object is actually alive with dancing molecules virbrating at a little less than the speed of light and thus appearing to us to be solid. Energy is the very stuff of the universe, and thoughts are a part of that 'stuff.' So when you are having a thought about something that you would like to see happen for yourself, remember it is nothing more than connecting the two frequencies together to make the reality happen for you. Keep in mind that if you are capable of conceiving the idea in your head as an image of something that you would like, then it is already here. And when you begin to doubt it, remember to ask yourself, 'Where else could it be if it's not here in our reality system?' The thought that I had in my head as a child of appearing on *The Tonight Show*, as difficult as it is for us to grasp, was already here. If time does not exist, then 1953 and 1976 are essentially the very same thing. If you know in your heart that your images are already here just by virtue of the fact that you can think them, then you will stop waiting around and start working on those images to make them your physical as well as your inner reality. 'Where else could they be?' is a wonderful question to ask yourself when you start doubting that your images are going to work out for you.

3 *Be willing*. Forget about the word 'determination'! Forget about perseverance! Forget about personal drive! These are not the concepts that will help you to understand the visualization process and bring it into your life. Over and over I hear, 'I gave it my best shot.' 'I really tried hard, and it still didn't work out.' 'I persevered for months, and still I didn't get what I wanted.' The key word that is

missing from these statements is *willing*. In order to make a visualization a reality in the world of form, you must be willing to do whatever it takes to make it happen. This is the single most important aspect of visualization and imagery. Everything that you can picture in your mind is already here waiting for you to connect to it. What needs to be added is your state of willingness.

When I left the university to pursue my dreams I was willing to do anything. If it meant moving to another part of the country, I was willing. If it meant borrowing money, I was willing. If it meant leaving my family behind for a time, I was willing, because I knew my family supported my dreams. If it meant working eighteen-hour days for years and years, I was willing.

When I give lectures on the subject of positive imagery and creative visualization, someone in the audience will usually say, 'I worked and worked at my dream and it still didn't work out. Why?' My answer to that person is a question: 'What is it you were unwilling to do?' The response is usually something like 'I simply can't uproot my family and move to a new area just to pursue my own dreams.' 'Perhaps,' I say, 'you need to examine how willing you are to do what it takes to make your dream a reality.' I believe that being willing to do *whatever* is necessary to achieve your dream is a key factor in the accomplishment.

Willingness is really a state of mind. It is an internal statement that says, 'I will *be* happiness and bring it to my undertakings. I will take the next step toward making my dream a reality.' This is not a principle that presupposes a long list of goals. Quite the opposite. It is an internal statement of *I will* do whatever it takes because that is what feels right to me.

I believe that willingness is proportionate to the rightness of your path. If you consistently find yourself unwilling, I suggest you examine your dream closely. You may be receiving an inner signal that this is not what you want. Otherwise, you will advance confidently and not stop regardless of what others say, what obstacles come along, or what evidence suggests that you will not fulfill your visualization.

In my office I have two framed posters. One is a picture of Albert Einstein, beneath which are the words 'Great spirits have always encountered violent opposition from mediocre minds.' The other poster is made up solely of words: 'I am grateful to all those people who said no. It is because of them I did it myself.' Great thoughts!

Inherent within this third principle of visualization is the notion of *openness*. When you are willing to do whatever is necessary to *formal*ize your images, your thoughts, you open your heart to all of the possibilities available to you as a human being. Nothing will be too absurd for you to undertake. No obstruction or discouragement will enter into your consciousness. You are open to it all. Furthermore, when you open yourself up to abundance, you begin acting in abundant ways. So many times along the way I had been told by 'experts' how futile were my efforts to tell the world about *Your Erroneous Zones*, but within my heart was the understanding that though their advice might in fact be true for them, it just made me more willing to do what I had to do. And I loved every step along the way, instead of viewing my efforts as some kind of torture path that I had to traverse in order to get to the picnic grounds. I would have my own internal celebration each time I overtook another obstacle. And I came to know that the future picnic ground was just an illusion, since the future does not exist at all, only the working unit of our lives, which is now.

Once you are truly willing to do what is necessary regardless of obstacles, your openness will lead to an internal harmony that will not let you give up. Being willing does not mean *having* to suffer, or *having* to do everything. The willingness itself is often enough, and willingness is a thought.

*

4 *Realize there is no such thing as failure.* Keep this in mind and you will achieve all that you conceive in your mind. You never fail, you simply produce results. Always results. If you make an attempt to hit a golf ball one hundred yards and it dribbles off to the right, you have not failed. You have produced a result. Your concept of failure comes from believing someone else's opinion about how you could have hit the golf ball. But in our reality, you could not have hit the golf ball any other way than how you hit it. You have produced a result. Then you either berate yourself or you place the ball back up on the tee and proceed from the result that you produced. If you do this two hundred times, you still have not failed, you simply have produced two hundred results. Thus, following the principles of visualization, if you want to be able to hit a golf ball down the fairway one hundred years or more in the air, you must be willing to do what it takes to make it happen. Very very simple. You do not do what it takes for your spouse, or for Arnold Palmer, you do what it takes for you. One hundred swings, two hundred, six thousand. If you want to make your vision a reality in the world of form, you must be willing to do what it takes, and remind yourself that you cannot fail at being yourself. You can only produce results.

Supposing you weigh 250 pounds and would like to weigh 125 pounds. You have not failed, you have produced massive results. Now apply the four principles of thoughts as things. See yourself as the 125-pound person. Get an image of this person in your mind and never, never let that image out. You will then begin acting on that image, and find your eating and exercising habits shifting to fit the image. Secondly, remind yourself that the 125-pound person that you visualize yourself to be is already here, even though he or she is surrounded by 125 extra pounds. Thirdly, be willing to do whatever it takes to bring about your visualization, to reach your objective. Not what worked for your sister. For *your* visualization. Finally remind yourself that you cannot fail at this process; you will only produce results.

If the results continually are that you do not lose weight, get to work to discover the belief system that is keeping you fat, because it is your thoughts that are creating the unwanted results. The most effective methods for doing this, in my opinion, are in the programs which emphasize that you have your own answers. Find the approach that suits you, an approach involving self-responsibility and understanding that what you believe is what you see. You might try dreamwork, whereby you pursue knowing yourself better by inviting solutions, answers, and clarifications to come to you from your inner consciousness through your dreams and meditation.

You are the Dreamer of Dreams

The you that is beyond form is eternal and alive in a formless world. A brazen statement, perhaps, but would you be convinced of that if you could leave your body, exist in a formless world, and then reenter your body and exist in the state that we call form? I suggest that you do exactly that every single night, and that you spend approximately a third of your entire time here on this planet doing precisely that. We call it dreaming, and much can be learned about ourselves as part of pure thought by seeing what happens when we leave our bodies and enter the world of dreaming.

Every time we go to sleep and begin dreaming, I believe we actually leave our body, and enter a new dreaming body. We convince ourselves that our dreaming body is real while we are dreaming; otherwise we would not be able to have the dream. Where would it take place?

Let's take a look at the rules that apply while we are dreaming, and see how different they are from the rules that apply while we are in waking consciousness.

First of all, in dreams, *time does not exist*. We can go backward and forward at will. We can be with someone who died many years ago and that person will seem very real. We can be a teenager again, and that too seems quite real while we are in the dreaming body. We can live an entire lifetime in a fourteen-minute dream sequence and it is all real to our dreaming body.

Secondly, *there is no cause and effect* while dreaming. We can at one moment be talking to someone we know very well, and in the next moment be on a bus talking to a stranger. We can engage in an activity that produces the opposite result from that which would occur in waking life.

Thirdly, *dreams can be without beginnings or endings*. We can shift in the middle of a sequence to another place, and then come right back again, years younger than we were a moment ago.

Fourthly, in the dream *every single obstacle turns into some kind of opportunity*. If in the dream we are driving along a road that suddenly ends at a cliff, we can turn that into an opportunity to fly over the terrain rather than crash into an abyss. In a chase scene we somehow develop the amazing ability to catch bullets in midair.

Fifthly, *we create everything that we need for our dream*. This is very important to my hypothesis. If we need a person to yell and scream in the dream we create that person as well as an episode of screaming. Everyone and everything that we need for the dream, we create. If we don't, who does?

Sixthly, *our reactions within the dream are manifested in our physical body, but the things that create the reactions are all illusions or thoughts*. For instance, if you create someone threatening you with a knife, your heart will start beating faster, and that is real. But the knife and the person wielding it are illusions.

And lastly, *the only way we know we are dreaming is to awaken*. If we dreamed twenty-four hours a day, that would be our reality.

We are convinced that the body is real, yet everything that we experience in the dream is entirely in the realm of thought. There is no physical reality, it is an illusion, we realize when we awaken. We spend approximately a third of our lives sleeping, and a large percentage of our sleep time in dream activity that is pure formless thought which seems very real before we awaken. In fact, we are capable of some pretty fantastic feats while in our dreaming body. We can fly, transcend time, create anything we choose; and male dreamers can even create the entire dance of life in this state of pure thought. What is a nocturnal emission or a wet dream but the ejaculation of the protoplasm of life? Pure thought creating the opportunity for the dance of life. No physical contact. Pure thought creating life. Quite an amazing process in the fabulously mysterious world of pure formlessness, of thought.

I am not addressing here the interpretation of the content of dreams. I am writing about the process of dreaming in order to encourage you to become a *waking dreamer*. That is, to help you understand that the rules that seem to apply only to your dreaming body can become applicable to your waking body as well. This lesson was advanced by Thoreau, who put it this way: 'Our truest life is when we are in our dreams awake.'

For purposes of comparison, think of three levels of consciousness. The level at the bottom we will call our dreaming consciousness; the next level up we will call our waking consciousness; and the third level we will call a higher level of consciousness. Now let's see what these various levels are like, and what they mean in our lives. I will use a personal example.

As a youngster I would often dream of shoveling snow, and sometimes I would mumble out loud about my shovel and wake up one of my brothers. He discovered that if he disguised himself as part of my dream, by speaking gently he could get me to hand him my dream shovel, which of course he thought very funny, and he would wake me up with his laughter. But as long as he masqueraded as part of my dream, I would cooperate from my dreaming level with him in his waking level. This I believe illustrates our ability to communicate between our dreaming and waking consciousness.

What if someone from a dimension higher than waking consciousness wanted to walk and talk with us? That person would also have to be disguised, and pretend to be one of us, though he or she would know that there was a much greater consciousness beyond the waking consciousness level. If that being was charismatic and convincing, many might listen and achieve a sense of the potential of the higher consciousness beyond waking consciousness. Such is, I believe, the process of highly spiritual masters who have come here to teach us about the dimensions that are there for us in the world beyond our form. What would be a good disguise? How about that of a carpenter who gives us an inkling of what is available for us, and who tells us while performing miracle after miracle, 'He that believeth in me, the works that I do shall he do also; and greater works than these shall he do'? How about a teacher, or a writer, or a gas station attendant? Yes, there are miracle workers out there who can lead us to the edge of our waking consciousness, to glimpse something more. The great spiritual masters who have lived among us and who continue to do so have transcended the rules of form that we believe are the only set of rules.

While we are in our dreaming bodies experiencing the part of our lives we spend in this world of pure thought, we can have transcendent experiences when we choose. We do not need any of our senses in this formless state. We need not touch or feel or smell anything using our senses to know that it is real. Thought is real.

By becoming a waking dreamer, you will enter that

higher level of consciousness beyond waking consciousness, the level that spiritual masters have let us glimpse through their teaching and their examples as human beings. But to do so you must challenge your reality-thinking belief system.

To become a waking dreamer you must learn to 'die while you are alive.' Let's start by looking briefly at the process of dying. It is my belief that (1) we cannot kill thought, and (2) all form is in transition. It follows then that death will be very much like the dream consciousness I described above. We, our thoughts, leave our body when we enter our dream, and then we (the thoughts we are) reenter the body for waking consciousness. Similarly, when we die our thoughts leave the body and can look back at this dream we are living now which we call waking consciousness, with the same kind of vision that we look back at our dreams. This is a powerful idea. It could free us from fearing death if we learn to internalize it. The reason we have difficulty accepting that this waking consciousness is a dream is that everything seems just too real. But go back to our dream consciousness. The same rationale applies here. While we are in the dreaming body we are convinced that it is real, but it is real only for the dream and becomes an illusion when we awaken. Everything that we experience in our waking consciousness is also real to us.

To die while we are alive gives us the only opportunity we will ever have to get outside of this package that houses us temporarily. An ancient parable repeated generation after generation by the spiritual masters of India illustrates this point:

A traveller from India went to Africa to acquire some local products and animals, and while in the jungle he saw thousands of beautiful multicoloured talking parrots. He decided to capture a talking parrot and take it back as a pet.

At home he kept his parrot in a cage and fed him wonderful seeds and honey, played music for his pet, and generally treated him well. When it was time for the man to return to Africa two years later, he asked his parrot if there was any message he could deliver to the parrot's friends back in the jungle. The parrot told his master to say that he was very happy in his cage and that he was enjoying each day and to convey his love.

When the traveller arrived back in Africa he delivered the message to the parrots in the jungle. Just as he finished his story, a parrot with tears welling up in his eyes fell over dead. The man was alarmed and decided that the parrot must have been very close to the parrot in the cage and that was the reason for his sadness and demise.

When the traveller returned to India, he told his pet what had happened. As he finished his story, the pet parrot's eyes welled up with tears and he keeled over dead in his cage. The man was astounded, but figured that his pet died from the despair of hearing of the death of his close friend back in the jungle.

The trader opened up the cage and tossed the dead bird outside onto the trash heap. Immediately his pet parrot flew up to a branch on the tree outside.

The trader said to him, 'So you are not dead after all. Why did you do that?'

The parrot answered, 'Because that bird back in Africa sent me a very important message.'

'What was the message?' the trader inquired impatiently.

'He told me that if you want to escape from your cage, you must die while you are alive.'

We must indeed die while we are alive in order to be able to look back at our waking consciousness and see ourselves trapped in our cage, which in our case is our body. And then we will see how unnecessary it is to remain caged.

Let's take a closer look at those seven rules that apply to our dreaming body and see how much more enchanting our waking consciousness will become if we learn to die while we are alive – to become an awake dreamer.

*

1 *Time does not exist.* Einstein's life study was devoted to the simple message that we exist in a completed universe. If time does not exist, except as a convenience for man, then eight hours and eighty years are the same thing. A dream of eight hours and a dream of eighty years are identical, and the only way we know we are dreaming is to wake up. In a dream, we can be a tiny baby or a toddler or an adolescent. We can get married, have children, pursue a career, go bankrupt, have grandchildren, move to a retirement community, and become old – all in a period of minutes. In the dream it is very real and we are able to reduce it all into a tiny segment of what we call time. While we are awake, in the waking-consciousness level, it is possible also to recognize that time is an illusion and redefine ourselves to include our formless and ageless natures.

2 *There is no cause and effect.* In the dreaming body we come and go freely without being restricted to the laws of cause and effect. In thought we are exactly the same. We can have a thought that is totally unrelated to the previous thought within a greater thought process. We can have a dream within a dream within a dream. In waking consciousness too we can choose to recognize that we need not be confined to the rules that determine form. The physical law of gravity does not apply in thought. In fact, just beyond our atmosphere even our form is not confined to gravitational restrictions. A waking dreamer can dream any thought without reference to the previous thought. We can flit from one thought to another and use only those thoughts which are useful. In waking consciousness we can understand that we are capable of shifting gears anytime in our life. If you trained yourself to .be a physician and it no longer applies in your life, you simply choose new thoughts and begin to apply the concepts of making your visualizations your waking-consciousness reality.

*

3 *There is no beginning and no end.* In our dreaming body we do not disappear or terminate, because it is only in form that there are beginnings and endings. We never die in our dream in the sense that we simply discontinue being. Nor do we in waking consciousness, and we must understand this if we are going to get over our fear of death. We cannot kill thought, and we prove this over and over every night. Your dead grandmother can be right there in your dream, at age fifty-three and eighty-three, unrestricted to the rules of form. When we go into our dreaming body we do not have to have a beginning for each dream sequence, we are simply there, pure and simple; there is no need to start out.

We can be right here now in waking consciousness as well, disregarding beginnings and endings, imagining forever instead. Within the concept of eternity, the notion of a beginning and an ending is an absurdity. Try imagining where the universe starts and ends, and you will see how foolish all of that is. Try imagining a thought having a beginning and end and you know that thought does not conform to such rules. The universe, and everything in it, including mankind, is thought, and the waking dreamer strives to comprehend rather than being preoccupied with where it ends and how it begins. Truly enlightened souls knew that they cannot die. They know that death is just a transition of form, and that the astral thought dimension experiences no such phenomenon as an ending or a beginning.

4 *Obstacles are opportunities.* Our dreaming body knows how to turn obstacles into opportunities, and when dreaming we all do this all the time. We are frequently transcending difficulties and shifting to new realities within our dreaming body. This is one of the lessons to learn about our awake state as well. Everything that we encounter in life has something to teach us. Every sickness has within it the seeds for overcoming the illness. Every relationship,

regardless of how noxious it may appear, has something to teach us. Every addiction has within it the power to overcome it, and every former addict I have worked with always says the same thing: 'I bless my addiction for what it taught me about myself and my own ability to transcend the trap that I created for myself.' The waking dreamer knows while it is happening that there is a blessing disguised in every problem he confronts, and gets better and better at seeing that blessing in the moment.

We can develop this waking-dreamer attitude by discontinuing our need to curse problems and instead pausing to see what we are about to gain from them. We must keep uppermost in our waking consciousness that everything that we fight or curse will only weaken us and hinder our ability to see the opportunity in the obstacle. We know all of this in our dreaming body. In fact, while in our dreaming body we may rage at someone and wake up still angry and tense. The lesson here is important. The anger is real and we experience it both in our dreaming and in our waking body, but the people or things that we were angry at are all illusions. What a great lesson to have. All of our anger will be experienced by us, but the source of that anger is not real at all, it is in a character that we created for the purpose of our dream.

5 *You create everything that you need for the dream.* In our dreaming body we create everything that happens. We create all of the people, the events, everybody's reactions, the time frame, everything. We also create everything that we need for our waking consciousness. Let it sink in for a moment! That is one of the lessons that spiritual masters have been trying to teach us since the beginning of recorded history. Take responsibility for it all! Imagine yourself dying and looking back at this level of consciousness from that dimension of formlessness so similar to dream consciousness. As you transcend your cage, your body, you will see that you created everything

you needed for the dream that we measure in years, rather than hours, but that is exactly the same if we understand that time does not exist.

Now try to recapture that notion while you are here in this body. Keep reminding yourself that you are a multidimensional being. From this perspective of being in the dimension of pure thought, creating all of your experiences, it will not seem like such an absurd notion. Look at everything in your life from the perspective of knowing that it is impossible to retain form when you transcend it, just as you cannot hold on to the things and people that you create for your dream when you awaken.

A bit weird? Yes! A bit scary? Yes! But imagine what a powerful and transcendent idea this could be in your life. You begin to stand away from your form, and view everything that you have and do not have, all of your possessions and all of your relationships, all of your business enterprises, all of it, as something that you have created for this dream. Now you can learn to have your creations work to make this the best dream anyone ever had, or you can become upset, immobilized, depressed, worried, and overstressed by things you have created for this dream. All over illusions! So why not begin to take responsibility for it all, and enjoy your eighty-plus-year dream?

6 *The reactions are real, the characters are all illusions.* While dreaming we have many emotional reactions. We feel ecstatic as a result of some thoughts, and our body reacts with changes in blood pressure, increased heart rate, blushing, erections, smiling, and the like. We feel hurt as a result of other thoughts that are our dreams, and our body reacts with frowns, tears, and other physical manifestations. Anger is produced by dream thoughts, and our body responds with clenched fists, fast breathing, gnashed teeth, even tears. But remember, we have created all of the characters and events and are acting them out in thought only, yet we are still having physical reactions.

The characters are indeed illusions, but the reactions are real. And so it goes in waking consciousness as well, though it may be difficult for you to accept the waking-dreamer concept in your life right now.

I have no desire to debate about what exists or does not exist in whatever reality is or is not. To me, the reactions, the manifestations of our feelings, are real. If those feelings are interfering with our enjoyment of this life, then we need to examine what we are allowing to interfere with our happiness. Whether the people or events are real or not is just a question of perspective. The value lies in examining what is happening to you, rather than whether what is happening is caused by something real or an illusion. Examine your anger, hatreds, or stresses in this new light. No one can create anger or stress within you, only you can do that by virtue of how you process your world, or, in other words, how you think.

So rather than debate who or what is real, focus on what you are doing to process your thoughts, your feelings. And just as in your dream, when you really awaken, you will see as you look back that only your reactions, the residue of feelings in your body, remain. Are you able to let those feelings and thoughts flow through without censorship as you do in dreaming consciousness? In waking life can you think what you think without judging it or repressing it or stopping it? In dreaming consciousness you feel and encounter the array of human experience without judgment. Try doing that in waking consciousness too, and you will become what I mean by an awake dreamer.

Consider the realm of love. Your reactions of love are real and you experience them in your wakeful body, but only you can create those reactions by your thoughts. The more you choose to have loving, positive, beautiful thoughts toward yourself and others in your life, the more you will have salubrious reactions in your body. We create it all, including the persons who are in our life. More important, though, is how we allow or disallow our inner reactions. This is the true essence of being a waking dreamer, to be nonjudgmental of how we react emotionally to all of the characters and events that are part of our lives. Focus on what you do with what you think and feel. If you learn how to die while you are alive, you will be able to look back at all of those externals and see that they are illusory, but that your reactions within you are very very real. In fact, those reactions are what you are, your thoughts pure and simple.

7 *The only way you know you are dreaming is to awaken.* If we dreamed twenty-four hours each day, that would be our entire reality. We know that we are dreaming only when we awaken. The same thing applies to this level of consciousness that we call wakefulness. Once we awaken, that is, examine the principles of the dimension of formlessness and thought, we are able to look upon all of our activities in the same way we look at our dream consciousness. From the perspective of awakening, it is pretty silly to be attached to things which we have to be asleep to experience. No doubt that is why my neighbour has a sign in her laundry room that says, 'After Enlightenment, the Laundry.'

It is unnecessary to allow the actions of others to control our thoughts when we have the capacity to process our world and the people in it as we choose. Awakened persons know deep within their souls that they are much more than a body, that they create everything that they need for their dream. By looking back at our dreams when we are awake we see how futile it is to be upset about the dream content which we created, and we can also see the folly of being upset about anything that we create in a wakeful state. The key to grasping that we are thought and thought is us is to wake up now, and use our new perspective to make this lifetime as glorious and harmonious and loving an experience as is possible. This does not exclude examining our dream contents and waking-life circumstances for greater self-awareness and understanding, though that is not the subject of this book.

Now I suggest that you reexamine the seven principles of being a waking dreamer and think of how you can apply them in your life. Use this new awareness to make this waking consciousness all that it can be, and also to free yourself of a fear of death. Use the potential of your own death as an awakening experience, and begin living the greatest life anyone ever dared to dream.

Why we resist

● We have become accustomed to thinking of ourselves as our physical body rather than as an inner energy. We look into the mirror and believe that what we see is who we are. We live in a culture that reinforces this belief. We are bombarded with messages every day to remind us to perfume, shave, cleanse, feed, rest, and decorate our bodies so that we can be happy, healthy, and successful. Many of us have been subjected to this philosophy since childhood and therefore treat ourselves as primarily a package whose contents are irrelevant. It is understandable that we would resist the idea that we also have a significant self which is invisible and impervious to the demands of an external world.

The story of the man searching for his lost key outside his home, under the streetlight, illustrates my point. When a stranger inquired if she could help him look for the lost key, he was most grateful. After thirty minutes of fruitless searching, the stranger asked, 'Where did you drop your key?' 'Oh,' he replied, 'I dropped it inside the house.' 'But why are you looking outside under the streetlamp if you dropped it inside the house?' she asked. 'I have no light inside the house, so I came out here to look where there is light.'

This is precisely what we do every time we look out-side of ourselves for the solutions to problems. We live inside, we think inside, our humanity resides within, yet we spend time ceaselessly looking outside of ourselves for the answers because we fail to illuminate the inside with our thoughts. We resist the principle that thought is everything we are, because it seems easier to look outside.

● It seems easier to define ourselves by the packaging rather than by the inner qualities we cannot touch, see, smell, taste, or hear. Taking the easier-appearing path is one of the predominant reasons for resisting the principle of thought as the basis for our humanity. Besides, when everyone else is perceived as defining himself or herself this way, it seems easier to go along than to be different. I notice this with the young people in my neighbourhood. When I suggest the possibility of thinking of themselves as separate from the crowd, they tell me, 'Then I would be seen as an oddball or weird.' They are concerned with how others perceive them, unaware that their thoughts are a crucial component of who they are. They do not realize that they can process their world in any way they choose, and they often opt for the easier-seeming choice of simply fitting in. Many of us choose to act as others do without examining our nonform reality. We may be unwilling to take the criticism that goes with thinking independently. We may resist seeing ourselves as something beyond that form, because we have totally indentified with this kind of approach to life. To change, we have to redefine our self and our priorities, to give ourselves permission to observe where we are without being defensive or judgmental about our point of view. We facilitate the next step on our path when we note our present position uncritically.

● By identifying with form we are able to function exclusively in the realm of things, excluding what may appear to us to be irksome thoughts. Acquisitions become a way to demonstrate our competence in life, while our nonform

72

nature is relegated to a closed cupboard. We behave as if we did not have a responsibility to the feelings and thoughts of others by insisting that they find happiness in the material things we provide. We justify ourselves by saying, 'I work hard, I pay the bills, I give them all that they want – what else can I do?' The what else we can do is to be receptive to what they are thinking, to talk with them about their aspirations, to touch them in that godlike space behind their form and encourage them to experience their life their way.

We work at accumulating, achieving, goal setting, and acquiring wealth and possessions. We identify success with the measurement of things, never knowing happiness within. We are continually striving, never arriving. I believe we are more, that we are intelligence within our form, just as the rose is an intelligence that delivers the fragrance and appearance of the flower. We can never create a rose by ourselves. We need the life force in the form that we call rose. Similarly, we need to touch the intelligence or god force behind the form that is us as well as that of those with whom we come in contact. We may resist simply because we are unfamiliar with this aspect of humanity and because the unfamiliar is frightening. Ask yourself if that is a worthwhile reason for you to remain exclusively in form.

• In the world of form, blame is a convenient excuse for why our life is not exactly what we would like it to be. We blame the world for illness, the stock market for financial conditions, the bakery for causing overweight, and parents for our personalities.

In the world of thought, though, we are responsible for everything. We think as we choose, and we are what we think. Not what we eat, what we think. If we do not want the responsibility for how we have created our self, then we ignore this self-creation aspect, and live exclusively in the form that we inherited. If we know that thought is capable of healing, of creating a happy life, and of making a difference in the lives of others, then we respond to life with our ability. We are then living responsibly. Once our focus includes the inner world of thoughts, we shift to a more responsible way of being in the world. Look within yourself to discover how you feel about being more responsible to the world.

• We may enjoy the dreaming part so much that we do not even want to consider that there is much more available if we awaken. Thus we choose to remain asleep, unaware of the grandness that is there for us in awakening. When we stay with the familiar we take no risks. If we do not risk we do not have to change. Avoid change and we can explain that the reason for our lack of growth is a multitude of external circumstances. It is a comfortable-seeming circle that keeps us safe, albeit stuck in place, and in a place that seldom serves us or those we love at a very high level.

Resistance is a basic part of the fear of changing. When we approach metaphysical or spiritual issues, we encounter a long history of relying on seeing is believing, and that becomes a stumbling block to looking anywhere but where our senses seem to point. I suggest we turn the stumbling block into a stepping-stone by revising our thoughts to: 'I'll see it when I believe it.'

Your way out of the cage

• Remind yourself of how to improve at anything you wish to accomplish in the world of form. For instance, practicing the piano for two hours a day will improve your piano playing. Hitting a bucket of golf balls each day at a practice tee will improve your golf game. Imaging is the equivalent of practice in the world of formless. Before going to sleep at night practice getting an image into your mind of precisely what you want for yourself. If it is to be more physically fit, practice seeing yourself exactly the way you would like to appear. Let the image get fixed in your mind. Remind yourself to do this several times during the day too. The work here is to use your thoughts to focus on positive images, to grow from the perfect person that you have chosen to be up to now to even higher levels of present-moment perfection. Do not think of yourself as imperfect. Get the image in your mind of precisely what you would love to be and you will find that you will automatically start acting on that new image. In other words, begin to act as if you already are where you would like to be, and the actions will follow automatically.

• Work each day on your thoughts rather than concentrating on your behaviour. It is your thinking that creates the feelings you have and ultimately your actions as well. So give this dimension of your being all the attention it deserves. Catch yourself when you verbalize thoughts that are self-defeating. For example, if you blurt out loud, 'I'll never be able to get out of debt,' or 'I simply cannot reach my mate no matter how hard I try,' stop and gently remind yourself that you are acting on your thoughts, rather than having your thoughts come from the conditions in your life. Now rearrange those thoughts and see yourself out of debt. Refuse to think indebted thoughts. You will soon begin acting upon the image of yourself as a debt-free person. You will find yourself tearing up your credit cards, or consolidating your debts, or working at an extra job and doing the things that flow from the imaging that you do in your mind. Similarly, with your spouse, rather than act from the image you have of being married to an impossible person, begin to act as someone who is going to resolve your relationship one way or another. Create an image of yourself in a relationship that is full of love and harmony, and you will act that way. If you do not receive the feedback that is consistent with the image, you may consider moving on along your own path alone, or with another who is more in harmony with you. But instead of being in turmoil because your spouse is unapproachable, you will begin to act on the image of you as a human being in harmony. If you work things out, that will be terrific, and if you do not, you will move along in peace. In either case you will be resolving your relationship rather than feeding yourself on the frenzy of a mental image of being in an intolerable situation. Make the situation perfect in your mind, and you will act upon that perfection. The quality of relationships is inseparably linked with our images and thoughts. What we *see* is evidence of what we believe.

● Remind yourself that your circumstances do not make you, they reveal you. Some people tell me that they think it is easy for me to give advice on how to be happy and successful because I am rich and famous. My reaction is that I feel that my circumstances reveal me. That is, I do not give advice because I am rich and famous. If I am rich and famous it is because I have followed this advice. I have lived these principles all of my life, and believe that this is why I have achieved the measure of wealth or fame that is a part of my life. Look at your life, whatever condition it may be in. Your relationships, your financial picture, your level of happiness, your state of health. Now try to consider that these circumstances *reveal* something about you. Acknowledge your involvement in your circumstances and view them as a reflection of how you have been thinking and consequently acting upon those thoughts. You can use that power of visualization to have the picture stay the same, deteriorate, or grow into whatever you illuminate on your inner screen. You are what you think about all day long. And even if you are thinking about the people who barely exist in squalid conditions, remind yourself that these people, more than any people on our planet, need to hear and believe what I am writing about. If somehow they could change their inner pictures of despair and hopelessness to an image of something grander for themselves, and if they steadfastly refused to imagine anything else, they would somehow begin to make that image a reality in the physical realm.

The evidence is overwhelming when you consider people who have escaped from seemingly hopeless conditions, and who report that their belief was the impetus for their accomplishment. Secondly, know that you are not that person. You are here, right now, the result of all the previous pictures you have painted for yourself, and you can paint new ones, including one of yourself assisting those who need help, if that is what you want to do.

•Remind yourself daily that thought is not restricted to the confines of time, cause and effect, beginnings and endings, and all of the other rules that govern form. There simply are no limits in the astral realm of thought. Armed with this awareness, you can begin to meet others in this realm. Relationships can exist in this area, and you can make them come about by reminding yourself that *everyone* in your life is a divine entity with an intelligence behind all form. Your loved ones share their bodies, just as you do, with God, or whatever you choose to call that perfect intelligence permeating all form. Relate to them in this manner, reach them in this new place, stay in touch with their perfection within their form, and you will find the quality of all your relationships improving dramatically. Furthermore, you can relate to strangers in the same fashion. See everyone as a part of the wonderful, mysterious, invisible force that is in each and every one of us. Treat other people like the divine creatures they are.

• Study the seven principles of becoming a waking dreamer by applying one to each day of the week. Here is a sample of how you can make this your own reality in the week to come.

1 *Sunday: time does not exist.* Spend some time today outside, in nature, looking straight up. Try to imagine

that up goes forever, since even our rational mind tells us that the universe cannot simply end. If it goes forever, then it is already complete, mysterious as this sounds. It is all complete. In a completed universe, time simply is mankind's way of helping organize the days and keep track of things. Eternity is forever, no time, only always.

Now, what can you do with this? You can eliminate preoccupation with time, aging, type-A behaviour, scheduling your life, and hurrying. It is all so perfect, this universe we are in. Slow down and enjoy it all. Your lifetime of ninety or so years is exactly the same as your dream of eight or so hours. I did not invent this notion of no time. Einstein gave it to us in a mathematical sense, and philosophers from the beginning of recorded history have reminded us of it. The Bible is replete with references to eternity. Your lifetime in form is to be honoured and celebrated, not calculated and compartmentalized. Go beyond your enslavement to time and live fully in this, the only time you have. In the *Now*, the working unit of your life.

2 *Monday: there is no cause and effect.* Today take time to comprehend what it means just to be. You are not a human doing, but rather a human being. While form follows all of the rules of cause and effect, formlessness is acausal, just like the time you spend dreaming. Now here, now there, your thoughts independent of each other. You can get past pure cause and effect by tuning in to your invisible humanity. You need not continue to do the work you trained yourself to do, simply because as a teenager, thirty years ago, you made some decisions about what you were going to apprentice or major in. You need not remain governed by the belief that past decisions cause you to be whatever you are today. You can be a creator without old rules governing your life. You can *be* anything you choose, regardless of what anyone says or does, and regardless of anything you have done or not done before. If you can imagine it, you can be it, and your imagination, your

thinking, is not restricted to the rules of cause and effect. Today, Monday, work at not being the *effect* of anything, but the *creator* of that which you imagine yourself to be. You do not need a consultant in this matter; you simply need to put your form in harmony with your thoughts and then just allow yourself to *be* it.

3 *Tuesday: there is no beginning and no end.* Practice living this day as if forever were all tied up in this day. This is forever right here and now. Without time as a factor in this metaphysical experiment, today and a million years are the same. You are eternal, and the invisible essence of you can never die. Knowing this, all of the petty, worrisome areas will melt into insignificance. Attachment to things you can never own will also diminish significantly. Look into the mirror on this Tuesday morning and say out loud, 'I am not my form. I am something much more divine than mere form.' The fact that you can come and go in your dreaming body independent of any time constraints gives you evidence that the dimension of thought is not something to fear, but something to savor. Today, Tuesday, live each moment as if it were the eternity that it is, savoring everything there is to appreciate in every moment. Make it a habit beginning today. One moment at a time. One eternity at a time. And be patient and loving with any fearful thoughts. Reassure your fears that you understand their need to warn you of what they think is danger, and invite them to experiment with you just today, to try this new way of thinking, safely and lovingly.

4 *Wednesday: every obstacle is an opportunity.* Today, welcome any disorderly or unpleasant behaviour toward you from other people, as an opportunity to remind yourself that they are only talking to your form. Know that they cannot have your divineness unless you choose to share it with them, and then, perhaps for the very first time, you will be able to see the divineness in them, inside the

form that is being unpleasant to you. Use the obstacle, the annoyance, as an opportunity to connect with your inner self. Today, see how many times you can take what would have been an uncomfortable reaction within you and transform it into a blessing for yourself and the other divine beings as well. Use the incidents as opportunities to practice and experience non-judgmental observation of what is happening in the world of form. Set judgment toward yourself and others aside, and instead observe what you are feeling, and let those feelings free you. Eventually, in this way, you will discover the blessing or opportunity in what previously you allowed to be an obstacle to harmony in your life. Today, Wednesday, you are becoming the waking dreamer, turning obstacles into opportunities while in your waking body, just as you do when you are in your dreaming body.

5 *Thursday: you create everything that you need for the dream.* As waking dreamers we know deep within that when we die our consciousness will live on in a new dimension, and that everything experienced on our present level of wakefulness will appear as an illusion. Thus, just as in the dreaming body, everything that we need for the waking dream is created by us, even the people whom we experience as difficult: they are in our life because we put them there. They have important lessons to teach us. Today, concentrate on asking yourself, 'Why did I create this in my life?' Take responsibility for everything that is in your life, believing that you created it all. Dedicate this Thursday to experimenting with this self-realization. Respond today as if everything that comes your way was put there by you, just as everything that you experienced in your dream last night was created by you. Everything that happens to us is in some way a mirroring of our inner beliefs. When you really and truly know that you create every aspect of your daily life, then you will learn to discontinue disharmony, or to discover its message. When you no longer need to

learn how to deal with disharmony in your life, you will stop creating it, and you will create love and harmony virtually everywhere you turn. Today is your day to keep this uppermost in your consciousness all day long.

6 *Friday: the reactions are real, the characters are all illusions.* Today is the day to soar in a transformational sense. Look at how you play out the reactions to all of the characters and events that you create for your life. Remind yourself that all of the feelings that you experience within you, the anger, joy, fear, stress, happiness, are all very very real for you, just as in your dream when you find yourself panting and breathing hard because someone has been chasing you, the panting and breathlessness are real, but the characters are your creation. Your reactions are the very stuff of which the quality of your life is made up. Today study how you are reacting to all of the externals that you have created for your life, concentrate on how you are processing your thoughts. Reactions to life are determined by our thinking. Begin today to study the self-defeating reactions instead of the event or person. Imagine waking up from your dream and being upset all day long because one of the characters in your dream did not behave the way you thought he or she should. You know enough to say simply, 'That was a dream,' and then get on with living, or examine this reflection of yourself. Today, you can use that very same strategy and refuse to be immobilized by the actions of anyone else.

7 *Saturday: the only way you know you are dreaming is to awaken.* Today you can practice awakening, that is, dying while you are alive, and look back at what you judged you needed to do for your life. Begin to realize that everything that you experience is a thought. The cookie that you want to eat but that will not help you is nothing more than a thought. The anger at your spouse or children because they refused to act in a certain way is only a thought.

You are awakening, and by doing so you are able to see exactly how all of your self-deprecating actions are really responses to what you are creating for yourself. From this perspective, you are separated from your body, and you are watching how you behave in a variety of situations. Like an actor on the stage, you see your body go through the hoops and roles that you have created for it, and you know that you are not exclusively that physical form. You are invisible and impervious to the senses for a day, and you can almost laugh at yourself for acting so foolishly as to immobilize yourself through the avenue of thought. As an awakened being you know that you can only give away what you have inside, and that whatever is inside is there because of thoughts. If you give away any hate or anger today, it is not because of anything outside of you, but rather what you have inside to give away. Loving, harmonious thoughts produce love and harmony to give away, regardless of what is coming at you. Disharmonious hateful thoughts produce the hate and anger that you have to give away. Both reflect your beliefs about your world. In this life, in this dimension of wakefulness, you simply cannot give away what you do not have. Watch what you give away all day long, and realize that the only way you will ever get a firm harmonious grip on how to live out this illusion is to awaken to another dimension and view all of your actions from the new perspective.

So ends a week of working each day at being a waking dreamer. Knowing that we only have moments to live, rather than weeks and months, we can begin to use this awareness to make our everyday lives a state of wakefulness as unlimited as that which we experience in our dreaming body.

Keep seven words uppermost in your mind and think on the wisdom that is behind them. From the Prince of Peace, 'As ye think, so shall ye be.'

3
Oneness

*You are at once a beating heart and
a single heartbeat in the body called humanity*

Take a few moments to study the word 'universe,' the
term that we use to describe this immense world of form
in which we find ourselves thinking and breathing, day
in and day out. Breaking the word down, we have 'uni,'
meaning 'one,' and 'verse,' a 'song.' One song! That is
our universe, my friends. Just one song. No matter how we
separate into individual little notes, we are all still involved
in the onesong.

This is one of the most difficult concepts for us to
grasp and apply to our daily lives, because we believe
so strongly in our separateness. We recognize ourselves
as one unit functioning separately among billions of
others. We identify exclusively with our own mind as
unique and separate from everyone else's on our planet.
We look out from our separateness and believe that
through it is the only way to interact with the world
and our reality.

A huge shift is required in our consciousness to include
the universal principle of oneness. Once we make that
shift and begin to recognize all of humanity as a beautifully harmonious song, magnificent changes take place
in our individual lives. But to make the shift you will
need to suspend beliefs resulting from the narrow perspective of a personal life history, and instead begin to
think about yourself in relationship to everyone else
who shares this planet now, who has ever been here
before, and, even more strikingly, who will show up in
the future.

A new perspective on our place in this onesong

Albert Einstein, a man I consider perhaps the greatest mind of our century, wrote these words regarding the perspective I am asking you to examine:

A human being is a part of the whole called by us 'Universe,' a part limited in time and space. He experiences himself, his thoughts and feelings, as something separated from the rest, a kind of optical delusion of his consciousness. This delusion is a kind of prison for us, restricting us to our personal desires and to affection for a few persons nearest to us. Our task must be to free ourselves from this prison by widening our circle of compassion to embrace all living creatures and the whole nature in its beauty.

Einstein was much more than a scientist; he was a deep-thinking metaphysician, with little or no regard for the established ways of thinking and doing. In the words I have quoted, Einstein offers us a challenge to free ourselves from our cages and to see how we are all connected, not only in a spiritual or astral sense, but in a linear physical real world sense as well.

I have my own way of making that concept take shape for me. First, to get a perspective for dealing with metaphysical matters, I ask myself, 'Can I get back far enough to see the entire picture?' I visualize being able to stand in a place and literally see the entire scope of creation. Since this is impossible to do in form, I try to look in the other direction, that is, toward the tiniest speck, and to magnify what is inside that speck, and so on to infinity. Victor Hugo put it like this: 'Where the telescope ends, the microscope begins. Which of the two has the grander view?' So I suggest that you temporarily put away the telescope on the entire onesong and take a look inward, at the one thing you know the most about, your own body.

Here we will see we are all an 'I that is we,' to borrow a phrase from Richard Moss's marvelous book of that title. Let's take a look through this metaphorical microscope.

We are teeming with life-forms, most of which are necessary to keep us in a state of aliveness. Our eyelids have many tiny organisms that work in harmony with the whole. The lining of our large intestines has hundreds of different kinds of microbes, all alive, all with their own unique characteristics, yet still very much a part of the whole person. Our scalp is home for tiny organisms, each one of which has a separate identity that can be examined with a powerful microscope. So too, our liver, pancreas, toenails, skin, heart, and on and on are brimming with life, all working in harmony with the whole that we call 'me.' Yes, indeed, you and I are a me that is we, and though those microscopic life-forms that reside inside our toenails will very likely never come into contact with those other very different life-forms that live in our eyeballs, they are both separate and unique and crucial to the survival of the totality that we call ourselves.

This became abundantly clear for me when I saw a documentary on the life-forms living within one raindrop. With a very powerful microscope, scientists documented that there were hundreds of life-forms in each raindrop, many of which had no physical contact with the other life-forms in the same drop. They were of different colours, shapes, and origins, each with unique physical characteristics, and were as far away from one another as we are from tribesmen in Afghanistan. Yet they all composed the totality called 'raindrop.'

In an endless universe, it is conceivable that our physical size is proportionately the same as that of the tiniest microbe within the tiniest microbe, within the even tinier microbe all within that drop of rain. The infinitely tiny life-form that resides within my toenail will never make physical contact with the tiny microbes in the inner lining of my retina in my eye, in that eye's socket, on the head of my torso, ad infinitum. At the same time it is a separate, unique part of the totality known as 'person.' From this perspective we can contemplate our self as a person in relation to the totality known as 'universe.'

With our narrow vision we can see that we are connected at the physical level, and we can validate this with physical measurement methods. But we tend to use those measuring sticks, which we have invented, as instruments to enslave us to a confining and narrow interpretation of our place in this onesong. We do this by believing that reality is only what we are capable of measuring, rather than both what we can measure and what is still unmeasurable. Germs and bacteria existed in our lives and bodies long before we could examine them under the microscope. The invention of the microscope did not create the germs! Just as we have created devices to measure what was previously there but unmeasurable, so too it is possible, and, for me, probable, that each of us is a part of a 'we' that is unmeasurable by contemporary man-made technology.

If we think of all humanity as one being, and ourselves as individual pieces of the gigantic being, and if somehow we could manage to get back far enough to see this entire life-form, we would notice immediately if one part of the being was missing. Our eyes would automatically go to the empty space. That space shows how important each of us is. You and I make the body of humanity complete. If we are not fully alive and working in harmony with the entire body, it lacks harmony and balance. And if enough of us are missing, the body will die. This is the perspective we must take in order to understand and begin to live the principle of oneness.

It is of course, a paradox to be unique and all-one at the same time. Nevertheless, it is our reality, and once we know how this principle of oneness works in this endless universe, we will begin to see how we can make the principle work not only for each of us, but for this entire song that we make up. The harmony will be felt within you, and it will radiate out to make the onesong a rapturous melody, totally in tune, harmonizing with all of the individual notes that make up this uni-verse! Let me tell you what a personal difference it has made for me in every aspect of my life.

My first contact with oneness

My mother's mother holds a very special place in my heart. When my mother was beset by so many difficulties after my father abandoned us, my grandparents took my oldest brother to live with them. And from my grandmother's role as a mother I got my first inkling of the concept of unity and oneness.

My grandmother had nursed each of her children and had been extremely protective of her young, including my mother. She had spent most of her time lovingly rocking, singing, cuddling, and caring for her infants.

My grandmother was in her ninety-fourth year when she began to lose some of her physical faculties. She needed constant help and care as she approached the age of ninety-five. I watched my mother taking care of her in those final days of my grandmother's life. I watched as my mother took clean clothes to her mother, and made absolutely certain that her undergarments were never soiled. And one day I watched my mother holding my grandmother and peeling a banana for her and actually mushing it up in her own mouth and massaging her mother's neck to help her swallow it. Then she helped her put on clean underclothes. She rocked her mother and talked to her almost as if she were a baby. As I watched, I asked myself the question that was swirling around in my head: 'Who is mother and who is child? Didn't my now-helpless child-grandmother once change the diapers of the mother-child and mush up her food to make sure that she was properly nourished?' Weren't these two human beings really fulfilling the same role for each other?

The oneness of it all struck me in an astonishing way as I watched this scene. I realized it is all one big circle, just as the universe is one big circle, and while we tend to identify ourselves with our separateness, when we can get a different perspective we see that it is all one, and that there exists in the onesong a large being called Human Being, and that each of us is born into that being.

My second encounter with this oneness concept came when I began to read some of the literature on collective consciousness. I had read Ken Keyes's *The Hundredth Monkey*, and I was trying to put it into a personally meaningful context. Very briefly, the hundredth monkey is a theory about how all of us within a species affect one another. A group of monkeys was being studied off the coast of Japan, and one monkey within the group began washing his sweet potatoes in a certain way in the salt water. Soon all of the monkeys began mimicking this monkey and doing the same thing. When a given number of the monkeys behaved in this fashion, the same behaviour began to appear in a group of monkeys hundreds of miles away, even though the two groups had had no physical contact with each other. The hundredth monkey symbolized what scientists call the critical mass within the species. It is theorized that once a critical mass number is reached, the same behaviour begins to show up in all of the other members of the same species. It seems to be true for all species that when a given critical mass of its members begins to think or act in a certain way, so does every other member of that same species. In Ken Keyes's book, he uses the example of nuclear war and suggests that if enough of us as members of the human species believe and act as if there will ultimately be a nuclear war, then when we reach that critical mass, we will of course create our own reality as a species. On the other hand, if enough of us believe and act as if such an occurrence were impossible, then we can create that reality for our entire species as well.

The invisible connection between all members of a species is more verifiable now than it was a few years ago. Physicists describe it as 'phase transition.' Scientists report that when atoms within a molecule align in a certain way and a critical mass number is reached, the rest of the atoms spontaneously line up the same way. Nick Herbert's *Quantum Reality*, Fritjof Capra's, *The Tao of Physics*, Gary Zukav's *The Dancing Wu Li Masters*, Lewis Thomas's *The Lives of a Cell*, and Rupert Sheldrake's *A New Science of Life* are a few of the books in the growing literature describing a connection between the principles of physics and a collective consciousness.

Just imagine the staggering implications of this fledgling scientific notion – a scientific basis for the oneness of it all, and the idea that if enough of us who share this life-form called human being begin to think and act in harmonious and loving ways, we can affect the *entire* being called Human Being.

The entire history of the Human Being is filled with war and disorder. How many mothers have wept for sons who have gone off to fight one war or another over the centuries? An endless cascade of terror and division marks this being that we call Human Being, and you have showed up in it! Do you support the divisions that have become a part of this being's history, or can you be one voice affecting the voice next to you and so on until we reach that critical mass where the entire being will align itself with the harmony that is the onesong? It is only the Human Being that has been out of harmony with the rest of the totality that is God or oneness or whatever we choose to call it. When the individuals within this total being align in a certain fashion, much like the atoms within a given molecule, then they can affect all of the beings within the one Human Being.

I have heard scientists in virtually all fields of study talk about the invisible forces that connect all members of a species. They report how when liquid matter crystallizes on one part of the planet, the same crystallization process occurs almost simultaneously in another spot without informational or physical contact. I have heard researchers talk about microbes in Europe suddenly behaving differently, while microbes on other parts of the globe demonstrate this new behaviour almost simultaneously without an exchange of information. The entire history of the Human Being seems to follow these unwritten rules of a collective consciousness.

I am not trying to make a case here for the scientific verification of this point of view, but to show that the idea of oneness enjoys credibility in scientific circles as a means of explaining what has previously been scientifically inexplicable. Certainly if enough of us begin to think in nonaggressive harmonious ways to reach a critical mass, there could be an end to war. As each being reacted harmoniously rather than with enmity toward the being adjacent to him, it would not be long before there would be no soldiers to follow the orders of the generals. Harmony would begin to reverberate in those who design the weapons of destruction. When the designers stopped creating weapons, government officials would stop contracting to purchase weapons of destruction, and the spin-off effects would begin to be felt in all fields of human endeavour. People who transport weapons would find this behaviour inconsistent with their own internal harmony and would simply refuse to participate. Advertisers would begin to feel the pressure to align on the side of harmony rather than of tumult. The transition would work within the Human Being, much as it does within a molecule. As more and more align in harmony, the pressure becomes overwhelming, and the oneness of humanity is the winner. And how does it all start? Symbolically, with that one monkey picking up that sweet potato and having the courage to behave differently, and then the next, until the critical mass is reached. One person with a conscience actually becomes a majority through this collective consciousness process.

I was running one day and thinking about this business of myself being a 'I that is we' when I noticed another runner about thirty yards ahead of me, and I asked myself a question that was to be a life-changing event for me: 'How can I possibly be connected to that being, whom I've never seen before and don't know from Adam and yet who seems to be doing the same thing I am doing?' Then I remembered the question of perspective. I thought about my feet moving one in front of the other, and all of the life-forms that are alive in and on me, that will never see one another and yet are inextricably connected and essential to make up this being that I call Wayne. I decided to project myself back far enough, and I realized for the first time that thirty yards in physical distance was absolutely nothing in an endless onesong that we measure in the distances that light travels in years. The other runner was no farther away from me than the microbe in my eye was from the one in my pancreas.

For the first time in my life, I saw myself connected to a being who previously seemed separated from me. It became crystal-clear to me that regardless of where any of us is on this globe, given a world that is round, it is impossible to choose up sides. I saw that we are literally all part of this being that we showed up in, with a mode of behaviour and a personality all its own, and that each of us within that being can make a difference in how the totality proceeds and exists. One small voice within that onesong can influence the entire being toward destruction or harmony.

It just hit me that day, and then when I got home and began to talk to my wife about this amazing realization, I opened a letter from a woman in Iran, a letter that was to crystallize it all for me.

An English-speaking person in Iran had read several of my books and had decided to translate them into Farsi and make them available to the peoples of Iran. She had translated the books and actually had five thousand copies of each book circulated, and then had elected to go into a second printing. At that point, the government decided to place a disclaimer in the book stating that my subversive ideas were inconsistent with the philosophy of the revolution taking place in Iran.

The niece of the translator got my address through the American publisher and wrote to tell me that my books had made a remarkable impact on her. Her letter arrived on the day that I had my stunning realization that I was not only connected to that runner some thirty yards away from me, but to all humanity as well. The letter from Mariam Abdollahi in Iran helped me to see that we are all connected as humans, regardless of the boundaries and divisions we have drawn to make us believe the contrary. Mariam wrote in detail how important my words were to her, and said that there was a growing awareness within Iran of the need for people to stop hating one another and come together with the rest of the world. She began to write regularly, and arranged for gifts to be sent to our children: tapestries that now hang in our home, books about peace and love. She showed us there was another aspect to the people who were caught in that vicious cycle of war.

One Friday afternoon I received a long-distance telephone call from Tehran, and there was Mariam, weeping in joy over some of the audio and video tapes I had sent to her, along with other gifts from this part of the onesong. We have since become friends, talking by telephone periodically, and she tells me that words I wrote and tapes made several years ago are now having an effect on people who speak Farsi. The oneness of it all again hit me dramatically. Then a beautiful letter arrived demonstrating anew the universality of us as human beings. Listen to Mariam as she writes from the other part of our circle, and realize how impossible it is to choose up sides on a circle.

Wayne

It was November 20, two weeks ago. I was a little tired of working for one week and wanted to rest.

My mom: 'Get ready, the guests are coming.'

'Oh, I'm tired. Tell them that I'm not at home.'

'No, this time is different. Get ready as soon as possible.'

I didn't know what was going on. The bell rang. I opened the door. My niece came. In her hand, I couldn't believe it. My package. Oh, how long I had been waiting for it.

'Aunt Mariam, this is for you.'

My brother had got the package and didn't tell me anything about it. I kissed the box lots of times. After a while my sisters, our friends, relatives came. 'What's the matter tonight?' I asked.

They wanted to take part in this celebration. My mom had invited them. There were about thirty people at this party. I told my sister, 'Oh, Layla, what did I tell you on Tuesday?' On Tuesday evening my sister and I had gone to buy some meat and milk. One can hardly get meat and milk at 7:00 P.M. but we had to. On our way I thought with myself, 'Oh, if we will get meat, it means that I will get my package. But if not, oh no.' This we call intention. I was afraid to intend but what about the risks that Wayne Dyer talks about in his books?

'You are very lucky. All our meat is finished, this is the last. Eight kilograms and four hundred grams, you are very lucky,' the man said. We wanted eight kilograms.

'Oh, Layla, I'll get my package, I'm sure.' When I told people that Dr. Dyer had sent me a video, everyone said, 'That time you were lucky to get your package. But this time you won't get it because they'll open it and won't give it to you.' Oh, Eykis must come here to make a list of worries such as if they arrest my son on the street and take him to the front, if today is our turn to be killed by Iraq bombs, or if I won't get my package!!

'Layla, I got it at last,' I told my sister and kissed the box.

'Open it,' people said.

'No, after eating cake,' I said ...

[Mariam describes her emotions after examining all the contents. She closes her letter with the following:]

'Listen, everybody, let's hear his voice. Okay? Suppose that he is here ...'

We listened to you on the tape: 'Either get out there and take charge of your life and be a responsible person and make things happen or be one more of the kids in the orphanage ... I have found that anything is now possible for me ... only because I believe I can do it. My work really reflects the notion that you become your expectations. Whatever you expect to become ...'

What a good night it was. I never forget it. It was two in the morning. 'OK, guys, go home. I have to wake at 5:30 A.M.'

'No,' they say, 'we haven't seen such a happy face, such a real, genuine laughter, such sparkling eyes for many years.'

My brother-in-law: 'I bet you don't sleep tonight and read the letter over and over and listen to the cassettes.'

Thank you for making some moments of my life, moments to remember. I enclose some pictures. Please send pictures as much as you can. The more the better. Is it the disease of more? Descartes, 'I think, therefore I am.' Mariam, 'I have a letter from Dr. Dyer, therefore I am!' Very grateful to you for sending me the book and also wish you Happy Holidays.

Love, Mariam

We can begin to fathom the potential magnificence of seeing the oneness of it all, without threatening our individuality. We can allow ourselves to feel genuinely connected, knowing that our thoughts, feelings, and behavior impact on everyone, even on those whom we have never seen. Each of us is a whole composed of an endless number of particles of life, and each of those life particles going inward continues ad infinitum. The reverse is true as well, when we shift from the microscopic point of view to the telescopic and see ourselves as part of one life-form in a larger and larger being which is oneness.

The great parable on this subject is *Gulliver's Travels*, wherein being a Lilliputian or a Brobdingnagian is a matter of perspective. Let's take another look at the entire business of oneness and how it applies to your individual body.

Getting a clear reference to the whole

If I turn my metaphorical microscope inward and look at a single cell within the totality that is me, I will find many many cell components, with fancy names like nuclei, mitochondria, DNA, RNA, centrioles, basal bodies, and the like. One single cell is a whole, a totality unto itself, and carries within it all that is required to reproduce the entire organism called me. One of your cells carries all of you. Assuming we have six billion cells, theoretically, any of those cells has within itself the capability of cloning another whole person. There is also, however, something else that makes up a cell, something that defies physical explanation and requires going beyond the physical to the metaphysical. Something that holds that entire cell together. That something we describe as the source, or as serenity, harmony, peace, or ease, or as my personal favourite, love.

Pierre Teilhard de Chardin put it this way: 'Love is the affinity which links and draws together the elements of the world . . . Love, in fact, is the agent of universal synthesis.' Love or harmony is that immeasurable, invisible ingredient that synthesizes and creates the form which we call our bodies and our physical world.

When a cell does not have internal harmony or ease, even though all of the inner parts are there in the proper proportions, that particular cell will behave in a nonharmonious way and affect the entire whole that contains it. Thus a cell with an absence of ease, a *dis*eased cell, is lacking a reference to the whole, including itself. A dis-eased cell lacks internal ease or harmony or love, or whatever we choose to call it. That cell has absolutely no reference to the whole, to the individual person. Consequently, it destroys everything in its way by refusing to cooperate with the adjacent cell, until it destroys the whole, and as a result it destroys itself.

What I have just described is the working of a cancer within a body. It is an organism with no reference to the whole, which does not cooperate with the other cells, and ultimately kills the whole and itself in the process. Because it lacks that reference to the whole, it puts itself on a path toward its own destruction.

Now shift your consciousness with me to the telescope and begin to look outward from that cell, and imagine the self as one single cell, among six billion cells in a larger body that we call humanity. The totality that you are is very similar to the workings of a cell. You have many component parts, and something mysterious and invisible that holds you together – the same thing that Teilhard described. Love is your universal synthesizer, if you are the universe. When you, as one cell, are composed of something other than that ease or harmony within, you are diseased, and you will react to the cells adjacent to you in the way that a cancer cell acts towards its neighbours. You will not cooperate; instead you will attempt to gobble up, or aggressively destroy, or insidiously judge your neighbouring cells. Thus a cancer in society is almost identical to a cancer in your body.

When an individual acts destructively toward another person it is because he has no reference to the whole. Without that feeling or belonging to the whole, he will act aggressively toward others and in the process end up destroying the self as well. We begin to see how a lack of affinity for the total unit or a lack of thinking in terms of oneness can produce a cancer in a cell, and in society as well.

Now let's turn the telescope up to a stronger focus. Think of the entire planet which we live on as one cell. I have never read a better description than Lewis Thomas's in *The Lives of a Cell*:

I have been trying to think of the Earth as a kind of organism, but it is no go. I cannot think of it this way. It is too big, too complex, with too many working parts lacking *visible* connections. The other night, driving through a hilly wooded part of southern New England, I wondered about this. If not like an organism, what is it most like? Then, satisfactorily for that moment, it came to me: It is most like a single cell ... Viewed from the distance of the moon, the astonishing thing about the Earth, catching the breath, is that it is alive. The photographs show the dry, pounded surface of the moon in the foreground, dead as an old bone. Aloft, floating free beneath the moist, gleaming membrane of bright sky, is the rising earth, the only exuberant thing in this part of the cosmos. If you could look long enough, you would see the swirling of the great drifts of white cloud, covering and uncovering the half-hidden masses of land. If you had been looking for a very long geologic time, you could have seen the continents themselves in motion, drifting apart on their crustal plates, held afloat by the fire beneath. It has the organized, self-contained look of a live creature, full of information, marvelously skilled in handling the sun.

How about that? The entire planet as a cell? And why not, when you shift your perspective to the enormousness of this entire onesong? All of the characteristics of a single cell, just like the cell that you are, and that cell inside the tip of your nose, and the cell within that cell in the tip of your nose, and inward, and outward to infinity. It is all one.

And what of the cancerous or disharmonious cell on our planet? Take a look at what we call the nuclear age. What have we done to our planet? Have we not in fact created weapons that have no reference to the whole, to our one cell called Earth? Isn't it working just like a diseased cell, gobbling up everything in its wake and ultimately destroying the whole and itself in the process? Should we ever explode one of those devices in aggressive warfare toward any of our brothers, wouldn't we in fact be destroying not only our neighbouring cells but ourselves and our planet as well? Without a reference to the whole, a sense of the oneness of it all, we can only act like a dis-eased cell. And what is a dis-eased cell but one that lacks internal harmony, serenity, or as Teilhard called it, love? The way to oneness seems to be through the path of inner harmony. The way to inner harmony is through thought. And what kind of thought? The thoughts of oneness and unity. The thoughts that all of us are connected. Though the bonds may not be visible to the naked eye, they are still there, just as they are within each individual cell in your own body.

Whenever you fail to see yourself as a part of this entire whole, related to all of us in this being that we call Human Being, then you lack inner harmony and became dis-eased. That dis-ease will manifest itself in aggressive, nonloving, and uncooperative behaviour toward your neighbouring cells. Thus, the problems of a lack of oneness in our world can really be traced to the individual cells that compose this body we call humanity. As we work at eliminating cancer in our bodies by teaching a sense of oneness and harmony and positive visualization, we also can help to eliminate the carcinogens in our society the same way. Each of us as a single cell has the opportunity to affect the entire being in either a harmonious and loving way, or in a dis-orderly and dis-eased way.

Up until now, the history of the Human Being has been one of far too many cancerous cells, and too few cells filled with harmony and ease. The body is wavering, and each of us must do what he or she can to make the shift toward higher consciousness and harmony reign supreme and make the onesong harmonize. This is not a job for others, it is for each of us to be involved and help the entire body heal and stay well. The Human Being has too long been divided, and it is our ultimate challenge to get a reference to the whole, to see ourselves as one, and stay a single cell within a larger cell that is working harmoniously.

It becomes clear, then, with this new perspective, that anyone who is acting in a destructive or aggressive way toward anyone else is actually a person who lacks inner harmony. We should examine all of our aggressive hateful behaviour toward others as a problem not with our neighbours, but with what we are sending out to those neighbours. Within this context, it is constructive to take a look at how we treat those cells adjacent to us who look a little different from us, or who speak a different language, or worship uniquely. We have created a large cell that is composed of many diseased cells, and we all know that the whole cannot long survive when it is made up of cells which are dis-eased. This was Einstein's warning to all of us when he reacted to the splitting of the atom by telling us that we were now on an unparalleled course toward ultimate disaster unless we could learn a new way of thinking, an alternative to solving our disputes through aggression and war.

A very brief look at the history of the human being

Ours is largely a story of division rather than unity. Study any book which chronicles the history of the Human Being, and we see one long story about how divided we are as a species. The most startling thing about our history is that we have always been at war with one another. We can measure our advancement in the sophistication of the devices we have created over the centuries for the purpose of killing off our brothers. We have evolved from simple weapons of destruction such as crudely fashioned knives and tomahawks to guns which can get the job done from a distance, to automatic machines which can kill many of our brothers at once. Now we have the twentieth-century term 'megadeaths' to describe the lethal capacity of our weaponry.

Reconsider the analogy of our own body and the billions of cells which constitute its physical totality. If we project that this one body was able to live for fifty thousand years, we would see that that entire period of time was devoted to creating microbes and bacteria within the body for the purpose of destroying the body quicker and more economically. We would see that we had now killed off the pancreas, the liver, the arteries, removed a few limbs, and were ready to have all of the component parts fighting each other in such a way as to complete the destruction of the entire body. And we have now created the ultimate cancer, a means of destruction which, if ever used, will destroy the entire whole once and for all.

The history of this being is also one of emphasizing our differences and divisions. Look at our history books, and see how we as a total being have behaved. The East against the West. The dark against the light. The old against the young. The Germans against the French. The civilized against the savage. Endless chronicles of dichotomies, of peoples figuring out ways to conquer one another, to outdo one another, to defeat one another. It is analogous to all of the life forms in your body choosing up sides based upon physical appearances. The liver cells against the whites of your eyes. The larger cells of your skin against the tiny cells within your blood. The liquid cells against those in the heel of the foot. The longer cells in the intestines versus the shorter cells in the eardrums. Division, division, division, until at last one group wins and kills off the entire body. You know how absurd it would be for you to try to live with this disharmony going on within you. You know without even having to think about it that all of the component parts that constitute you must work in cooperation and with a reference to the whole that is you if you are to survive for ninety or so years.

Well, the being that is our Human Being simply has a longer life span because it is so much bigger (a question of perspective), and consequently you must take a look at how the individual beings within this Human Being have been behaving, and then ask how it is possible for the being to survive with all of this division. The answer is that we either help to change the behavior and attitude of the beings that make up the Human Being, or it will destroy itself. Listen to Paramahansa Yogananda writing in *The Divine Romance*:

I believe there will always be wars, until perchance we all become so spiritual that by the evolution of our individual natures we will make war unnecessary. No matter what their differences, if great minds such as Jesus, Krishna, Buddha, Mohammed, sat together, they would never use the engines of science to try to destroy each other. Why must people feel it necessary to fight? The power of guns evokes no wisdom, nor has it ever accomplished lasting peace.

Our history is replete with references to how we have divided ourselves and brought the entire human race to the brink of destruction as a result of our emphasis on enemies rather than allies in this miracle of life. Some of the greatest minds who have been among us know that oneness is more than idle thoughts of philosophers and metaphysicians, that it is the very essence of our reality.

In the oneness that is humanity we have practiced division to the detriment of the entire whole. Yes, we have had some shining lights who have attempted to help us see the folly of our ways, but essentially we have not been able to transcend our physical forms and see that our humanity is in our thinking, and that the totality of our thinking has always been that of divisiveness and separateness. There is much for you, as both one single cell in this body called humanity and as a functioning whole composed of a multitude of individual cells, in the application of this principle of oneness to your own personal world. One of the best places for you to begin to put this principle to work is in how you function in relationship to all of the other humans within the onesong. You can be either an instrument of cohesion and leadership, or one of the beings that unconsciously brings your unit down.

Cultivating a reference to the whole

Not long ago as I was running through the neighbourhood, I noticed a tree-trimming service at work on a neighbour's lawn. Since I had a large overgrown tree in front of my house, I stopped to ask the worker if he could give me some information so that I might use the trimming service. His response gave me a great deal of information about how he sees himself, both within his company and within his world: 'Look, mister, I can't stand here and talk, my job is to get the trees trimmed. I don't know a damn thing about the front-office end of this business.' He proceeded to turn up the volume on his chain saw and dismiss me entirely. He was so preoccupied with his own little compartmented responsibilities that he failed to see how his actions affected the whole business, and that if he displayed that attitude on a regular basis, he would be alienating himself from the whole and contributing to its downfall, and therefore his own downfall as well. It is akin to a waiter in a restaurant responding to a diner's request for the time by saying, 'Sorry, that's not my table.'

In the world of business, two attributes stand out clearly in distinguishing leaders from followers:

1 *All effective leaders have a reference to the whole.* In any given day I could count hundreds of examples of people I encounter who have no concept of the whole, who in fact act just like a single cancer cell in the totality that is their business enterprise. 'It's not my department – you'll have to talk to accounting.' 'I'm only doing what I'm paid to do.' 'I'm sorry, that's someone else's responsibility.' 'I can't take responsibility for how others do their job, I can only do one thing at a time.' Your hear it from a teller at a bank, a cashier, a telephone operator at a large

department store, a clerk at the driver licensing bureau, and so on and on. No reference to the whole. No sense of belonging to the entire unit, no understanding that one must cooperate with those adjacent to us in order for the unit to survive. All on a self-destructive trip each day in their contacts with the public they are being paid to serve, breaking down the effectiveness of the entire unit because they see only the very narrow, it's-not-my-department picture. A leader always sees the whole and knows that each individual impacts on everyone.

2 *All effective leaders have a reference to the larger whole.* Yes, I said the 'larger' whole. Keeping in mind that time is not a construct for those who are truly transformed, we then have to look at our business enterprise as a totality outside of time, measured by the instruments we have devised to keep track of the whole. Thus, we see that true leaders understand in their hearts that a customer alienated today by an employee is also someone who is impacting on the business days, weeks, and years down the road. The leader is in this endeavour for the long haul and knows that a mistreated customer will affect the whole not only today, but forever. In addition, that dissatisfied customer will tell ten other people about his experience and they will impact on the whole down the road as well. Thus, the effective leader knows that every single contact between any employee and a customer is a total moment of truth. The big picture is now and forever, the whole now and the grander whole of all time. The typical follower employee is unconcerned about whether you ever return. His attitude says, 'I only care about getting this over with and getting home, and having my paycheque arrive on time.' He does not have it in his consciousness to care that that customer will inevitably select a competitor next time, and will do so for a long period of time, because of the surly treatment by the employee with narrow vision. Those employees with no reference to the larger whole are sabotaging the entire unit

in the same way that a diseased call gobbles up everything in its wake.

If your job involves business recruiting, I suggest that you look for these variables in your future employees. If they view themselves as belonging to the whole and are aware of how their individual pieces of behaviour impact powerfully on the whole, you have a potential leader. A leader is alert to how every single piece of human behaviour affects the whole, and knows that the whole cannot survive with cancerous cells doing the work. The effective leader knows that future business is determined by how each customer is treated in that specific moment of truth when contact is first made. When I encounter a person who has no reference to the whole, I sense that that particular business or unit its in serious jeopardy. The clerk who lets me know that I am important and is willing to do whatever it takes to produce results is the employee who makes me want to return to that business. That clerk is one of the harmonious cells that will make the entire body function effectively today and in the future as well.

Within the confines of our own family unit we need each member to be a single individual, functioning alone, and at the same time working in harmony with all who share the same unit or household. This can be said of communities, cities, states, countries, and yes, even the biggest whole of all, humanity.

When we encompass this concept of oneness and apply it in our daily life, we begin to feel a sense of being a part of the human race rather than of fighting it. We begin to sense that we are all truly in this together and that each and every individual piece of behaviour impacts in some way on this body or being called Human Being.

In the panoramic picture, oneness becomes abundantly clear. Truly great world leaders know that we cannot stay divided and survive. They know that all of the divisions of mankind, whatever those divisions may focus upon, contribute in some way to the destruction of the whole of humanity. Sadly, it is quite difficult for people who think this way to get elected. Voters are predisposed to vote for those who favour their particular divisions, and not leaders who are working toward a harmonious objective for all mankind. A Jesus Christ could hardly have been elected in his time, nor could a Mother Teresa today. Yet still we have seen some leaders emerge who understand the totality of mankind. Certainly the United Nations is one small step forward using cooperation rather than aggression to solve the disputes that arise over the borders and divisions we have created in our attempts to carve up our onesong. An Abraham Lincoln surfaced when unity was called for in the previous century. Perhaps there will be another Lincoln in this next century to assist humanity toward harmony.

From the smallest individual cell, up through you as one cell, and outward to all of the units that we see emerging within our social structures, to our largest units which we call countries, and outward even farther to the entire universe, the message is the same. When we sense the oneness in all of this, and we behave as individuals with the highest regard for that totality, we allow the whole to survive and flourish. When we act without respect for the totality, we contribute to the downfall of the whole, and to our own destruction in the process.

Seeing the oneness is not simply a metaphysical exercise; it is a way of being that transforms life. When we have harmony within, it becomes automatic to see it in the larger context of how we relate outwardly. We will give away only what we have. When we see it within and vow to have it there, then we will be one more cell seeking oneness, and keeping the self flourishing as well.

Oneness and the dream

I would like to go back to the perspective of your dreaming body to remind you that while you are dreaming you are in a world of pure thought in which you create everything

you need for your dream. You do not need your senses
to see, hear, smell, touch, or taste. Everything that you
experience while you dream is reacted to by your body.
The characters that are a part of the dream are simply
illusions; they are your creations to act out your dream.

All of which leads to the biggest lesson of all, and the
most difficult to grasp while you are in form.

There is only one dream! Read that again. There is only
one dream. Granted, there may be a thousand characters
in a dream. The dreamer creates many different life
situations that have nothing to do with time. There may
be automobiles, airplanes, boats, knives, bombs, beds, or
anything that the dreamer wants, but there is only one
dreamer and one dream, and that is *you*. In the state that
we call dreaming consciousness, there is only one dreamer
and one dream.

Now for the hard part. In Chapter 2 I described three
dimensions of consciousness, which I called dreaming
consciousness, waking consciousness, and higher-level
consciousness. Masters of the higher-level consciousness
state have disguised themselves as ordinary people and
have walked among us letting us know that what we
experience in dreaming consciousness is also possible for
us in waking consciousness. Jesus told us that even the least
among us could do all that he had done, and even greater
things. Imagine a truly higher level of consciousness in
which all form is an illusion, as it is in your dream. In
this scenario too there can be only one dream. Yes, waking
consciousness can be seen as one big dream, taken from
the perspective of a level of consciousness higher than this
one, if you perceive yourself as one of the characters in
this larger-than-life dream.

Who is the ultimate dreamer? Call it as you will: God,
higher consciousness, Krishna, spirit, whatever pleases
you. But try to let this possibility in. From the perspective
of the next dimension, one level of consciousness is all that
there is, and all of us are characters in that dream. Our

form is as real to us as it is to the characters we create in our dreams, but from an expanded awareness we can see that they are all illusions in our one dream.

One dream, one dreamer, billions of embodied characters acting out that one dream, and the disembodied spirit leaving the waking-consciousness level and the illusions of suffering that form is subject to. Your true essence is that you are part and parcel of the one big dream.

Now from this perspective, try to view your own death. In the waking-consciousness level of existence, we view death as something fearful and the ultimate in suffering. In fact it is quite the opposite. You cannot suffer in the astral or thought plane. Suffering is played out in form. The pain that we experience, the aging process, the various diseases, the cuts and bruises, and the relationship difficulties are all sufferings that we experience within form. With the death of form, suffering is no longer possible.

With this understanding I am unable to make death the great melodrama that most people do. I truly see it as a reward rather than a punishment. I know that transcending my form means an end to suffering, and also that I am capable of doing just that while I am in form if I live in the consciousness dimension where there are no limits. Viewing the entire next dimension of higher consciousness as one dream, and one dreamer, with many characters in the level beneath that, helps us to recognize death as transformation rather than punishment and to see the great oneness that is our onesong.

This is the quintessential message that is available from all of the spiritual masters. The way to glimpse it is through the mystical world that you are able to create for yourself and live out in your dreaming body. You, the dreamer ... God, the dreamer. You create all the characters and situations that you require. God does the same. Your characters are real for you while you are in your dream. So too are God's characters real. In fact, you are one of them. All form is nothing but an illusion in your dream, though the reactions are very real. In God's dream, the characters are illusions also, though His dream lasts ninety years and ours ninety minutes, and the reactions of thought are real. When you wake from your dream you look back at the folly of being upset over the illusions, and you get on with the next level of living. When you wake up in God's dream and look back you see the folly of holding on to the illusions, and you get on with the next level. You see from a new perspective a grander wider-lensed view which encompasses it all.

There is only one dream and one dreamer. How you live out your one dream character role is entirely up to you, as a character in the dream and as a dreamer. It is a monumental paradox, one that once accepted allows us to see with new eyes. However, it is no more of a paradox than the fact that we contain billions of cells, and that we are also encompassed in any one of those cells at the same time. I assure you that when you truly know that there is only one dream and that you are connected to everyone in that dream, you begin to think and act as if you are connected to it all, rather than attached to your separateness. This can provide an eternal access to happiness and success. You will feel unthreatened by anyone or anything forever after.

Ask yourself the question 'What happens to the characters in my dream when I awaken?' Now try to see that it is not a place at all, but a new dimension. They are not waiting in a room; they have demonstrated their multidimensionality. You too can enter this ever-formless dimension at will.

Why you may resist the principle of oneness

• This is an easy principle to spend an entire lifetime resisting. Why? Because we have been taught that separateness is the essence of our humanity. We believe in boundaries, limits, labels, and traditions. We have learned to look at 'others' as distinct from us, and, in many cases, to regard literally half of humanity as our enemies. We have been raised to treasure our ethnicity, and to regard anyone different as 'not of our clan.' Our labels have become our self-definition. What happens over a lifetime of this conditioning is that we identify ourselves as French, male, female, Protestant, tall, dark, conservative, athletic, middle-class, and on and on. These are all labels that separate and classify us, making it difficult to think of the onesong and to become enlightened.

• Oneness is an admittedly abstract and therefore difficult concept to grasp and then live out. To truly believe and see this principle in action requires a view of the physical world from a grander perspective than we can conceive even with our imagination running at full throttle. We must be able to suspend our narrow view, and this is not an easy thing in a world which requires living within the confines of narrow physical boundaries. To get a big picture requires suspending our conditioned way of thinking. It would be similar to asking a cell within the liver, which has only seen the liver environment, to abandon the belief that the liver is all that there is and see itself as a part of an entire human body it does not know exists. All it knows is liver. All it has ever seen or experienced is liver. Yet it is expected to see how it functions in conjunction with a whole that can only be speculated about. This is where you are, with one exception – you have a mind that is capable of perceiving how the whole thing fits together. You are part of that universal mind. Even so, it is a monumental task to imagine how it all works while you are in physical form, and in the boundaries inherent in the world of form.

• It is easier to choose the world of boundaries. Even though we can understand the metaphor using our own body as a whole, it is difficult to make the shift from the microscope to the telescope. We are inclined to take the narrower road, and to defend the boundaries and limits. It is easier, though far less rewarding, to live in a world where the lines are all drawn, often by people who lived thousands of years ago. Where and how to worship is mandated by birth, and it seems easier to follow that path. It is easier to go along believing our enemies are who we have been taught they are, rather than to resist the vision that creates enemies in the first place. It may seem easier to continue a family business or tradition that contributed to disorder than to incur the wrath of the others who have gone along. It is simply easier to be a cell that lives its life out that way, ignoring the long run and the overall picture.

● Defending our separateness gives us a tremendous opportunity to practice blame as a way of life. When you believe in and live oneness, blame literally becomes impossible, for we are all connected, and therefore life energy is directed to finding solutions for the good of the self *and* the whole. When separateness is the goal, we tend to view others as responsible for whatever is lacking in our life. 'They' are easy targets for blame. You may not be willing to give up this business of blaming 'them,' particularly those who reside in a completely different chorus of the onesong, whom you will likely never see in person, and who look so different from you. It is up to you to decide if it feels more convenient for you to have enemies and people to hate and blame than to feel that we are all one. As long as we need others to take the rap for the problems in our lives, we will find this notion of oneness easy to resist.

● Those who personally profit from separation will find it easy to deride the concept of oneness. Anyone in the business of manufacturing or marketing weapons designed to kill our brothers and sisters will scoff at this 'nonsense' of unity and oneness. Anyone needing to hold on to traditional ways of living and being that separate us into superior or inferior categories will resist what I am saying in this chapter. Your business or religion or any enterprise you are involved in which is designed to remind you to judge others will find unity a discomfiting notion indeed. In truth, anyone who spends life energy on the side of disorder, even in a small way, finds unity a troublesome notion.

A simple review of history gives us the clues. Many leaders who believed in and preached the notion of man as one have been assassinated. Those who strive to eliminate war are often derided as silly idealists. Those who write songs asking us to *imagine* that the world could be as one are somehow destroyed for their efforts. It is convenient to forget the whole in the name of profiteering. It is threatening to many who want to promulgate separateness.

These are a few of the reasons that we resist this universal principle. Yet our very survival and evolution as a species are dependent upon enough of us shifting to the idea of unity. I am convinced that this will, in fact, happen. As surely as the universe is a onesong will mankind ultimately hear the message of the need for unity. It is coming closer each and every day. Below are a few suggestions to speed up your own transform-ation to this wondrous principle of oneness.

Some suggestions for applying the universal principle of oneness in your own life

• Suspend your thoughts of separateness for one hour today. During that hour, regard everyone that you meet as connected to you in an invisible way. You will find that once you start to think in unity ways it becomes much more difficult to be angry or spiteful toward others, because it is like behaving that way toward yourself. See yourself as connected, as sharing something with every-one you meet, or even hear about. What you share with everyone else is your humanity, and the less you are inclined to separate yourself from others, the less you are inclined to experience the dis-ease that flows from separateness.

● Examine the labels that you apply to yourself. Every single label is a boundary or a limit of one kind or another. If you are of English or African origin and you apply this label to yourself, you have placed a limit which does not allow you to experience anything which is non-English or non-African. View yourself as human. No labels necessary. Thoughts cannot be broken up into neat little compartments. You are not old or young in thought, only in how you label yourself in form. So too for political ideology, and physical attributes. In thought you can be anything and everything. Keep reminding yourself that only the tiniest aspect of you is form, that form is only the packaging that embodies the real you. Attempt to think globally and act locally. See yourself as one cell among billions of cells in the one large cell called humanity. When you see yourself as connected rather than separate, you automatically begin to cooperate. This is what the healing process is all about.

When I was a young teenager and a girl told me that she loved me, I asked her what she really meant by that. I said, 'Supposing I suddenly turned into a frail, wrinkled-up, ninety-nine-year-old man – would you love me then?' She was perplexed, but she answered, 'No, that wouldn't be you.' I can remember telling her, 'I am not this body, and if that is what you love, you don't really love me. I am that ninety-nine-year-old man too.' Mostly when we love something or someone we refer only to form, neglecting what is inside. Recognize labels as part of the outer life of form. Decide to pursue your inner life also.

● Realize that the journey and the goal are the same. You are never going to be formed. You will never reach an ultimate goal. Life is transition and growth. Paradoxically, you can realize all of your goals in this perspective of oneness. Every step along the path, every day of your life, is both a singular experience and a part of the whole called life. There are no ordinary moments. This one moment that you are alive right now is a totality and not something separate from your entire life. Keep in mind the old saying 'Life is what happens to you while you are making other plans.' This helps focus the oneness of everything and keep you focused there, instead of on the artificial ways in which we have carved up the one.

• The members of your immediate family are a daily reminder of the humanity you share with them. You are all a part of this great body referred to as mankind. Whenever you find yourself striking out verbally toward those you love, use that moment to visualize them sharing the same life energy that you do. Our uncontrollable anger toward others is propelled by a denial or a fear that we are the way we are judging the other to be. We can only give away what we have inside. If you have regard for yourself, that is what you will give to those whom you love. If you have self-contempt, it will be reflected in how you treat those closest to you. When I find myself having difficulty with something my children are saying or doing, I try to imagine the invisible force connecting me to them within humanity. I see that their behaviour is mine and vice versa, and I am able to be more understanding and loving toward them.

• Consider those whom you regard as enemies. The same logic and reasoning applies to them. This is the lesson of spirituality. Because human beings look different or live in a different part of the world, or think in different ways, does not mean that they are not part of the whole, part of the humanity that is you. Do not let anyone else, or the trivial factor of geographical placement, determine for you that you are going to have enemies. You do not have to buy into any reasoning which demands you think in terms of

113

enemies. This does not make you an unpatriotic person. You can love your country enough to want it to survive for our children to live in peacefully. This means doing everything within your power to make sure that we all see oneness. Know that one cannot choose up sides on a round planet. It is a question of perspective, and you have the tools available to you to grasp the infinite view – the oneness view.

• If you are in a position of leadership within an organization, create options for the individuals who work with you to feel a sense of reference to or belonging to the whole. Celebrate each individual's contribution to and participation in the well-being of the entire organization with enticements such as profit-sharing, recognition of the leadership, and pay incentives. Do not compartmentalize and specialize so much within your organization that individual members are excluded from contributing to the larger vision. Be attentive to how each person can contribute to the whole, and gear your training programs toward an understanding of the overall impact of pieces of behaviour. At the same time, support individualism and individual choice-making. Each cell within any unit must have a degree of autonomy in order to feel important as an individual. One cell gone awry contributes to the downfall of all. One cell that has harmony within contributes to the health of the entire unit. Individualism and a sense of wholeness only appear to be mutually exclusive. Living with this paradox and understanding that two seeming opposites always function within a harmonious whole is integral to enlightenment.

• Make every effort to send love out in response to hate. This was the message of Christ. If you have love within, it is what you will have to give away. All hatreds, even our seemingly justified hatred in reaction to aggression, is a part of the cancer that destroys humanity. The more we send out harmony and love to others, regardless of their behaviour, the more we are living in oneness. Certainly we need jails and other means of protection from those who transgress toward others. What we do not need is hatred as our response to their antisocial behaviour.

• Try viewing everyone who comes into your life as a teacher. See every other person as the part of you that is ready to grow. In relationships, it is not an accident that sustaining partnerships are combinations of opposites. We often love someone who represents an undeveloped part of ourselves. Instead of judging others as people who should or should not be behaving in certain ways, see them as reflecting a part of you and ask yourself what it is you are ready to learn from them. Love the seemingly opposites in your world, treasure their way of being as a gift to you. And remember, those who seem to cause you the most anguish are those who remind you of what you feel is either lacking or wanting in yourself. If you did not react at all, it would mean that you were totally indifferent. The fact that you do react, while preferring indifference, means there is something inside you that gets hooked when you encounter that provocative behaviour. It is your learning situation, not their problem. The entire planet is a collection of differences, living at once in form and nonform. Forget wanting others to be like you, and start relishing their uniqueness as the variety that makes up this glorious onesong.

No one can tell you 'how to' become more connected and less attached. You control your thoughts. I can simply help you to initiate your capacity for thinking in terms of oneness. Perhaps I can help you to open a few doors that are closed because of the conditioning processes, but only you can make the decision. But once you decide to process your role in this thing called onesong, no one can make you stop. It is your path that you are taking, and you can traverse it in any manner that you choose.

What you can ultimately expect from adopting the principle of oneness is a new sense of personal harmony that removes most conflict from your life. A glorious payoff indeed. You cease questioning your role in anything and instead radiate outward to the oneness of all life. You become part of the energy of love, first in your inner life, then in your outer life in family and personal relationships, on to business and community, and ultimately to all of humanity. You develop a sense of appreciation for all aliveness. You no longer identify with difference and know that differences are only in form.

Three words can symbolize our invisible connection to one another. They are 'alone' and 'all one.' The only thing that separates them is one letter, the letter *l*, which I think of as standing for love. 'All one' and 'alone' are identical concepts. Within every cell in the universe there is a sense of aloneness, as well as a sense of all-oneness, existing simultaneously. When Paramahansa Yogananda was receiving his training in the way of the spiritual masters, he was told:

It is the Spirit of God that actively sustains every form and force in the universe; yet he is transcendental and aloof in the blissful uncreated void beyond the worlds of vibratory phenomena ... Those who attain Self-realization on earth live in a similar twofold existence. Conscientiously performing their work in the world, they are yet immersed in an inward beatitude.

I wish for you to have that twofold experience as you learn of your connection and participation in the oneness: performing in form, and inner grace. Truly you are alone and all one, all at the same time.

4
Abundance

*It is a simple procedure to calculate the number
of seeds in an apple. but who among us can EVER say
how many apples are in a seed?*

The reason that no one can say how many apples are in
a seed is that the answer is infinite. Endless! That is what
the abundance principle is all about: endlessness.

It seems a paradox, because we as human forms seem
to begin and end at a specified time, and so endlessness
is not a part of our experience in form. But it is difficult
to imagine that the universe has any boundaries, or that it
simply ends someplace. If it does, what's at the end, and
what's on the other side of what's at the end? And so I
suggest there is no end to the universe, and there is no
end to what you can have for yourself when this principle
is part of your life.

We have already seen that a large part of who we are
as human beings is formless, that this part – thought – is
without boundaries. And I conclude from this that we are
therefore endless as well.

Consequently, abundance, with its absence of limits
and boundaries, is the very watchword of the universe.
It applies to us as much as it does to everything else in
the onesong. It is the universe's response to our belief in
scarcity. We should be conscious of abundance and prosperity and not make scarcity the cornerstone of our lives.

If we have a scarcity mentality, it means that we believe
in scarcity, that we evaluate our life in terms of its lacks.
If we dwell on scarcity we are putting energy into what we
do not have, and this continues to be our experience of
life. The theme of so many people's life story is 'I simply

117

do not have enough,' or 'How can I believe in abundance when my children don't have all of the clothes that they need?' or 'I would be a lot happier if I had—.' People believe they live a life of lack because they are unlucky, instead of recognizing that their belief system is rooted in scarcity thinking. Yet as long as they live with a scarcity mentality, that is what they will attract to their lives.

Everything that it would take to eliminate this life situation is already here in the world that we live and breathe in every single day. Where else could it be? The truth is that there *is* enough to go around, there is an endless universe for us to work in, and we are a part of that endless universe. Once we truly know this, we will see it working for us in thousands of ways. Everyone that I have ever met who moved from a life of scarcity into a life of abundance has discovered how to believe and live this principle. I mean *every single person*, including myself. But how do we get rid of a scarcity mentality.

Transcending a scarcity consciousness

The first step toward discarding a scarcity mentality involves giving thanks for everything that you are and everything that you have. That's right – give thanks, but not in some meaningless charade. Truly appreciate the miracle that you are. The fact that you are alive. That you have eyes, ears, feet, and that you are here right now in this marvelous dream. Make an effort to begin focusing on what you have, rather than on what you are missing.

Nothing is missing. How could anything be missing in a perfect universe? When you begin to focus on being thankful for all that you have – the water you drink, the sun that warms you, the air you breathe, and everything that is a gift from God – you will be using your thoughts (your entire essence) to dwell on abundance and your humanity.

Keep in mind that you are one cell in a body of humanity,

and that cell requires harmony within in order to cooperate with the adjacent cells. As you do this, your energy will shift to the miracle of your being here. While you are focused on the miracle that you are and all that surrounds you, you cannot be focused on what you are not, and what seems missing from your world.

As you practice being thankful, expand the list of things that you are thankful for. Friends and family. Clothes and food. Any money that you have. All of your possessions, every single thing that has come into your life for you to use while you are here. I mean every single thing. The pencil, the fork, the chair, everything. Begin to focus on how thankful you are to have these things in your life now, when you need them. Think of them as yours to use temporarily before sending them back into circulation.

Once you have trained yourself to begin the process of being thankful for everyone and everything that comes your way, as well as being appreciative of your very humanity, you are on your way toward eliminating a scarcity mentality.

Whatever you focus your thoughts on expands

Read it again. It really is quite logical. Whatever you tend to think about is what you will focus on, and create more of. For example, if you have some debts and some principal, and your entire focus is on what you have, then you will expand your principal. If your principal is only five hundred dollars and your debts are five thousand, and you focus on the money that you have, you will begin to do something with it. Whatever you do with it in a positive way will help it to expand. Conversely, if you focus all of your thoughts on your indebtedness, always reminding yourself how poor you are, and making that the locus of your emotional life, that is precisely what you will expand. This is very clear when it comes to minor illnesses. If you focus on your cold, always talking about it, always complaining to everyone you meet about how lousy you feel, you will expand what you focus on. That is, your energy will flow to the cold that you are so proud of. But if you focus on all of you that is not sick, and tell others how great you feel, you will expand wellness.

We act upon our thoughts. These thoughts literally become our daily life experience. Consequently, if you spend a great deal of your life energy focusing on scarcity, that is what you are going to expand in your life. I can give you a real-life example of how this works.

I have a dear friend name Bobbe Branch who lives in Wenatchee, Washington. She is a spectacularly alive, higher-consciousness person who is a true joy to be around. In virtually all areas of her life she has mastered the principles of abundance. Yet in the area of her career she continually focused on what was missing in her life. Bobbe is a very talented singer and songwriter and wanted to produce an album of her songs, but she was convinced she did not have the financial ability: she was operating from a scarcity mentality when it came to money. And this scarcity mentality took over when it came to her performing in front of an audience: she was sure she could not.

We talked for several hours one evening about her belief that she would never have an album unless some angel suddenly emerged to provide the funding. I tried to help her see that this belief was the very thing that was keeping her from actualizing her dream of recording her own songs.

I invited Bobbe to sing her beautiful music at some of my speaking engagements. In spite of her fears, she performed beautifully to standing ovations and began focusing on what she could do rather than what she felt was impossible or difficult. The more she thought about singing in front of an audience, the more that very thing expanded in her life, and after a year or so she was accepting singing engagements. Then came the big challenge for Bobbe: to view herself in a prosperity manner. In a phone conversation she told me that she had finally mustered the courage to inquire how much it would cost to produce an album using one of the finest arrangers and musical directors in the Northwest. The total was more money that she had ever accumulated in her life. I told her to begin focusing her thoughts on prosperity, and never allow a 'lack' thought into her consciousness.

She began to get the message. One evening I received a long-distance phone call from Wenatchee, and Bobbe announced, 'I've been thinking about nothing else but having that money at my disposal. I never let in a scarcity thought.' She then said that she and a friend at work were discussing ways to make it happen. Bobbe had said to her friend, 'What if I asked fifteen of the people I know to invest one thousand dollars in me and my music? I mean, people who really believe in my singing?' To her delighted astonishment her friend said, 'I would love to invest in you,' and Bobbe realized that she was already one-fifteenth of the way there.

In three days she had drawn up investment portfolios and signed up the necessary investors, all of whom invested one thousand dollars to be repaid within one year. She was ecstatic that she had finally overcome her belief in scarcity, for when she focused on abundance, that is precisely what expanded for her. Within two months she had produced her album, *Happiness is the Way*, with three songs on it that were conceived around Eykis, the lady about whom I have written a book.

Now Bobbe is busy promoting her music and happily working at making it a big hit. Focusing on abundance rather than scarcity is paying off handsomely for her. She has repaid almost all of her investors and is in a second run of the album. Her dedication on the album reads: 'To my friend Wayne Dyer; I appreciate all you have done to encourage me to dare to risk.' All I really ever did was help her focus on what she wanted to expand in her life.

The same is true for each of us. To experience anything

other than abundance in your life you actually have to deliberately resist if by focusing on scarcity!

When you live and breathe prosperity with a belief that everything is in huge supply, and that we are all entitled to have all that we can, you start actively treating yourself and others in this fashion. This principle applies to the acquisition of wealth, personal happiness, health, intellectual pursuits, and everything else. It relates to the ancient Biblical promise 'To him that hath, shall more be given.' It truly works. This universe is an incomprehensibly large enterprise, too big for any of us to begin to comprehend from the perspective of our limited bodies. Abundance reigns everywhere. The only limits we have are those that we encourage with our belief in those limits.

You are it all already

You are already whole, already complete. You are not going to *get* it all, you *are* it all already! Give this some serious personal consideration. If you are not enjoying your life right now, with what you have accumulated, with your current state of health, and in your present job and relationships, you will not appreciate and enjoy new or different life conditions. Our ability to enjoy life comes from how we choose to process life, rather than from externals. Nothing outside of ourselves has the power to bestow happiness or fulfillment on us. What determines the quality of our life is our choice to be fulfilled or not, based upon how we think, how we view ourselves and our place in the universe. Consequently, if you are a person who needs more in order to feel complete, then you will still feel incomplete when you have acquired more.

Thinking in terms of the abundance principle means believing an inner dialogue: 'I love who I am and what I have attracted to myself up until now. I do not need another thing or even one tiny change in order to be happy or complete. I know in my heart that I am not going to get it all, but that I truly am it all already. The universe is endless, I am the universe, and therefore I am without boundaries.'

Creating and believing your own affirmations demonstrates your readiness to tune in to abundance. There is the story of a man who went to a guru asking for the essentials he needed to have perfect happiness and success for the remainder of his life. The guru left him with nothing, implying that he already had everything that he needed. Happiness and success are inner processes that we bring to life undertakings, rather than something we get from 'out there.'

When we operate from the principle of scarcity, we generally believe, 'If only I had something else, *then* I would have a lock on happiness and success.' A close look at this logic shows that what we are really saying is: 'I am not complete right now. In some way I lack what I need. When I get that, then I will be complete.' If that is our belief, then we are relying on a disabled incomplete person. This kind of scarcity thinking assumes that we are not yet complete, happy, loving, total human beings, that we do not already have the missing pieces in abundance within ourselves. Thus we operate from a thinking process of deficiency, and end up trapped in the belief that 'I've got to have more before I can be happy.' This is the very thing that keeps us from tuning in to the abundance that is everywhere.

You are it all already. You already possess exactly what you need for happiness, success, fulfillment, and all of the lofty general goals that so many of us aspire to. If our basic needs are met, and we have food, water, and air, then we have within us the ability to be blissfully happy. As Gandhi said, 'God comes to the hungry in the form of food.'

We can value and celebrate the magnificent miracle that we are. We can process everything that comes our way without judgment. Our world is abundant and endless, and how we think about it is totally our choice. Even in a prison, our corner of freedom is still how we choose to think. No one can take that away. Ever! Once we know this, we can relate to abundance as the watchword of our entire existence.

Yes, indeed, you are it all. Everything that it takes to have abundance in your life, you already are. Tune your antenna in to making it all work for you.

You cannot own anything!

Abundance is not something that we acquire. It is something we tune into. This thought is paramount to making the abundance principle function in our lives. Keep in mind that there is an infinite supply of energy in the universe, and that everything, including your very form and all of your accumulations, is essentially energy. Everything vibrates. We call that vibration energy, and our universe is infinite in its supply of energy. This energy is what constitutes aliveness.

The energy that each of us emits is determined by our thoughts and how we choose to process our world. Process it through eyes that see only scarcity and that is what will expand. Process it through eyes that see unlimited abundance, and that is what expands. If we need to own things, like it or not, we are filtering our universe through scarcity eyes. Our needs to own and possess things is a reflection of our belief that we do not have enough. Our need to accumulate and own literally keeps us from tuning in to the abundance that is there right in front of our 'lack-filled eyes.'

All the things we think we absolutely must have in order to be happier are indications that we are controlled from without, rather than from within. This assumption leads to believing that we are incomplete and lacking somehow, and that we can complete that incompleteness by having more things. An endless trap! One that we can never escape as long as we think that ownership of something is going to fill the void.

How can you possibly own anything? Think for a moment about all of the possessions that you have in your dream – the cars, boats, money, toys, or whatever you possess while you are in your dreaming body. When you awaken, you immediately realize that all of those possessions were illusions, and you only needed that temporarily for the dream. Now try to put this whole thing into perspective in relationship to the dream that you are now in, which lasts eighty or ninety years. Imagine yourself awakening and being able to look back at all of your possessions. How could you ever have owned anything at all? The best, I mean the very best, that we can do is to have temporary possession or our toys for a tiny speck of time, and then, like it or not, we awaken and realize that they are of no use. Since the major part of our living is in the astral dimension of thought, things are of no use in this state of formlessness.

If we have a void it is because we are thinking nothing-ness thoughts, and that kind of thinking always broadens the emptiness. We can expand in a more satisfying way, by focusing on completeness, and realizing that we cannot own anything, ever. This does not preclude taking great pleasure in anything that we accumulate or take title to temporarily. But remember, just as nothing in our universe is ever formed, neither are we. Everything is always in a state of trans-formation, including the title that we hold to our property, all of our toys, our family, our money, every-thing. All in transition. All circulating, landing in our lap for us to enjoy momentarily and then get it recirculating. Once we internalize this notion of not being able to own anything, ironically it frees us to have anything that we choose, without being attached to owning or possessing it. We soon discover the joy of passing it along and sharing it.

The paradox is, of course, that when we stop chasing and accumulating, we find all that we ever wanted or needed is available. The fear of not having enough prevents many from seeing that they already are enough. We cannot own anything, and a lifetime spent believing in scarcity and lack is a violation of the universal principle of abundance.

A life of abundance does not mean a life of accumulating, but instead developing a spiritual sense of awe at the 'limitlessness' of it all. Take, for example, your very own body. It is a portrait of unlimited abundance, capable of extraordinary accomplishments, and restricted only by thoughts which focus on its limits. Your brain with its trillions of cells can direct your body to sleep or dance, to meditate or create, to build airplanes and submarines. You – yes, you and the body you inhabit – are an example of exquisite abundance and perfection. Its possibilities are indeed endless. Its existence as a self-sustaining entity is so much a miracle that it boggles our mind even to consider how it got here, and how it all stays alive, and thinks, and dreams, and so on through an endless catalogue of miracles.

You yourself are abundance in action. But the body that you call you cannot own anything or take anything with it when you leave it. That body functions by forces and energy that transcend accumulations. All of the 'stuff' of your life has arrived to serve you, rather than to make you a servant to the stuff. Try keeping this principle in mind as you read on. Everything that was 'owned' by someone only a few years ago is now serving someone else. The land that was thought to be owned is now serving others. The jewelry now adorns others. And so it goes in the entire spectrum of life. Nothing gets owned, and the sooner we realize this and stop trying to own things and people, the more we will be able to tune in to this wondrous principle of abundance.

The secret is to stop focusing on what we do not have, and shift our consciousness to an appreciation for all that we are and all that we do have. With this change in consciousness, service become a natural part of the abundant life. Gandhi said it beautifully:

Consciously or unconsciously, every one of us does render some
service or other. If we cultivate the habit of doing this service
deliberately, our desire for service will steadily grow stronger,
and will make not only for our own happiness, but that of the
world at large.

Or read Albert Schweitzer on the same subject.

I don't know what your destiny will be, but one thing I do know;
the only ones among you who will be truly happy will be those
who have sought and found how to serve.

These two men were saints among us in many respects,
and we cannot expect to emulate their total dedication to
the service of others. But there is much to learn from
studying their lives and even from reading these two brief
quotations. The meaning is in finding our true sense of
fulfillment beyond success and accumulations.

Tuning in to abundance

Abundance is not something that we manufacture, but
something that we accept and tune in to. If our mind
believes in scarcity, expecting only a small portion of
life's abundance, then that is what our life experience
will be. We receive that which we are willing to let in, and
what we block is not from unavailability but from scarcity
beliefs. When we conceptualize abundance and prosperity
as something we are deserving of, we notice a significant
shift occurring. First the thoughts about what we deserve
change, and then slowly our behaviour changes. Eventually
we know and believe that whatever it is we want is already
here, and our belief will cause it to manifest. Again and
again I say, we expand what we focus upon.

But how can *you* tune in to this abundance that constitutes the entire universe? By changing around your

perception of what is available for you and how you choose to recirculate that which flows into your life. Start by examining three questions:

1 *What do you think you are worth?* You are a divine creation in this endlessly perfect universe. You are it all. As Walt Whitman declared, 'The whole theory of the universe is directed unerringly to one single individual – namely to YOU.' This is not a selfish proclamation. It is perfectly sensible within Whitman's world-view. You are at once all of humanity *and* at the same time an individual human. You, like every other person in the whole of humanity, have complete and total perfect value. As part of that complete perfection, worth is measureless and abundant. How could anything be more perfect that a human being? How could anything have more value?

2 *What do you think you deserve?* If you feel that you deserve only a minimal share of happiness, then that is what you will expand. If you know that you are worthy of it all, and your intention is to keep abundance circulating and serving others, then you will attract high levels of happiness into your life. If you think you deserve very little, you will attract this to yourself. If you feel self-important, taking what you think you deserve, at the expense of others, the results will be the same as if you felt you deserved very little. In both scenarios you are undermining yourself in the process. Believing you deserve nothing, or that you deserve it all at the expense of others, is a self-destructive path that not only leads away from abundance but toward scarcity in your life. Know that you deserve it all, and so does everyone else, and that in the process of helping others to get it all, you serve yourself and all others simultaneously.

3 *What do you think is available for you?* The totally honest answer to this question is central to how much is out there for you. If you focus on what you do not have or simply

can never get, that is precisely what will expand in your life. At the end of a talk one evening, a woman asked, 'Dr. Dyer, what do you think are the limits to my achieving all the success and happiness I would like in my life?' My response was instantaneous: 'Your belief that there must be limits.' It is not what is available or unavailable that determines your level of success and happiness, it is what you convince yourself is true.

A report on participants in a study of visualization techniques related to job-hunting demonstrates the impact of personal expectations. Three participants were instructed to visualize the following: availability of the work they wanted, their entitlement to that situation, and working at the new job. The participants' previous jobs had paid them annual salaries of $10,000, $25,000, and $250,000, respectively. Within a matter of weeks each of them began working in precisely the same pay range as they had in their previous employment. Each of them was limited by what he believed he deserved, and could not visualize himself in a higher-paying position. The abundance that came into their lives fitted perfectly with what they imagined for themselves and no more. This is true of virtually everything. The belief in scarcity is what creates scarcity and helps it to rule our lives. The same principle applies with abundance.

Freedom and abundance

The concept that the universe is onesong, ever-expansive, without restrictions, other than those we choose with our thoughts, has built within it the notion of freedom. Boundaries and lines restrict freedom, but such boundaries are all created by man. The universe simply flows. The water goes to the edge, and the land flows right out from it. The air and the water are not separated by boundaries, they coexist and flow into and with each other in perfect harmony. Space goes on and on, uninterrupted by boundaries. There is a freedom to all of this that transcends any walls or restrictions that man has invented.

So freedom is what abundance is all about. Freedom is the absence of restrictions. In nature it is the bird deciding to put his nest wherever he pleases in harmony with the entire environment. It is the whales swimming wherever their hearts and instincts take them. Abundance in humans can only come about when the mind of mankind is likewise uncluttered by imagined limits. Learning to rid ourselves of the freedom-defying belief in limits is one way to create an abundant world for ourselves.

How I made the major decisions in my life

Even as a very young boy, I would use my mind to centre on what I wanted, rather than on what other people had, or what was missing in my life. It always worked for me, and continues to do so today.

The essence of all of my decision-making, as I look back, seemed to be in the direction of having more freedom in my life – freedom and control over my own destiny. I disliked having to be in a specific place each and every day, or having someone tell me how to dress, what to do, how to act, what to say, and how much money I would be receiving. And I wanted to go in a direction that would expand the freedom that I cherished. This is what the principle of abundance it about – tuning in to the vastness that is there for us beyond all of the boundaries and controls that others would impose upon us.

My first real job, other than cutting lawns and shoveling snow, was my paper route. From age ten to about age fourteen, I delivered the *Detroit Times*, the *Detroit News*, and the *Detroit Free Press*. I loved going to the local newspaper office and getting my papers, folding them, putting them on the handlebars of my bike or in saddlebags over the back. I was free, I made all of the decisions, and no one told me how to run my route. But the one area in which I was not free was collecting from my customers. Each weekend I had to knock on doors and collect the money for the weekly delivery. This took a great deal of time and had to be done every single week or I did not get paid. Many many times people were not home, and I had to return over and over to collect my money. I felt trapped by this weekly ritual of collecting money, putting aside the amount I owed to the company, and then trying to collect the rest so that I could realize a profit.

My very first decision to change jobs came about exclusively as a result of wanting to have more freedom over how I received my pay each week. I took a job working at Stahl's Market, a small grocery store in my neighbourhood on the east side of Detroit. The first thing I wanted to know was how I would be paid. I discovered that each Friday evening, at the end of the day, I would be paid for the hours that I worked that week. This was a new measure of freedom for me, and one that I treasured. I felt a new sense of control over my life. Of course, I also had many new restrictions imposed on me: I had to report to work when Mr. Stahl said to. I had to wear an apron. I had to work the hours that he decided were appropriate for me. But I did not have to traipse through the snow and slush hoping that my customers would be home so that I could collect my earnings.

I stayed at Stahl's all through my high school years, working as an assistant manager after a few years, closing up the store and taking responsibility for the safe and the money tabulations, working as a butcher if needed, and generally being in charge. I gained more freedom over my working hours and what I could do as I progressed from bag boy to cashier to produce manager to butcher to assistant manager. My weekends were always six hours on Friday evening, twelve hours on Saturday, and six hours alone on Sunday to handle everything in the store. I was making good money and enjoying the work, but I knew this was not to be a career position for me.

After graduation from high school I enlisted in the navy. I knew I had a military obligation, and I also knew that I did not want to be marching in a column and carrying a gun in preparation for learning how to become a potential killer. I could not have done it then, and I could not do it today. I tested well and was assigned to communications schools and ultimately to the island of Guam in the South Pacific. Each job that I managed to get while serving four years in the service was in the direction of more freedom.

But the very first time I had to participate in a personal inspection, I experienced an internal revulsion that is impossible to describe. To have a young officer staring at me, inspecting my shave, critically examining my uniform, and telling me that my shoes were not shiny enough turned my stomach. I knew that I could not handle being in that situation for the next four years, and so I figured out in my own mind how I would avoid future inspections. For four years, I never was inspected again. Ever! No one knew about this internal decision I made, not even my very best friends. I simply moved toward more freedom by getting assigned to the kinds of positions that were exempt from inspections. I became a cryptographer, a supervisor of a message centre. Even within a system that is thoroughly regimented, I was able to extend a large measure of freedom over my life.

After four years as an enlisted petty officer, I knew that I had to make some dramatic changes in my life. Reenlistment was out of the question. I had watched each payday as many of my contemporaries drank themselves silly, spending all of their pay as soon as it arrived, and passing the rest of the time reading comic books and generally being broke, both financially and in character.

I had made a commitment while on Guam for the last eighteen months of my enlistment that I was going to college. I knew that I did not have the necessary funds, so for eighteen months I managed to live on 10 percent of my salary and to save the remaining 90 percent. That's right. I saved 90 percent of my salary for a year and a half, and I had it all put into a bank account for the purpose of paying my tuition for the full four years of school. No one in my family had ever attended college, but I focused on attending Wayne State University in Detroit. No one in my family had ever accumulated the money necessary for school, but I concentrated all of my thoughts on what I had, which was a bank account that was growing steadily every two weeks. I expanded what I thought about, and what I thought about was what I had, rather than what I did not have, or what the history of my family had been.

I made the decision to become a teacher because I loved being in front of an audience, I loved young people, and I especially loved being off every day at three o'clock and having my entire summer free. The freedom aspect of teaching was a major consideration. I knew that I would be able to do pretty much what I wanted once the classroom door was closed. I knew that I would have a lot of spare time for attending classes in the evening. I also loved pursuing a college degree, even though I was twenty-two years old and a mere freshman, when most people my age were either college graduates or well on their way to a working career.

Once I started teaching I loved what I was doing. But it was not long before I began to notice how much of my freedom had been stripped away from me. I had to be in the same classroom every single day, for the same time period, for an entire school year. I had administrators imposing a lot of curriculum rules on me, telling me what committees I had to serve on and when I had to go to faculty meetings. My life became exceedingly scheduled. I disliked the fact that I was going to have to be in room 223 every single Wednesday for the next forty weeks at 2:00 in the afternoon. More and more I found that I was having less and less control over how I spent my days. In the name of a job, I was giving up a great deal of the freedom and abundance that I treasure so much.

I noted at this time that the school counsellors had much more freedom than the teachers. They had their own offices, were free to schedule appointments at their convenience, and could leave the school for lunch, since they did not have a class and time schedule to adhere to. They also were able to work one-on-one with students and pretty much could come and go as they wanted. There was a lot of important work to be done, but it could all get accomplished on the counsellor's own time schedule.

So I went for my master's degree to become a school counsellor. And I loved counselling. I loved my studies. I loved being in a school setting with young people everywhere. I loved the freedom that I had in contrast to teaching. My day was what I wanted it to be, and I did not have to live and breathe by the school time schedule. However, I noted that the college professors who were teaching me to become a counsellor had to come into the university only two or three days a week, and that their schedules were much lighter than mine: they had a great deal of free time to write and do research. I still had to be in that school office five days every week, forty weeks every year, and my days were filled with school duties. I wanted still more freedom, and I immediately enrolled in my doctoral studies to prepare myself to become a college professor.

Teaching at the university level is a wondrous experience, and I thoroughly enjoyed it for six years. I was able to work it out so that my office hours and class teaching assignments were completed on a three-day-a-week regimen. Fantastic! Three days for the college, and four whole days for me to write, to counsel, to have control over my own life and my own destiny. The relative freedom in comparison to working for a school system was like night and day. But I was still dependent upon the university for a paycheque. They still set my school calendar and gave me my teaching assignments. And they began to give me more and more committee assignments. I was assigned to doctoral study groups and research assignments.

I knew in my heart that it was going to be necessary for me to assume total control over my days if I was ever going to experience the abundance that I am able to write about today. But of course, I had all of the concerns that everyone has about money, bills, and family.

When the day came for me to leave college teaching, it was not because I was dissatisfied. In fact, I was thrilled and proud to call myself Professor Dyer. I was very proud of having gone from my humble beginnings in Detroit to the academic world of college professor in New York City. I loved what I was doing, but I wanted to do it all on my terms. I did not want to be told how to dress ever again. I did not want to be told when to be in what building or on what committee at any specific time. I wanted freedom, complete freedom. I made the decision to leave a marvelous teaching assignment at a wonderful university in order to have that control over my life.

Again, I point out that never once did I entertain the idea that I would abandon my responsibilities and obligations. As I have said, I place an enormous amount of importance on being responsible for the choices that I have made in my life. My family comes first, and I have always met all of my obligations as a father and a husband. And I have been blessed with supportive family members who always encourage me to pursue my own dreams, regardless of how 'crazy' they may seem at the time. They have always known that Wayne was the kind of person who could not survive if he had to run his life by other people's rules. In turn, I respect the need of my wife and of all my children to take risks and to trust the universe to provide as long as they are acting out of love for themselves and for all others. This kind of mutual respect for the rights of all of us to follow our dreams is of paramount importance in creating an abundant life. If your loved ones are fighting you, then everyone is weakened. When you are being encouraged, everyone is empowered.

I continue to make decisions wherein I have more control over my own destiny. Being a writer requires tremendous mental and physical discipline. But I am the one who decides when I write and how I write, and if I want to write nude in the middle of the day on Wednesday (which is right now, and which I am right now), then that is precisely what I will do. I probably put in more hours speaking, writing, producing tapes, consulting, researching, and reading than I ever did before, but I am free to do it at my own whim. I honestly do not know the difference between a Sunday and a Tuesday. I live each day, doing what I love, and always focusing on what I have, rather than on what is missing. I have always pursued freedom because that was the focus of my thoughts. I did not run away from bondage – I lived joyfully through the years when my schedule was governed by other people and events – but I always focused on what I wanted. Freedom. The small amounts of freedom that I had were so thoroughly blissful for me that I stayed focused on those, rather than commiserating about my lacks. And through all of it, every single step along the way, money was never an issue. I never went for a better-paying job. Ever! And irony of ironies, paradox of paradoxes, each succeeding position provided me with more money.

Abundance and doing what you love

I do not want to be the least bit equivocal here. In order to experience abundance in your life you must transform yourself in such a way as to be doing what you love, and loving what you do. Now! Yes, today. It is that crucial. Doing what you love is the cornerstone of having abundance in your life. Robert Louis Stevenson said it this way in 1882: 'If a man loves the labour of his trade apart from any question of success or fame, the Gods have called him.' I would like to help you receive that call to follow your bliss.

Remember, our days are the precious currency of our life. In effect, how we spend our days is a measure of the quality of our life. When our days are spent in unsatisfying tasks in which we feel ungratified, simply spinning our wheels to pay the bills, we are working to satisfy something outside of ourselves, like our financial obligations. If you choose to satisfy financial debts by doing work you dislike, you are constantly thinking about and centered on what you dislike. In fact, a third of your entire life becomes focused on thoughts which are negative. Since what you focus on expands, you are going to find this negativity enlarging in your life. Your life literally becomes focused on what you dislike. When you are experiencing your daily life doing work which you do not love, you are operating from a scarcity consciousness.

Why do people spend their lives doing things that they do not love? Because they believe in scarcity rather than abundance. They will tell you, 'I don't have enough to do whatever I want, so I have to do the things I do.' Or 'I can't afford to do what I love.' Or 'I have no other choice – I've got to pay my bills.' Or 'I don't know anything else.' Look at these reasons very carefully. They all imply that there is a scarcity of what is needed to survive. The person feels forced, by virtue of this scarcity, to continue in whatever work he is doing to fulfill his outer needs. However, if you understand that what you focus on expands, then you begin to see the folly in ever trying to fill in the gaps by doing what you loathe. The loathsomeness is what continues to expand, because that is where all of the energy is centered.

Think about this for a few moments longer. You cannot feel fulfilled unless you feel authentic to yourself. Authenticity comes from acknowledging the needs of both your outer and your inner selves. If you hate or are indifferent to your work, then those life moments are phony in a metaphorical sense. That is, you are behaving in form inconsistently with who you really are in thought. Ninety-nine percent of you is disappointed while the remaining 1 percent carries out the charade that you are living! If you live like this for a long period of time, you will learn to focus on scarcity. Why? Because you feel incomplete, and the incomplete part of your life is what we label as scarcity, and that is what will continue to expand. It becomes a vicious circle from which you cannot escape, unless you are willing to do what it takes to begin doing what you love and loving what you do.

You are probably thinking how impractical this is when it comes right down to living your life every single day, and paying bills and meeting all of your obligations. Let me say that your skepticism is duly registered, but that I regard it as part of the scarcity consciousness that can be overcome. A recent incident in my life illustrates this.

One of my dearest friends is named Joanna. I have known Joanna for twelve years, and she is godmother to two of our children. She is one of the brightest, most sensitive, best-read people I have ever known. When Joanna and I first met in 1976 she had been working as a flight attendant for a major airline for sixteen years. She had an apartment in the same building as I did in Fort Lauderdale, and we had many occasions to talk. Often she told me how dissatisfied she was with her job as a flight attendant. My reaction was always: 'What do you love to do?' Consistently, her response had to do with her love of books and ideas, and an attraction to the publishing field, which she would not consider because of low pay and the necessity for a move to New York. Joanna continued to fly because, as she told me, the benefits were good, the hours were great, and she could not imagine giving up all those years of seniority logged toward a retirement that was twenty years away.

I encouraged her to leave, to take the risks that go with doing what you love, and assured her that abundance would flow into her life. She liked the idea, yet she was not ready to make such a move. Meanwhile, she managed from paycheque to paycheque, never seriously in debt, still always short of the money that she needed, regardless of how many extra hours she flew. The more she worked, the higher her income-tax bite and the more she felt that she was not working for herself, but simply to keep ahead of the game. Meanwhile, her life was going by.

After realizing her phenomenal skills, I began to hire Joanna to do some work for me. She started out by typing my manuscripts for magazine articles and doing some editing work. Eventually, she became my personal editor, and worked on my previous three books, editing, rewriting, line editing, typing, doing research, and generally becoming indispensable to me. The acknowledgment at the beginning of this book is testimony to the important role that she has played in its development.

As the years went by and Joanna continued to fly, her dissatisfaction intensified, and unusual things began to 'happen' to her. She injured herself rather seriously on three different occasions, all of which required her to take time off from flying. Illness became a feature of her life. She tried relocating overseas, but still she continued to have personal and physical difficulties. She was losing the excitement for life that had always been her trademark, and she was increasing the scarcity in her life. Her bills mounted, and though she managed to stay ahead of the creditors, she was experiencing anything but abundance.

Recently the breakthrough happened. During a phone conversation about some details of this book, Joanna said, 'Remember back in the seventies, Wayne, when you used to tell me and my friends that if we did what we loved doing, money would literally fly in the windows?' Joanna was laughing as she continued, 'We used to laugh and tell you that was easy for you to say. It was flying in *your* windows from the popularity of your best-selling books, but we were convinced that *we* had to keep flying to keep the money coming in!'

'I don't think I realized then how sincerely you were speaking from a self-knowledge,' she said more seriously. 'From your discovery for yourself of the rewards of doing what you truly loved doing. These past few months, working on this book and not flying at all,' she continued hesitantly, 'I've gradually identified my exhilarated feeling as what you described then as "doing what you love."' She sounded determined as she added, 'It has dawned on me that the difference between being a flight attendant, with those guaranteed benefits, and losing myself pleasurably in doing what I love doing is a difference in a way-of-being-in-life that simply makes flying no longer an option for me.'

I wondered what had caused the breakthrough as she excitedly continued, 'This morning I was happily immersed in thoughts and books and your words and ideas, working on the manuscript with a cup of hot tea next to my typewriter. As I was staring at the tiny new buds on the lilac bush outside my window, I saw the mailman drive up. And he was delivering my third large cheque from you!' she said triumphantly. '*For doing what I love doing!* When I got back to my typewriter, it really hit me. Here I am, reveling in the awareness that is is possible to feel this good about work, when the money appears at my window! I didn't even have to go out and pick up my cheque!'

I chuckled, as she explained, 'It seemed to me exactly what you were describing years ago, and here it was happening to me. I realized,' she said in a steady voice, ' there is no question about my going back to work as a flight attendant. Actually, the money only confirms the rightness of doing what I enjoy.'

The words 'You'll see it when you believe it' drifted through my thoughts as Joanna concluded, 'I feel such an inner sense of joy at honouring and encouraging this part of me, rather than listening exclusively to the part of myself that logically dictated all the advantages of working for the airline. "You'll see it when you believe it" are mere words in comparison to the feeling!'

Putting it into practice

It does not matter what your occupation is or even if you have one. It does not relate exclusively to your employment. Whoever you are, wherever you live, whatever your life circumstance, you are doing something every day. Those days can be experiences of abundance or scarcity. The ideas below may help you to begin doing what you love. The actual implementation is, of course, up to you.

1 *Reexamine your resistance to doing what you love.* I was going to call this 'Take the risk!' – but I truly do not believe it is necessarily risky to begin doing what you love. If you label it a risk, it means that you must somehow muster up the courage to make a change. But as you become more awakened, you will see that the risks are nothing more than thoughts – which you have convinced yourself are impossible to implement. Instead of thinking 'risk,' which has scarcity built into it, think: 'It will be absolutely great to be doing what I love, and I know that whatever I need to handle my life affairs will come into my life. I know it!' Stop focusing on all that will be missing, unless that is what you want to expand in your life.

Your resistance to doing what you love is based not on the world of abundance and unlimited opportunity, but on a belief that work and play are separate parts of your humanity. The belief is that work is painful and entails suffering and that play is fun. But it does not have to be that way. Imagine yourself doing exactly what you love doing. Composing, drawing, engineering, being a florist, being a beautician, having your days to be with your children as a homemaker – the list is endless. Imagine what gives you the most pleasure and makes you feel purposeful. What is it that when you finish doing it, you feel immeasurably fulfilled, and while you are doing it, time just seems to be nonexistent? Invite that into your consciousness, and then proceed to follow your bliss.

Know that you are not stuck where you are unless you decide to be. Know that if you use your mental energy to see yourself spending your days doing what you truly love, and if you keep that thought uppermost in your mind, that is what will expand for you. It has to.

You were very likely taught that you choose your career in the early part of your life, and then you live out your life doing what you were trained to do. But is it sensible to continue doing something that someone eighteen or twenty years old chose years ago? Would you go to an eighteen-year-old today for vocational counseling? Continuing to do regularly what you dislike is going to expand scarcity in your life. You will never escape from the trap unless you are willing to shift the internal focus of your thoughts to what you love doing. Put that thought in your mind and make it the central feature of your thoughts, even if you refuse to make the move today. Stay with the thought. The more you focus on it, the more it will expand.

Virtually everyone I have ever met who has gone on to live the kind of abundant life I am discussing here has been willing to do what it takes to make it happen. They all quit jobs that were not personally fulfilling and pursued their dreams. *There is no scarcity of opportunity to make a living at what you love, there is only a scarcity of resolve to make it happen.* Whatever you love doing more than anything else has built within it an opportunity to make a living at it, even though you may not believe it. Your fears of doing what you truly love are based on a belief that you are going to go broke and be unable to pay your bills and meet your family responsibilities. Not so! Those who love you will support you in every way if you take the opportunity to pursue your dreams. If you have always paid your bills, why would you suddenly become the kind of person who does not? If your entire history speaks to being responsible, why would you ever consult an imaginary fear-based history to make your real-life decisions? Moreover, you may find that many of your extraordinary expenses are simply the result of a life-style in which you have been doing what you loathe.

Simplify your life and you may find that you reduce your expenditures and obligations considerably. If you truly want to live out in the wilderness, or travel across the country, or open up a small business in another part of the world, you very likely can make it happen. I have talked with numerous executives who made the decision to alter their stress-filled lives and begin to slow down and 'smell the roses' and still pursue a dream of doing what they really loved. Interestingly, in many cases it took a near brush with death to bring this change about. Your fears of doing what you love are mostly rooted in unenlightened conditioning. All of those fears can be recognized as nothing more than fearful 'thoughts' which you can change.

2 *If you refuse to change what you do, practice loving it each day.* This little Zen proverb sums up my message in this section:

> Before enlightenment
> chopping wood
> carrying water
> After enlightenment
> chopping wood
> carrying water.

Enlightenment has very little to do with your daily activities and quite a lot to do with how you view those activities. You are still going to chop wood and carry water in some fashion, only the awakened person is no longer going to curse the wood and the water, or even his own lot in life. Whatever you are doing now can become a labour of love if you are willing to make it that way. You do not have to hate your work or anything that you are doing. Hate is a choice that comes from having hateful thoughts. Hate is not caused by having to change a dirty diaper twenty times a day, or clean toilets, or live in a prison cell, or collect garbage, or sort out accounting forms, or attend committee meetings all day in which nothing is accomplished. The circumstances are irrelevant. The loathing exists inside of you, not in the external world.

If you decide to continue in your present activity, shift your attitude toward that activity and allow abundance into your life. You can perform whatever tasks are required of you with an entirely different perspective. Joanna, my editor and literary specialist extraordinaire, previously a flight attendant, did precisely that while she continued to fly. She worked on her attitude while in that uniform, and brought a kind of love to a job that many others find routine and unpleasant. She practiced loving the passengers and going out of her way to serve them. It was her dissatisfaction with not feeling personally authentic that eventually won out. But for the years that she was flying she preferred loving what she chose to hating it. Thus she could 'chop wood and carry water' in a radiant manner while on the job.

It really boils down to a very simple choice that does not require a genius to figure out. You can either change and take all of the attendant 'risks' that go with doing what gives you the greatest satisfaction, or you can develop a new attitude toward what you continue to do. This new attitude can convert a stifling job situation to one of joy. It is entirely your doing. It may be done by providing more service to others, which will almost always contribute to personal satisfaction. You can make chopping and carrying a joyful enterprise or a spiteful one. It is truly up to you. No matter how much you convince yourself that your job or life situation is boring, routine, or hateful, the fact is that those are thoughts that reside in you. Somewhere there is an individual who will do what you are doing and bring joy and fulfillment to it.

The truth of this maxim is evident to me every week when a beautiful woman who is originally from China comes to our home to help with the cleaning. She laughs and smiles her way through chores that others consider onerous. She stops to play with the children, brings them small gifts from her native country, and genuinely contributes her own sense of joy to what she is doing in our home. She is a treasure to have with us. She reminds me every time I see her that cleaning house for someone else can be loaded with either misery or joy. The job does not contain anything demoralizing within it, only people do.

3 *Whatever you are currently against can be restated and rethought so as to promote abundance in your life.* Everything that you are against blocks you from abundance. Everything! Decide to get your life working in a positive rather than a negative style. If you are against terrorism and war, you become part of the problem. You are one more soldier fighting for what you believe in. And fighting always weakens you and brings more scarcity into your life. Instead of being against terrorism and war, try being *for* peace. Once you are for peace, you will start directing your thoughts and consequently your actions in that direction. You will become a peacemaker simply by not being against anything. This may sound like semantic juggling, but it is much more than that. Once you are focused on something that you favour, you will expand that in your life. Whatever you tend to be against puts you right into a fighting mold, and consequently expands dissension in your consciousness.

This same principle applies to the work you are doing. If you are *against* your boss rather than *for* improvements, you will focus your energy on the things about your boss that you dislike, and those things will expand. If you focus on what you dislike about your work, that will become your centre of thought and those things will grow. This is a very powerful philosophy that I am asking you to embrace. Everything that you are against work against you. Everything that you are against can be restated in a way that puts you in support of something. When you are able to state what you are for rather than what you are against, you are focusing on the potential for positive change. Once that is in place, you will find whatever you are focusing on expanding.

Instead of hating illiteracy, be for literacy and you will be working to help improve literacy. Instead of being against drugs by joining another war on drugs, be for helping children to discover life-enhancing ways of having positive highs. With enough of us working to help children make positive choices there will ultimately be fewer customers for the purveyors of artificial highs. Instead of being against your company policy, be for an improved policy. Instead of being against your spouse's outbursts or alcoholism, be for your spouse's gentleness and sobriety. You will help to expand all that you are for or against, so it is simple to know where you want to be aligned. Doing what you love involves restating how you choose to align yourself each day. On the side of personal order or disorder. On the side of worldwide order or disorder. Tell me what you are for and I will show you what is going to expand in a positive way. Tell me what you are against and I can show you what is going to expand in a destructive way.

When you find yourself loving what you do, you will begin to notice how effortlessly you do your work. Once you are at a place where you use love as your guiding principle for your daily activities, you will see that abundance is really there just for the tuning in to.

Why you may be resisting the principle of abundance

• We are raised in a culture which emphasizes scarcity rather than abundance, and it is difficult to overcome this background. We have heard statements such as 'I'm getting mine while the going's good,' or 'If I don't take it someone else will,' or 'There's only so much out there and you have to fight to get your share of the pickings.' We have learned to believe in limits and scarcity. The haves and the have-nots seem to be a reality in our culture. There are indeed a large group of have-nots and fewer haves. We are not taught that abundance is truly available for everyone, that there is plenty of everything to go around. Through our conditioning, we believe quite the opposite. We will never activate this principle of abundance as long as we believe that what is missing is of primary importance, and focus our life energy there. A mentality of 'I never have enough' is a reason for living for many people. They spend their lives striving, fearful of ever arriving. Focus on what you have, no matter how insignificant it seems.

• People do not want to take responsibility for the scarcity in their lives. It is much easier to blame circumstances, others, events, or even God for the things that they have failed to acquire or achieve. They justify their place in life and reject responsibility for those limited life circumstances by believing that they have been assigned a life of scarcity. Continuing to believe this guarantees they will remain in this experience. Releasing the binding restrictions of scarcity as a belief system can create an opening to a new level of abundance consciousness.

• Resistance may just be easier for some. On one level, it is less challenging to stay in a scarcity mode than to experience a lifetime of abundance. This is because those who actually live the abundant life I have been describing know that they already have enough and that they themselves are all there is already. They no longer strive and accumulate to feel positive about themselves and their life mission. Without such striving, many feel lost and directionless.

• People may prefer to elicit compassion and sympathy from others. Many people constantly elaborate on how they were cheated, or how hard they worked without getting ahead of the game. Since there are many other people out there willing to tell the same story, they can milk this melodrama for all that it is worth. They will not have even a smidgen of a chance to transcend the scarcity mentality as long as they seek sympathy from others who feel victimized and short-changed. Still, it gives them a powerful reason to avoid abundance.

• The 'I don't deserve it' pattern keeps many people stuck in their scarcity life-style. This is generally a strong indication of low self-regard. They convince themselves that they are unworthy of the abundance that the universe provides. A 'poor me' belief system gives them a convenient rationalization for focusing their life energy on what is missing. They convince themselves they deserve no more.

• Some have grown so comfortable with scarcity and fear that they really would not know what to do with a life of bountiful abundance. Those who are comfortable in a real or metaphorical prison cell find it very difficult to go beyond their four walls. With bare necessities provided, they do not have to worry. They withdraw from the complications that they imagine would accompany abundance in their lives. The longer one maintains a scarcity consciousness, the more one finds reasons to avoid changing.

Some ideas for bringing abundance into your life

Remember that I do not believe that abundance is about accumulating a lot of stuff. I believe it is about looking at life and knowing that we have everything that we need for complete happiness, and then being able to celebrate each and every moment of life. It is about knowing that we do not need anything else and that whatever we need will be there when we focus on what we want to increase in our lives. It is about knowing that scarcity is a set of beliefs and actions that emphasize what is missing rather than what we have. Here are a few ideas to help you challenge any scarcity consciousness in your life. They have worked for me in my life, and in the life of almost every happy and successful person I have ever known.

• Be *against* nothing! Make an effort to state everything that you stand for in positive rather than negative terms. For example, instead of trying to *lose* weight, try being *for* the image of yourself that you have in your mind. Rather than attempting to *quit* smoking, try being *for* yourself as a tobacco-free person. I saw a sign outside a gift shop on Maui which illustrates this point perfectly. It states: 'Please enjoy your cigarettes and soft drinks outside of the store.' Emphasize what you want, rather than what you dislike or what is missing.

• Make an effort to be thankful for what you have and who you are each day. Do this even if you want more and dislike who you are. Being thankful upstages greediness, and focuses your thoughts on abundance. The universe seems to provide abundantly when we are in a state of gratefulness. The less we need to have more, the more we seem to get!

• Take some daily time to observe the ways in which you are using your mind. Assess how much of your mental energy is focused on what is missing. How much of your time do you spend wishing that you had more, or commiserating about your sorry state of affairs? Be scrupulously honest with yourself. You may discover that a surprisingly large chunk of your waking hours is spent thinking this way. If so, make a concerted effort to shift that consciousness for a specified amount of time each day. Shift your thought processes to what you truly want to expand. This can eventually develop into a lifetime habit. To make this shift of consciousness, you must first become aware of how much of your thinking, you life, is spent on feeding that which you really do not want to grow.

● Practice this in personal relationships too. Much of the time, problems in a relationship occur because each person is concentrating on what is missing in the other person. If you are angry with someone you love, shift your focus to something about that person that you truly love. Then allow that person to be what you love *and* also at times something that you find difficult to accept. When you focus on what you love about someone, that focus will grow in your relationship. This is also a phenomenal way of being with children. Catch them doing things right!

● Make a personal commitment to do what you love and to love what you do. Today! I cannot overstress how important this is as a strategy for experiencing abundance. If deep within you you would love to try another occupation or to change locations or whatever, then you will sooner or later do that. It is the only way for you to be authentic to yourself. It is virtually impossible for abundance to replace scarcity while you feel inauthentic. As you begin to do what you love and love what you do, you will find life opening to you in ways you never dreamed. And if you are not ready to change jobs, avocations, locations, or whatever, then change your thoughts toward those disliked daily activities. Search for the joyful part of what you do and be thankful for having the mind, body, and spirit to do something productive. Abundance flows when we love what we are doing.

● Whatever you enjoy receiving in your life, remind yourself, 'I deserve this.' It is okay to feel deserving. And you will if you believe the self that is receiving something is worthy and important. Abundance is related to how you feel about yourself. If you feel that you are important enough to ask, and divine enough to receive, receiving will be your reward. If, on the other hand, you feel unworthy, it will be almost impossible for abundance to flow into your life. Think of how a tree unfolds to all of its magnificent potential, always reaching for the sunshine and growing and flourishing. Would you ever suggest to a tree, 'You should be ashamed of yourself for having that disgusting moss on your bark, and for letting your limbs grow crooked'? Of course not. A tree allows the life force to work through it. You have the power within your thoughts to be as natural as that tree. I often remind myself of this by recalling something Lao-tze said, thousands of years ago: 'The snow goose need not bathe to make itself white.' Neither need you do anything but be yourself.

● Softly and kindly remind yourself, 'I cannot own anything.' It is a valuable thought to keep in mind as you struggle to improve your financial picture, worry about investments, and plan how to acquire more and more. It is a universal principle which you are a part of. You must release everything when you truly awaken. Are you letting your life go by in frustration and worry over not having enough? If so, relax and remember that you only get what you have for a short period of time. When you awaken you see the folly of being attached to anything.

● Use affirmations as a regular part of your life. Use every technique that you can to attract abundance. Walls, mirrors, the refrigerator, your car, are all great spaces for displaying written affirmations. A positive affirmation helps you to shape your thoughts around your wants. A positive affirmation helps you to be authentically aligned with your thoughts. Your beliefs need to be affirmed regularly in order for you to see them in the world of form.

● Whenever you are tempted to give less, try giving a little extra instead. When you find yourself living out the old stingy habit, it helps to stop yourself on the spot, 'in your

mind,' and then exhibit a completely new way of being.
You will be shocked at how much more begins circulating
back into YOUR life; to say nothing of how much better you
will feel inside because of the special effort you extended
to another person. It truly feels good to give a little extra.
As they say, 'It is never crowded along the *extra mile*.'

Abundance is a universal principle that many of us do not
experience because we misinterpret it. We believe it means
having things and striving for more of those things. But
abundance really means understanding that our eternity
and our universe are endless. It is a different way of
seeing. I have always loved the following little fish story,
which illustrates beautifully the intent of this chapter.

'Excuse me,' said one ocean fish to another, 'you are older and
more experienced than I, and will probably be able to help me.
Tell me: where can I find this thing they call the ocean? I've
been searching for it everywhere to no avail.'
  'The ocean,' said the older fish, 'is what you are swimming
in now.'
  'Oh, this? But this is only water. What I'm searching for is
the *ocean*,' said the young fish, feeling quite disappointed.

We, too, are already immersed in total abundance. We do
not have to keep trying to find it. No matter how far that
little fish swims, he will never run out of ocean. It is as
universally abundant for him as our universe is for us.
  Decide how *you* are going to live each of your days. Abundance is yours for the asking. It is not something that is
available only for a lucky few. Abundance is a part of your
very humanity. It is there for you to tune in to right now.
Whatever you are thinking right now is expanding for you.
You will ultimately take action on those thoughts.

5
Detachment

*Detachment is the only vehicle available to take you
from striving to arriving*

You would think that in a land where everything is bountiful, the people would have an eternal lock on happiness
and fulfillment. It seems only logical that we here in the
affluent West should indeed be the happiest people on
the planet. We consume a large percentage of the world's
natural resources. We have the highest standards of living
in the history of mankind. We have abundant supplies of
refrigerators and television sets and automobiles. These
things, which we have come to think of as necessities, are,
in fact, luxury items for some 90 percent of the world's
population. Relative to most other people on the planet,
we are rich beyond their dreams. Still, we are not blessed
with contentment, happiness, and joyousness. How can
this be?

It seems to me that the more materialistic we become,
the less trusting we are as a people. The more we
have, the less we are inclined to focus on communicating basic human values. Instead we shift our
emphasis to the wallets and possessions of ourselves
and others.

When we have very few possessions we are compelled to deal with each other and look directly into
one another's eyes, there being nothing of a material
nature to distract our gaze. As we accumulate more
and more, our eyes shift to our possessions and away
from one another's humanity. Consequently, in the most
materialistic society in the history of humanity, we have
very high levels of loneliness and despair. As we have

shifted our emphasis away from human interaction, we have also produced one of the most violent cultures in human history. Loneliness and violence seem to be the natural offspring of an excessively materialistic society.

The most important questions you can ask regarding your place in this culture are: How can I be a happy, loving, fulfilled human being and still function within the materialism that seems to define all of our social structure? Is it possible for me to live my life with inner joy and harmony within a larger context of greed and accumulation? How can I accomplish a daily life of love and harmony, and, yes, success, when I seem to be surrounded by people who beget loneliness and violence in their perpetual pursuit of more?

I believe the answers can be found in detachment.

Detachment is an unwritten fact of the universe which is always operating. The question is whether or not you are willing to tune in to it, make it operative in your daily life. In our highly materialistic society, detachment is a principle that is easily rejected by those who are still chasing more and more success. It is something that many scoff at because it challenges the very fabric of their lifelong traditions and beliefs.

Please understand that I am not contending that the accumulation of material wealth and possessions is evil. Having attained wealth after impoverished beginnings, I delight in the harvest that has come from having made a great deal of money. It is satisfying and lovely. I am proud of my accomplishments and do not feel apologetic for being able to purchase whatever I choose as a result of my labours. Detachment is not about denying the joy of achieving abundance. Paradoxically, it will bring more abundance into your life, rather than require you to shed all of your material goods. However, you will probably find it quite easy to divest yourself of your possessions if that is your choice.

Understanding what detachment means

Throughout this book I have referred to the duality that we are, our form and our formlessness. A large part of our being is formless, a part that includes all of our thinking, spirituality, and higher consciousness. Thought is one essential dimension in which we do literally all of our living, and where our higher consciousness and spirituality reside. All of our attachments are in form. I use the term 'attachment' to describe holding on to something, or defining our life purpose in terms of things or persons external to ourselves. Thus an attachment is something in the world of form to which we have applied so much meaning that we are emotionally attached to it. We feel we must have it or some of our essential humanity will be lost. But keep in mind that our essence is in thought, where it is literally impossible to have attachments. In the dreaming body it is possible to have attachments in thought, but the moment you awaken you realize that the things and people to which you were attached are illusions created for the dream.

When you *truly* awaken you will see the insignificance of any attachment to any of your stuff. Imagine yourself after leaving this plane (dying), looking back at all of your attachments. You can see how unimportant they will then be. Think of this principle of detachment in a like manner. Detach yourself from the *need* to hold on to things and people. In essence you can never own anyone or anything. Every attachment is an impediment to living at a higher level of consciousness. On another level, attachments are responsible for reduced personal happiness and success. The more you can let go of people and things, the fewer obstacles you have for your life journey.

The ability to be detached from all things and all people and yet still see yourself as a part of the whole of humanity is one of the greatest paradoxes of the spiritual journey. At this point in my own life I truly know that I am connected to all other human beings in oneness, and at the same moment I know that I no longer have to be attached to (that is, have to hold on to in order to make me complete) anyone else, in this body called humanity, nor is it necessary for me to accumulate anything else in order to feel whole. What I have I value and celebrate.

Thus, my detachment from needing any thing or any person in order to feel whole and complete allows me to flow and simply be in life, rather than to fight life or demand anything from anyone. Detachment is the absence of a need to hold on to anyone or anything. It does not mean not having things. It is. a way of thinking and being which gives us the freedom to flow with life, as does everything that is given to us by God.

Detachment is accomplished in the dimension of formlessness or thought. It is a cleansing process that ultimately leads to freedom from a need to live so much in the world of form. It is not being a slave to the attachment of all of those things that you are accumulating. It is arriving rather than a life of striving. It is experiencing what it feel like to row your boat gently *down* the stream. To flow without impediments. It is a portrait of the perfection of the universe. Flowing down the stream.

Flowing as a means to detachment

The more we are attached to people, things, ideas, and emotions, the less we are able to experience these phenomena authentically. Try squeezing a handful of water and see how quickly it disappears. But relax and let your hand flow in the same water and you have the experience of the water as long as you like. This is the principle of detachment and flowing. Allowing things to flow naturally is the way of the universe. Everything in the universe – yes, everything – is energy, and that includes you. Energy must have a free flow in order for it to be most efficient.

Allowing things to flow naturally is the way of the universe. Air flows around the planet without interruption. Water flows throughout the entire physical plane with the path of least resistance. The earth itself flows perfectly without interruption on its axis, as do all heavenly bodies in the universe.

The entire universe may be said to be one large energy system, flowing around any efforts to bridle the movement of that energy. It works in harmony with all of its components without any demands, or attachments to how things should be going.

Keep in mind that human beings too are an energy system. We too are part of the life force that is onesong. And since all energy wants to flow unimpeded, it seems only natural to conclude that in order for us to function perfectly in our universe, we too need to be flowing uninterrupted by attachments. The fewer impediments to the energy flow, the more efficiently we fit into and harmonize with the entire energy system called the universe. Attachments which cause us to believe we must have more things, and more control of others, are impediments to higher consciousness and living the awakened, transformed life. Detachment is one of life's great lessons for those on the path of enlightenment.

How your form functions in the universe

You are one exquisitely perfect energy system. Yes, you! You are not working at making your body do what it must do in order to sustain life within you. You are not attached to the actions that your body performs every moment that you are in your form. You are not trying to make your entire system function. It is working perfectly without any direction from you. In fact, if you tried to direct your bodily functions you would become an impediment to its perfectly flowing energy and systematic working. As an example, imagine yourself eating a salad and swallowing the lettuce after chewing it up. Look at all of the chores that you and the one piece of lettuce must perform in order for it to do its job of nourishing you. Saliva automatically enters your mouth to help with the chewing process. You are not busy salivating, it just happens. Then when you start to swallow the chewed-up lettuce, you do not actively work the peristaltic muscles of your throat in order to make the lettuce go down instead of up. It happens without any help of interference from you. You do not direct the lettuce mulch to enter your bloodstream. The digestive process causes the lettuce to do precisely what it is supposed to do and go exactly where it is supposed to go, and transforms the lettuce into nutrients to provide the precise amounts of lettuce nutrition wherever they are needed. The nutrients from the lettuce that are needed for your pancreas never mistakenly go to your big toe. Never have you had to do one thing within the system that is *you* in order to make it all work perfectly. You have absolutely no attachments to anything having to do with the lettuce once you have chewed it up. The journey of the lettuce does not require your attention. You are never busy talking to and working on your digestive, respiratory, or elimination systems. They all simply work without any interference from you.

On a similar note, your heart beats thousands of times each and every day of your life. When did you ever spend time trying to beat your heart? It works automatically and perfectly, and the less attached you are to how it is working, the less likely are you to have trouble from it. You see, there are many many functions being performed at all moments of your life that you have nothing to say about. They all work perfectly because they are in harmony with higher universal principles. There is no need for you to interfere. More likely, any interferences on your part would inhibit the natural flow of these functions.

This, then, is how you as a system of systems function within the largest system of all, our universe. The energy flows just as it is supposed to. The food goes in, your perfection takes over, and everything works as it is designed to do. Interference by you will only curb that natural flow, and consequently do damage to the perfection that you are.

Now I want you to shift your perspective away from the microscope that has been examining you and look through the telescope to see the bigger picture. The universe is a system of systems similar to the perfect systems that function in a human being. It too works on many principles that are beyond our control, that work independent of our opinion about them – work even if we do not understand them. And, most important, they work best when we do not interfere and simply allow the energy to flow unimpeded. I like to compare this process to the lettuce (which is nothing more than energy) making its way throughout your system, dropping off the precise amount of nutrients where it is supposed to. You, like the lettuce, perform your functions perfectly. This is the intelligence that is behind all form. This is the force, or the god, or the spirit, or whatever you choose to call it, that is a part of all form. Working in harmony without any interference or attachments.

Now for the big leap! A moment ago you were the system that was using the lettuce. Now imagine yourself as a giant piece of lettuce. Shift outward and become the metaphorical lettuce that is a part of the biggest picture of all, your place in the universe. You too are a large chunk of energy flowing perfectly within a larger system and within a larger system to infinity. You too can do exactly what you are designed for, as long as you do not interfere with your role within this perfect system. You do not have to try to do what you think is your role, you have to be like the lettuce and let everything work perfectly. You need to understand that every attachment you have to how things are *supposed* to be interferes in some way with your perfect functioning within the larger system. You need to understand that every possession that you become attached to has the same effect on this perfectly functioning energy system, as if the lettuce in your intestines had picked up some baggage that it had to take along with it on its journey. You know what would happen to you if that lettuce somehow decided that it had to have more in order to function properly. It would affect not only the lettuce, and your stomach, and your respiration, but eventually your existence as well.

Obviously I realize that we are much more complex than a piece of lettuce. But the analogy serves to remind us that the universal principles work perfectly without any interference or assistance. When you apply the principle of detachment to your daily life, you will discover that you are functioning freely, and flowing with the energy system that is the universe. Even more significantly, you will discover you are allowing the energy of the entire universe to flow uninterrupted through you.

The more that you are able to flow without the attachments, the happier and more contented you will feel. Moreover, the things that you previously chased after endlessly, always ending up wanting more anyway, will now arrive in your life in the precise amounts necessary to take care of you and your loved ones. Combine this with the practice of the principle of abundance, and you will find more and more flowing into your life in an almost effortless fashion. You will eventually keep the energy flowing by circulating and giving away all that you do not need. Then, miracle of miracles, the more you give away, the more you have.

It is a gloriously perfect system when you allow it to work without any interference. Our interference is due to some kind of attachment that we have grown to believe we cannot possibly live comfortably without.

How I learned to apply this principle

In the fourth through the eighth grades I would sit in my seat in school silently pining for Earlene Rentz, the love of my life. I thought she was beautiful, yet I could never seem to muster the courage to tell her. We lived in the same neighbourhood, and I was friendly with her older brother, so I would see her quite regularly. She always held a special place in my heart.

Recently I received a letter from her telling me that she had read some of my books and that she had seen a story about me in the Wayne State University alumni magazine. On a lark I decided to call her.

Earlene and I talked for about forty minutes. I told her of my youthful love for her, and she replied, 'I knew that.' I couldn't believe that she knew all those years. During our conversation she said, 'Wayne, the thing that stands out the most about you in my mind is that you were never very concerned with possessions, and you were the most generous person in our class.' I was somewhat surprised that this was Earlene's most prominent memory, and yet when I look back, I believe her assessment was correct. Somehow I knew that being attached to something was the surest way to be certain that one never appeared to have enough of it. While many of the other children my age would talk about wanting something, I was generally quite content with what I had. In fact, I would help my friends figure out ways to get the things they seemed to want so desperately. When I was a teenager and a young man, my friends had souped-up drag racers and would talk endlessly about wanting this or that fancy car, yet I was in love with my 1950 Plymouth with its profusion of rust spots and its deficiencies. It never seemed to matter. As I look back, I see that I was comfortable with detachment even then.

I have very few of the items that seem to decorate the lives of wealthy people. Fancy clothes play no part in my life, and hoarding a lot of expensive possessions does not even enter my consciousness. Yet, paradoxically again, I seem to have acquired the ability to have all of the things anyone could ever desire. It seems the less I concern myself with acquisitions the more they arrive in my life for me to use and recirculate. There is something very profound in the seeming paradox 'More is less.' For me, having more means having to insure it, protect it, polish it, worry about it, try to double it, brag about it, price it, maybe sell it for a profit, and on and on.

Of course, one can appreciate the beauty in any object and truly receive enjoyment from it, but that is not attachment. That is simply allowing the energy of your appreciation and love to flow through the object and back into you. If you wonder about the difference between attachment and enjoyment, ask yourself how you would react if suddenly an object you value was gone – stolen, broken, lost, or whatever. Would you be distorted with anger and worry? Would you become immobilized and unable to function effectively with yourself and your loved ones? That is attachment. The need that is attached to the object gives it some degree of control or power over your emotions. I truly know in my heart, as does my wife, that if any object that we have suddenly disappeared, I would say something like 'It is now where it is supposed to be. I hope that whoever is using or observing it is receiving some kind of joy and happiness. It is just a thing and I am not attached to it.'

This is not to suggest indifference to thieves and careless people. It is a suggestion that you not allow your stuff to own you. Be able to detach yourself and your humanity and life purpose from mere things that only have the value we ascribe to them. If we can ascribe value to a thing simply by a thought process, then of course we can detach ourselves from that value-added process equally efficiently through a different process.

A perfect example of this presented itself while I was writing this book.

After a three-hour radio talk show in Miami, I made an impulsive choice to accept a long-standing invitation. Marie Provenzano, whose business is providing luxury facials, had written me numerous letters describing how

162

she had benefited from my tapes and books. Over the years she had invited me to her studio for a complimentary facial treatment as her way of showing her appreciation. For whatever reason that was operating in the universe, I decided to stop on my way home from Miami and have my very first facial.

As I settled in for this new experience, Marie told me she had had a mild stroke several years earlier and she felt she had cured herself through repeatedly listening to my tapes. It felt very good to hear that I had played a role in helping someone overcome such an affliction. She showed absolutely no signs of ever having had a stroke. Marie explained to me that prior to the stroke, she had always been concerned with being a 'perfect person.' She described how she loved to entertain, yet made it a stressful experience for herself because everything had to be exactly 'right.' She created evenings which were showcases of expensive gowns and jewelry, food of the finest gourmet quality, and table decor that displayed the originality and taste for which she wanted to be known. She loved the compliments she received for these perfect evenings. Looking back, she said she now realizes that much of her life was concerned with meaning derived from attachments. One of these 'perfect' evenings became a turning point in her life.

Instead of lavish compliments, a female guest said, 'Marie, aren't you tired of all this show, and having to do everything perfectly?' Marie told me that she simply broke down crying. The woman walked with her over to the couch, put her arm around her, and comforted her for two hours. They talked about the real Marie, the person behind the baubles and the fancy dinner tables. They talked about how easy it is to disguise oneself in external 'stuff' and how lonely it is to end up caressing your jewels, rather than looking into the eyes and heart of a fellow human being. They talked about ways to rechannel energy to serve others and to get back to the real person inside the cage of possession. It was the beginning of an authentic friendship.

Marie suffered her stroke shortly after that, and her new friend helped her to transcend it. Together they studied the literature of love and harmony, and Marie began teaching a course on my materials at a community college in the area. Today she has forty-five students enrolled in a life-enrichment class that is growing faster than Marie can believe. She begins her classes by describing how her attachment to things and possessions had blocked her ability to see the beauty and joy available in human relationships. How an evening which began as one more 'perfectly attached' dinner party changed her life and led to a discovery of how to live better and even how to cure herself of the effects of a stroke.

Marie is one of the happiest and most delightful people I have ever met. She was thrilled to share this transformational story with me, and blurted out, 'I just can't believe that you are really here in my studio! You, my guru, the man I've listened to for hundreds of hours, actually here with me.' I reminded her that she had as much to teach me as I her. I said, 'The guru is you, not me.' Not only was my face tingling after an hour of strange and wonderful gels, vapors, massages, and creams, but my heart was tingling as well.

Why am I writing about Marie and how she came to know the meaning of detachment? In part because I believe Marie's story could be a catalyst to help others to recognize the hollowness in attachments. But also because I believe that I was flowing with an energy that directed me there, on that day, to hear that story, so that I could share it with you.

Attachments do not always take the form of possessions. Attachment to things is a common thread that winds its way throughout our materialistic culture, tying people up in knots because they are focused on ownership. However, there are other significant attachments, such as attachments to other people's opinions and to how we are perceived by others.

I feel that my writing is able to flow because I have become unattached to what anyone else says or thinks about it. I simply allow it to flow, knowing and trusting that it will all be just as it is supposed to be. I am open to improvement, but I cannot think about that while I am writing. If I do, my focus shifts to what I should be doing, instead of what I am allowing to happen. Writing is energy, just like all human activity.

Ralph Waldo Emerson expressed it well: 'The good writer seems to be writing about himself, but has his eye on that thread of the universe which runs through himself, and all things.' This is what I do even at this very moment. I write about myself, but I know that I am a part of you as well, even though we may not have met on the physical plane. These words flow through me to you. I do not own them, nor do you, and the less attached I am to the entire process, the easier and more pleasing it is. Do what you do for yourself, unattached to the outcome in the sense of being emotionally attached. Or as Carlos Castaneda says:

Thus a man of knowledge sweats and puffs and if one looks at him he is just like any ordinary man, except that the folly of his life is under control ... His controlled folly makes him say that what he does matters and makes him act as if it did, and yet he knows that it doesn't; so when he fulfills his acts he retreats in peace, and whether his acts were good or bad, or worked or didn't, is in no way any part of his concern.

This is a tough one for many of us, because we have grown up believing that what we do really matters. Most of us do not get the folly of our lives under control. We worry about how it will be perceived. We focus on external opinions, and consequently cannot simply just be. Castaneda and others encourage us to cultivate an attitude of allowing the energy to flow through us without any judgment about it, and yet at the same time participating in it as if it really matters, and then being able to detach and turn away in peace when it feels finished. If it sounds paradoxical and inconsistent, it is because it is. Nevertheless, the detachment will help you to appreciate and enjoy what you have, rather than worry about gathering more.

I experience the same feelings about speaking. I do not use notes when I go up before an audience, and I haven't for years. When I gave up my notes and spoke entirely from my heart, my speaking improved significantly. I am not attached to having to please an audience, to saying it right, to anything at all. I generally meditate for a thirty-minute period before speaking, and I visualize everything going smoothly and my audience and myself enjoying and appreciating the entire experience. The absence of attachment allows me to flow for hours onstage, often in front of several thousand people. While I am in this state of mind onstage, I find myself in an entirely new sphere of living, a different dimension. Time ceases to exist. My memory for recall is more phenomenal than at any other time in my life. The words flow, without even a hitch or a pause, and it all fits together perfectly.

When I gave up my attachment to perfection about speaking, paradoxically, a kind of perfection seemed to enter into my performance onstage. The internal excitement and nervousness before speaking is my intense desire to be out there in that magical space where I am doing what I love and allowing myself to just be, and experiencing the energy flowing through me unimpeded by any attachments to the outcome. This free-flowing energy is the highest place I know about in the physical plane.

In these two areas of my life where I am doing what I love, writing and speaking, I have come to understand that detachment from the outcome and detachment from external opinions are the keys to allowing me to flow freely and perfectly. No trying, no worry, no anxiety about it –

I simply allow myself to be, without interference from my mind about any part of it. I know somewhere deep down inside of me that I am making a difference, but that it is not necessary for me to do so. I know that even making it matter is a judgment of sorts, so that in the largest analysis, it really does not matter, but I behave as if it truly did. Yet when I am finished with my speech or a book, I never look back. I know that it is over, and that regardless of anyone's opinion about it, it is still done just the way it is. So I move on to the next challenge, unimpeded by attachment to what I have already finished. I learn from the previous experience, and go on to the next project. This new project does not truly matter, but I act as if it did. The process involves, as Castaneda said, having the folly of our lives under control. The way to do that is simply to be, rather than having to be the way others think we should be. Be detached and enjoy each moment of energy that flows through you.

My wife and children are the dearest people in the world to me, and I have truly transformed my thinking toward them, and have altered many of the attachments I previously held in my life. This is a major transformation for me, and one which has brought us a new sense of love and serenity.

I love my wife deeply, yet I know that I do not own her in any way. My inner knowingness recognizes that she is on her own path and that being married to me is a part of that journey she is on. I am most grateful that we share a big part of each other's life. It has taken me quite some time and some bitter disappointments in other relationships to enjoy the experience of loving someone without having to control her in any way. I can allow this person that I love simply to be, even though that may be diametrically opposite to what I am, or to what I may prefer her to be.

For me, this is the essence of the marriage relationship at a conscious loving level. The ability to suspend judgment about how we feel our loved one should be conducting his or her life, and to love that person as is, is a valuable exercise in detachment. Suspending judgment means honouring her need and right to be on her path according to her own inner directives without my uninvited input. Suspending judgment also means honouring my need and right to feel what I am feeling without judging my feeling as right or wrong. This is unconditional love for myself and my loved one. Unconditional love does not demand that one of us be 'right' and one of us 'wrong.' When you are strongly attached to judging anyone, you are *not* defining him or her, you are defining yourself.

My wife and I are very different from each other. In many respects I would describe us as opposites. Love often seems to work this way, allowing us to have in our loved one some of the qualities that we have not elected for ourselves. We do not seem to fall in love with those who have identical qualities. Perhaps that is because we already live with those ways of being in all of our waking moments, and to choose them in another would make for a redundant relationship. I have stopped judging and fighting the differences, and instead remind myself to be grateful for the new flavour that she brings so deliciously into my life every day. We lovingly and playfully acknowledge that we do not have to please each other all the time, nor do we even have to understand each other. This is the quality that detachment from ownership in a relationship brings. It allows us to truly appreciate the opposite 'strange' qualities in each other. When a need to convert her appears, I remind myself that I fell in love with this woman for what she was. As I was falling in love I was not saying, 'If only she had a different point of view I could love her more.' It was our unconditional love that made our love flourish and grow. If the need to change her in some way nags at me, I look inward for what it is saying about me, I find relief from the need to change *her* when I discover what it is about that trait that *I* am disowning.

On other occasions I admit to being inwardly perplexed by her views and actions, but can also shift instantly to loving her for that, rather than having an internal dialogue which tries to make her wrong.

I have found that by being this way in my marriage, more and more I automatically behave in this same fashion toward all others. I know from my own personal experience that any attachment to being right automatically defines me and says absolutely nothing about other people. I finally realized that other people are going to be exactly the way they are, independent of my opinion about them. This allows me simply to be in my relationship toward all others. No judgment, no anger, no hostility – simply to be.

Since I have become less attached to making others wrong and consequently making myself right, it is much easier to be with people who view life differently from the way I do. When I do slip into judgment I find that I am much gentler and easier on myself. I allow myself to have that burst of inner anger for a fleeting moment, and, again paradoxically, when I allow the feeling of anger to be, it usually leaves. If it persists, I nonjudgmentally consider the issue here. Ironically, I find I have much greater impact on people who are mistreating another, or behaving in prejudicial ways, since I am more detached. My detachment from needing to be right almost catches them off guard, and instantly they see that I am not going to get myself all worked up simply because they decide to act or think in their own way. The peaceful person, unattached to converting others or to making them wrong, is far more powerful in helping to bring about constructive loving behaviour than the person who judgmentally and angrily demands change in others.

Recently, at the club where I play tennis, several people were engaged in an angry discussion. They were divided on a racial issue, with one side criticizing an ethic group, and the other side criticizing the first side for their lack of compassion and love. One person stopped and said,

'Wayne, what do you think? I never see you upset about these things. You must have an opinion.'

I responded, 'I am sitting here sending all of you my love. If you could do that to each other right now, there wouldn't even need to be a discussion about who should love whom.' They stopped and looked at me as if I were a bit weird, but they also discontinued judging each other for those few moments.

This approach to loving everyone, even those who seem to be so different, started in my marriage, and has extended outward. It becomes easier and easier to be unattached when you are at peace with yourself. That kind of inner peace contributes more to the world than being one more combatant in the endless feuds that arise out of a lack of respect for the differences in others.

I have found it is much easier to be an effective parent since I have truly understood and adopted the words of Kahlil Gibran in *The Prophet*.

> Your children are not your children.
> They are the sons and daughters of Life's longing
> for itself.
> They come through you but not from you,
> And though they are with you yet they belong
> not to you.

That is a powerful message of detachment for all of us. Nothing drives our children farther from us than the attitude that we somehow own them simply because we are big and they are not. To be able to teach them to be responsible and yet not be personally attached to that outcome is a great lesson. I love my children as much as it is possible to love anyone. I would instantly lay down my life for any one of them. I am sure of this. Yet I am not attached to their success or lack of it in life. Each of them knows that I am not going to have a nervous breakdown or ruin any of the present moments of my life because they fail to do their homework, or come home late, or do any of the thousands of things that young people do or do not do. I teach them to be responsible both by my actions and my words. I teach them to value themselves by presenting them with a father who does the same, and encouraging them as much as possible. But I will not be emotionally or spiritually attached to the decisions that they make as they proceed along their life paths. They have to live their lives. I cannot do it for them in any way. They are learning to assume responsibilities that quite often are usurped by parental attachment.

When we let our energy flow through our children and do not impede them by imposing our will on them, they become more responsible. And why not? They have no one to fight. They do not have to be obstinate to prove that you cannot control them.

My detachment does not mean that I am uncaring. I care immensely. In fact, I care so much that I allow them to make their own way along their path, guiding them here and there, helping them to make responsible loving choices, catching them doing things right as much as possible, and always reminding myself that I do not own them, they own themselves.

My personal growth on this road of detachment has led me to a place where suffering has been eliminated from my life. I have learned in my relationships to others, to myself, and to the accumulation of stuff that the less I am attached to needing a certain outcome, the more I enable energy simply to flow through me and outward wherever it goes. Detachment is a big factor in eliminating suffering and in nurturing a sense of inner peace. Having things in life is wonderful, but needing them is attachment. Having loving people in life is phenomenal, and it is important to value and celebrate them every day, but owning or controlling them is attachment. If you are suffering in your life right now, I can guarantee you that it is tied up with some kind of attachment to how things should be going.

Detachment is the only way out of suffering, as a passage from the Bhagavad Gita explains:

A person who is not disturbed by the incessant flow of desires – that enter like rivers into the ocean, which is ever being filled but is always still – can alone achieve peace, and not the man who strives to satisfy such desires.

The ocean is always being filled, yet it is always still, with the exception of a small amount of surface vibration. We too can be continually open to new growth and remain still, unless we choose to be disturbed by all of the things that are perpetually entering our consciousness. The perturbances are caused by our attachment to an idea that somehow, some way, things should be different than they are. Our suffering, regardless of the form it may take, is caused by the mind – by a mind that insists on having preferences, and will not allow others to be just as they are.

Our most common attachments

Suffering can take many forms and is always played out in form. Our attachments to externals are unlimited. Here are seven of the most common kinds of attachments and the reasons why you may be treading a path of suffering.

1 *Attachment to stuff.* Most of us in the Western world identify ourselves and our relative degree of success or failure by the quality and quantity of stuff that we accumulate. When we make such a connection we are attaching our very worth as human beings to the acquisition of things. Consequently we set ourselves up for suffering when the stuff is not in our lives in sufficient quantity. We become our stuff.

When you adopt such a stance you set yourself up for perpetual frustration. What you are really saying is that you are valueless, incomplete, and worthless. You must continuously replenish your supply of material items in an effort to feel valued. The thesis 'I am lacking value without stuff' leads to an endless pursuit of more. Striving for more things leads to the realization that you cannot ever fulfill yourself from the outside. This position prevents you from knowing that you are already whole, that you do not need anything else to be complete. It leads you to hoarding and ceaselessly comparing yourself to what others are accumulating. It takes your human gaze away from the eyes and hearts of those that you encounter, to their wallets and material possessions. The more you attach your value and humanity to those things outside of yourself, the more you give those things the power to control you. And when you are controlled by things external to yourself you are a slave to those externals, making suffering the only available course for you. Granted you may suffer in comfort, but still the agony is within you as long as those attachments remain.

2 *Attachment to other people.* This is one of the stickiest attachments, and it will create a great deal of suffering until you learn to overcome it in your life. I am not saying that it is inappropriate to love someone else, to value another person's presence in your life, and to celebrate your connectedness. These are all very positive results of creating unconditional love relationships in your life. I mean wanting or needing to own another and feeling useless, immobilized, and hurt if that person is not a part of your life in the way you desire. Such feelings are attachments. These are the relationships in which you give power and control over your own being to another, and they will always lead to suffering.

All human relationships can be happier from a position of detachment. This means loving people enough to allow them to make their own choices without any flak from you, even thought those choices may not be consistent with what you think they ought to be doing. It means having enough confidence in yourself not be threatened when others fail to live up to your expectations. In lover/spouse relationships it means loving the other so much that you forget about your own needs and simply accept and love the other for what he or she is, which is, after all, what you fell in love with in the first place. In family relationships it means being detached enough to allow your relatives to be what they choose to be, and feeling secure enough within yourself not to judge yourself based upon what others decide to do in their own lives. It means forgetting about any evaluation that you might make and instead listening and loving the other family members for what they are, offering advice when asked, and otherwise sending them unconditional love. In your parenting relationships it means constantly reminding yourself that your children are on their own paths and they are not going to live their lives the way you decide they should. It means guiding them, helping them to become self-reliant, and always letting them know that you unconditionally love them, even when they behave in ways that are self-defeating

Detachment in human relationships does *not* mean an absence of caring. It means caring so much that you suspend your own value judgments about others and relate to them from a position of love rather than attempting to control or judge them. The person who is detached in this sense is one who will avoid all the unnecessary suffering that most people experience in their relationships. You send love, decline a victim role, and exhibit an infinite supply of caring for yourself and your loved ones. And you are detached metaphysically. Your detachment allows you to have the 'un' in unconditional love.

Attachment carries with it a subtle implication that somehow you must please me in order to be loved by me. When you learn to let your loved ones be and love them for what they choose to be regardless of your opinion about what they choose, you are detached. Once you reach this state of detachment, you will not want or need to own or control another human being, especially those who are in a close relationship with you. Paradoxically, the less you attempt to own and control someone, the closer you become.

Detachment actually encourages you to grow closer in your relationships and to intensify your love. You reduce the likelihood of suffering in your relationships because you have so much unconditional love for others that your love is going to show even if they choose to leave you. In learning to become less attached you also learn a fundamental truth about loving relationships. *Love is for giving, not for taking!* This is the true essence of detachment in all human relationships.

3 *Attachment to the past.* Learning to be detached from the past and the traditions that are an important part of many people's lives is one way to eliminate some of the suffering that exists in our world. Take a look at all of the people who are fighting in wars around the globe today, and you see them suffering and dying in the name of tradition. They are taught that what their ancestors believed is what they must believe. With this logic they perpetuate the suffering in their own lives and in the lives of their assigned enemies. Many of these battles between ethnic groups have been waged for thousands of years. With the kind of attachment-thinking that is taught within these cultures, the battles will last forever. The minds of those in such cultures are not their own. They are living in form only and dying for a tradition that guarantees enmity and hatred for generations to come.

We participate in attachment to the past when we attempt to determine for others what their spiritual choices should be, based on what we were taught to believe. What education we seek, what vocation we choose, who our friends will be, how we will vote, what we wear, how we speak, and even how we choose to think are often determined by attachments to traditions – traditions that are so overwhelmingly powerful that to ignore them often means complete ostracism from family or neighbours. 'You are a —,' say your parents. 'This is what you were born into, and you have no choice about it.' Such a sentiment has no place for the enlightened soul. How is it possible for anyone to grow if you always do things the way you have always done things? As we learn about universal principles, we know in our hearts that we are not our form. Our package may look a certain way and have a certain history, but it is by no means who we truly are. It is only the cover for the real I, which is formless and has no need for labels determined by the actions of the past.

Attachments to the history of your form as representative of your ancestors and relatives will only cause untold amounts of suffering. Learning to be detached from traditions often takes a great deal of courage, and for those who do detach themselves, there can be a terrific price to pay. However, the price for remaining attached is far greater, and paying it creates much more havoc in your life. The disapproval of those who are addicted to the history of their particular form is far less costly in the long run. Anything to which you are attached owns you in a fundamental way. It is tantamount to tightening the chains and shackles each day to make certain that you do not have a mind of your own. Ralph Waldo Emerson reminded us, 'Be not the slave of your own past – plunge into the sublime seas, dive deep, and swim far, so you shall come back with self-respect, with new power, with an advanced experience, that shall explain and overlook the old.'

Think about that as you consider eliminating suffering in your life that is related to attachment to the past. We can respect and even appreciate the past and the ways of our ancestors. We can love them for having chosen to go their own way. But to be attached to having to live and think the way others before you did, because you showed up looking like them in form, is to deny yourself enlightenment. This is how people and their institutions have controlled others for thousands of years. Demanding and instructing children to live only by the established rules can turn them into unthinking servants of anyone in authority. Attachment to a past is responsible for giving guns to little boys, turning them into killers, telling them who their enemies are, and conditioning them in nonthink conformity. They grow up with the belief that to be unattached to the past is dishonorable in the eyes of God. It is easy for us to see this extreme example in other lands, and it is a lesson for us to be alert to how we cultivate attachment to the past.

4 *Attachment to your form.* If you believe that you are only your body, and as it goes, so go you, then you are inviting a lifetime of suffering. Wrinkles, hair loss, weakening vision, and all indications of physical change will create a sense of suffering in direct proportion to your attachment to remaining the same. This attachment to your body can create a life-style of artificiality and fear that will prevent you from being on your path and involved in your destiny.

Attachment to your body as the means of fulfillment in this life results in an endless preoccupation with appearance. It is an attachment to the packaging that contains you, and it disguises the knowledge that your body is a temporary form that you are occupying. Being exclusively involved with outer appearance makes it difficult to see that your true essence is a formlessness that resides inside the body. The more you are attached to the body and how it appears, the less your chances of being able to stand in back of your form and see the divineness that is truly you. Addiction to form keeps many from ever considering the formlessness that makes up the largest part of humanity. Paramahansa Yogananda, writing in *The Divine Romance*, said it this way:

The saints say this is how you must treat the body, as a temporary residence. Don't be attached to it or bound by it. Realize the infinite power of the light, the immortal consciousness of the soul, which is behind this corpse of sensation.

I like that phrase 'this corpse of sensation.' That is your body, a slave to the rules of form, hindered always by the baggage of pains, aches, bones that crumble, and pimples that break out. But inside, where you are that formless astral thought, you are pure and devoid of the obstacles that rule in form. Attachment to your body is like having an attachment to suffering and being unwilling to let it go.

Detachment from your body does not mean a disregard for the perfection of your form. In fact, paradoxically, it almost always results in your taking better care of the covers that house your soul. I have found that I take much better care of my body, maintaining a healthy weight, exercising, getting enough rest, eating fewer nutritionally empty foods, since I am less attached to my appearance. I can now stand back and watch my body go through its aging mechanisms without feeling that my being, my Self, is deteriorating. Since I am less attached to this body I am not alarmed by any of its infirmities. There consequently seems to be very little need for them to surface. As a result of this detachment I have fewer and fewer difficulties with my body. Thus I celebrate my form and its perfection, and I know that I am more than this body. I have love and respect for, but am not identifying with, my physical self. 'Being in the world, but not *of* it,' as Jesus said. I am in my body, but not *of* it, and ironically it helps me to be in my body much more effectively than when I was exclusively *of* it, only a few short years ago.

5 *Attachment to ideas and being right.* This is one of the most difficult attachments to discard. 'Being right' could be considered a terminal 'Western disease.' I listen to talk radio for several hours each day in cities all over North

America. It is my observation that virtually everyone who calls to a radio station to discuss a current topic is attached to his or her idea and to the notion of making someone else wrong. It seems to be unheard of for someone to listen to another point of view with an open mind. The callers almost always are quiet and polite for a few moments while the other party is talking, and then ignore everything that was said and state their own position. Seldom do I hear anyone say, 'You make a good point. I'll rethink what I believed before I made this call.'

This attachment to being right creates suffering, because it is almost always a useless device for communicating with other people. If you cannot communicate effectively, you are going to suffer in your relationships. People do not want to be told how they should think, and that they are wrong if they disagree with you. When people encounter such a stance, they automatically shut you out of their consciousness, and a barrier has been erected. If you are the one being shut out because of your inability to listen, it is because you are so attached to what you already believe that you insist on making everyone who disagrees with you wrong. Attachments, like these make loving relationships almost impossible to sustain, because boundaries are continually being erected.

For every idea that you absolutely know is right, there are millions of people who believe that you are wrong. This dichotomy of right versus wrong gets people into a mess of trouble metaphysically. When you encounter someone who believes something quite different from you, and you try to explain how wrong he is, all you have done is define yourself. Your position will most likely make him more adamant about his beliefs. So encounters of this nature almost always end up with each person more firmly convinced than ever of the rightness of his position.

To be detached you must know that all right-versus-wrong dichotomies are the invention of people. Right does not exist independent of man. The universe simply is the way it is, running on the principles that we have defined, but still running independent of our opinion about it. Certainly it is fine to have strong opinions about anything that you choose, but the moment you become attached to these ideas and thereby define yourself by them, you shut out the possibility of hearing another point of view. This attachment to ideas and to making others wrong is the history of the being called Human Being, and it accounts for untold wars and misery since the beginning of recorded history.

Seldom do people stop and truly hear what the other person has to say. Seldom if ever do we change our mind based upon solid ideas presented by others. And virtually never are we able to hold two contrary opinions and beliefs in our mind simultaneously. Yet this is precisely what is required of you in order to awaken to a new level of human consciousness: an internal awareness that an opposite point of view can be held simultaneously with your own, and no need to make others wrong. This is something highly enlightened beings speak about. One of America's great novelists, F. Scott Fitzgerald, said:

The test of first-rate intelligence is the ability to hold two opposed ideas in mind at the same time and still retain the ability to function. One should, for example, be able to see that things are hopeless and yet be determined to make them better.

This is truly what it means to be able to be detached — to allow opposite points of view to reside within you at the same time, and to see the exquisite beauty in such an attitude.

6 *Attachment to money.* This attachment borders on being a full-fledged disease in the Western world. It is important to understand that I am not suggesting a distaste for money. I strongly believe that having money is a benefit in life, and I have nothing negative to say about money. Money is fine, and working to make money is part and parcel of living

in modern times. What I am writing about here is an attachment to money such that it becomes the controlling factor in your life.

To be detached from the acquisition of money is a difficult undertaking. It is, however, important if you are to feel a strong sense of authentic choice-making within your life. I have found that those who are able to do what they love and keep themselves focused on living that way have the amount of money they need come into their lives. They seem to keep that money circulating, using it to serve others, rather than letting the accumulation of capital and cost of things be the dominant themes in life. They do not suffer from the *more* disease that is so prevalent in our culture.

To be detached from money means to shift your focus to doing what you love and what makes you feel purposeful, and to let the money arrive in your life without being consumed by it. Detachment means an awareness that *you* are not your bank account. If you feel that you *must* have money in order to feel happy and successful, then you are attached to it. Your need to have more means that you do not feel whole now, that *something* is missing. That something you are calling *more money*. That missing part will keep your mind focused on getting what is missing, rather than being here now, and doing what you love. And, of course, what you think about will expand.

Since what you are seeing right now in your life is precisely the result of what you believe, you may want to change those beliefs if they do not serve you when it comes to money. Ask yourself: 'Has money brought me the satisfaction I believed it would?' If the answer is no, and you cannot seem to change those beliefs, then examine what the beliefs are attached to.

One way to do this is by centering and/or meditation. Ask and trust your inner self to reveal what that belief is. It may not be an attachment to money at all, and most certainly is not when you feel dissatisfied in spite of your money. An analogy would be believing you are hungry and after eating still feeling the hunger. Believing food is the solution creates an attachment to food that can never satisfy the hunger. Attachment to food or money in this type of situation intensifies a fore-doomed attempt to fulfill a yearning. When we are obsessively attached and would prefer not to be, because it is unsatisfying, it is a signal to examine what that attachment represents.

7 *Attachment to winning.* Winning is almost an addiction in our culture, and as long as we are attached to the need to win we will experience some suffering as a result. Once again it is important to emphasize I am not against winning. I love to win as much as anyone, particularly when I engage in athletic contests. But the test of awakening in this area is the ability to be detached from the *need* to win. When we are attached to winning, it becomes an obsession, and we suffer when we do not emerge as the winner. A great test of character is how we react when we lose. If we play competitively and our opponent scores more points or 'wins,' what have we really lost? Absolutely nothing! We simply went out and played a game. If we truly know this, we find it easy to congratulate our opponents and feel just as good for them as we would have felt had we emerged victorious. Attachment to winning makes many many human beings feel like losers. Maintaining that attachment means feeling like a loser a large part of our lives, since no one can always win.

Winning is a judgment. When we buy into it, we are agreeing to guidelines that other people have decided determines winning and losing. Seeing it as only the outcome of rules established by others can be a way of playing the game without being attached to winning. We can still relish our successful actions and learn from our not-so-great ones, and simply be in the process of participating. Winning or losing can be viewed as just one more rule that we can choose to agree with or not. Attachment to winning means we are the score or performance. Suffering results when we feel like losers.

Paradoxically, the more detached we are while actually playing the game, whatever it is, the greater our likelihood of winning. That is, the less focused we are on winning, the greater our chance of doing just that. Read some of the excellent research on the inner game, the Zen of archery, and the like. Outstanding performers are not trying to win. Those people are allowing the action to flow, totally in the moment. Their competition is more like a meditation than a contest. They are in harmony with their body and mind. Great dancers simply let it happen, trusting instincts and intuition to allow their forms to flow with the music, and when they are able to be completely in that inner place of perfect harmony, winning is not even on their minds. The moment great gymnasts or platform divers think about the score, they are unable to function in the perfection that their trained bodies are capable of. Winning becomes next to impossible. This is another paradox. If we think about winning and are attached to it, we lower our ability to function at the level that winning demands.

An attachment to winning almost always goes hand in hand with a need to fight our opponents. The language of competition is similar to that of warfare. Fight team fight. Beat them back. Stomp them, crush them, annihilate them, blitz them, kill them. When we have our minds focused on winning at all costs, our performance level deteriorates. We become tense and nervous, and ultimately defeat ourselves. Why? Because fighting weakens, while harmony strengthens and empowers. When we are at harmony within, our bodies perform at the highest level. When we are tense within, we perform at a lower level. This is the essence of detachment in the game of winning. Stop making it important. Permit yourself just to be, enjoying fully what you are doing in harmony with body and spirit, and your detachment will lead you to the highest levels you have ever reached.

*

Examine each of the above attachments carefully and see if they apply to you. Remember, it is possible to love things within each one of these categories and still be detached from them. Practice letting go, and allowing it all to circulate in a network of harmony and inner peace. As we transcend attachments we learn to shift our consciousness to networking and giving power away, and we discover the metaphysical luxury of living peacefully and productively.

Networking: a helpful means to detachment

Most of us are familiar with organizational flow charts. Such a chart starts at the top with the chief executive officer, then spreads out one level lower to a series of vice presidents, then down farther to middle management, then to lower-level managers, and finally to clerks, secretaries, and other support personnel. Persons entering an organization with such a flow chart generally plan to inch their way up the ladder. At each level they acquire a bit more power and prestige, until they reach the pinnacle where they will have the supreme authority and all of the trappings of success that go with such a position.

This is the way educational, religious, governmental, and charitable groups and even many families are organized. The powerful person is at the top, collects as much power and authority as is possible within the organization, and delegates that authority down through the flow chart. This is the model most of us have been trained to respect. Such an organization of people is called a bureaucracy. It is the least efficient way to get things done. A less-known but far more effective system is called networking. I espouse this system because I believe it contributes to a more awakened and enlightened society.

A network is the exact opposite of a bureaucracy. In a bureaucracy the purpose is to collect power and distribute it down through a flow chart of underlings. In a network the purpose is to give power away. It works like this: Think of a huge telephone network with no central source of power, but instead with every single terminal connected to the next terminal and on and on endlessly. The communications network has as its purpose to give service to the next terminal, and it then passes the services along to the next. No one in the network is interested in amassing power, but only in passing it along.

Human beings can work this way as well. Rather than being obsessed with gathering influence and seeing how many people we can control, we shift our objective to giving away our knowledge and acquisitions to the next person, and then to the next, and so on. If networking had a flow chart, it would be horizontal rather than vertical. It means sending out into the system what we have and what we know, and having it return to recirculate continually through the network. It means giving things away without any expectations. Again, the paradox surfaces. Giving and being unattached to that act will increase the flow in your life.

I find networking to be the most effective way to get the word out about anything that I want to share. I have sent a copy of one of my books, *Gifts from Eykis*, to everyone who has written to me over the years, simply as a gift, with no expectations attached. Moreover, I have sent it to thousands of people in all walks of life simply as my way of circulating the ideas that I so strongly believe in. The *sales* of *Gifts from Eykis* have increased since I began *giving* it away! The more I give away, the more people buy, and the more my mail overflows with the return of those thoughts and ideas from Eykis, elaborated and discussed by readers who keep the book circulating in a network of affirmative response. Additionally, I have received over one thousand books and tapes from people all over the world in response to my sending them a book! A movie is going to be made based on Eykis, and the book continues to grow in popularity. That old saying 'What goes around, comes around' is my working principle.

A networker finds it easy to give a great deal more than is expected, and understands that the way to feel successful and enlightened is to surprise others by giving them more than they expected. Networkers never try to accumulate power; they circulate all that they have, and encourage others to do the same.

Many businesses are starting to network. The essence of the recent trend, described in the fastest-selling business books, is to develop a win/win approach; to forget about your own quotas; to focus exclusively on how best to serve the customers. Growing numbers of employees and employers are discovering that reintroducing exceptional service into their organizations and reconnecting to a spiritual side of themselves and others are a pleasanter and more successful way of doing business. When the organization begins to function at this level, the networking principle of detachment creates an environment in which the customer and the members of the organization are all in a winning situation.

From allowing yourself to simply flow, to examining your attachments, and finally to networking. This entire universal principle of detachment is troublesome for those of us reared in the part of the world that prefers to count the trees rather than to contemplate the forest. It is important therefore to look openly at any resistance you may have to developing a more peaceful, detached view.

Why you may resist detachment

Below are the most common reasons why many people in our Western culture find it difficult to be detached.

● Detachment means to trust the universe to provide for us as we travel our path of enlightenment. We have not been encouraged to make this kind of commitment to a metaphysical principle. We were taught to get as much as possible, hold on to it before the other guy takes it away, and always scramble for more. Examine whether you want the controls of your inner life to be based on people, things, and events external to yourself. Consider how it would feel to have self-determination for your inner life.

● We work hard at a given profession, climb the ladder of success, deny ourselves for a majority of our years, and hope for a future reward. We believe that suffering in some capacity is what we must do. We have never had a course in applied metaphysics in all of our formal schooling. Our educational experiences centre around what we know rather than how we feel. I suggest that you diligently examine what you believe about being successful. Is it really wealth accumulation, ownership, profits? You may want to abandon some entrenched beliefs to make detachment a workable philosophy of life.

● Many people conclude that detachment means not having anything and consequently having to sacrifice all that they have worked for up until now. In short, giving up the good life. But detachment means freeing yourself from *needing* attachments. It does not mean sacrifice. Success as an inner process cannot be measured by accumulations. When you use external acquisitions to measure your inner worth, it is impossible to feel detached from them. You can incorporate the principle of detachment in your life and continue to enjoy all the abundance that you choose.

● The idea of being detached from loved ones may trouble you. You may feel that it is promoting a noncaring, indifferent attitude. But detachment as applied to loving relationships means quite the opposite. It means loving people deeply and unconditionally for what they are, without judgment when they choose to be what they want to be. With children, detachment does not mean allowing them to follow their instincts and disregard their responsibilities. Children are happier human beings when they have learned how to include respect and responsibility in their lives. But they learn this from adult behaviour that demonstrates respect and responsibility. An attitude of detachment will prevent children from manipulating parents into emotional slaves to their conduct. Attachment, not detachment, will victimize you and contribute to a breakdown in your relationships.

• You may be thinking of detachment as an absence of conviction and purpose, and feel that one needs to get out there and rattle some cages in order to survive. I suggest, in response to this misunderstanding, that those who experience a great deal of success are those who know how to flow with life rather than fight it. They experience inner peace rather than inner turmoil. Flowing rather than fighting is a sure way to avoid a stressful approach to life in which you are always struggling to row upstream.

If your resistance to the detachment principle is strong, if you find it difficult to comprehend, I suggest you nonjudgmentally and lovingly embrace how you feel. Do not try to force yourself to feel what does not feel right to you. Do not feel that you are judged by yourself or others. This unconditional love for yourself will always lead you in *your* right direction. You are on your path. Believe it, and you will see it!

Implementing detachment in your life

Detachment involves a kind of surrender to the force or intelligence that is behind all form, including your own. Once you completely trust in this energy that makes all form work perfectly, you begin to slow down and work in harmony with this intelligence. The word 'surrender' is a good one to keep in mind. It reminds us to stop the fighting that creates a battleground of life. With surrender, we relax into the natural intelligence and flow of life and can ignore the impulse to be attached to things and people, as they wind in and out of our lives.

Here are some ideas to help you with the surrendering process – ideas that will make you stronger, since fighting and attachments weaken you and you gather strength when you flow unimpeded.

● Flow with what you encounter rather than being inwardly critical. Learn a new way of processing or thinking about everything that you encounter. For instance, rather than judging the way the driver ahead of you is behaving, send a loving thought and practice believing that what you are encountering is exactly the way it is supposed to be. Detach yourself from the idea that a slow driver is somehow wrong and that you are right to be upset. Set aside an hour to flow with everyone that you meet. Allow everyone to be who and what he or she is without your being attached to an idea that someone should be different. Do the same thing while watching the news on television. Do not pretend to love what you despise, but see if you can let the news flow through your awareness without being hooked by compulsive judgment. Detachment will give you a sense of peace about what you hear and see. You will discover the simple yet elusive truth that the world is working exactly as it is supposed to. Your attachment to how you think it is supposed to be working only makes you a victim.

● Try replacing some of your competition with cooperation. Rather than viewing yourself as in competition with anyone, try viewing others from a universal perspective. See them as a part of Human Being. See yourself as someone who functions much more effectively and happily when you do not have to defeat anyone in order to feel good about yourself. Remember that when you need to defeat another in order to feel total, that other person controls your life. Compete athletically and in business if you choose to, but cooperate at the same time by detaching yourself from the eventual outcome. This loosening-up process is detachment in action. Let every single move you make in a competitive encounter be something unique unto itself, something to enjoy and live fully in that moment. Remember that if you are concentrated on what the eventual outcome will be, your attachment to winning will paradoxically make it less likely that you emerge with the better score. Detachment works by seeing yourself in cooperation with all of humanity, including your adversaries. Detachment from needing to win frees you up to flow with every single moment needed in the competitive process. Enlightenment is not in whether you win. It is in seeing yourself as fully human when you do not win and treating others respectfully whether you have won or lost.

• Keep things circulating in your life. If you have not used something in the past year, regardless of how attached to it you are, pass it along. You have used up its usefulness to you. By circulating it to someone who will be able to use it now, you ensure that this process continues. Go through your garage and discard as much of your 'thens' as you can bear to right now. Remind yourself that it is impossible to run out of 'nows,' so you do not need to store away those 'thens' as a safeguard. Keep everything circulating. Letting go of attachments is a rewarding way to feel positive about yourself, and to keep things flowing back into your own life as well. It works – it really does – but you will see it only when you believe it.

• Talk to yourself about your attitude toward ownership. How can you own a watch, a diamond, a house, or anything? The best you can get is a temporary lease to enjoy them. Ownership is impossible. Your pleasure is a result of your thinking, not of your possessions. An object is just that. Your pleasure in and enjoyment of it come from how you choose to think about it. Close your eyes.

Now the object is gone from your consciousness. Has your happiness and success disappeared as well?

Things flow in and out of our lives just as frequently as we open and close our eyes. The less stuff you need to convince yourself of your happiness, the higher your consciousness, and the less potential you harbour for any suffering. If you attach yourself to all of those possessions you can be assured that you will experience a great deal of suffering as those things wear away or begin to disappear from your life. Remind yourself that everything that serves you today – your home, your automobile, your jewelry – will someday soon be serving others.

● Work each day at simply allowing loved ones to be, without any attachments on your part. The more you detach yourself from any ownership conduct toward loved ones, the closer you will become to those people. With your love partner, practice celebrating the differences between you. Let your partner make mistakes without a long lecture from you. Respond to your partner from a sense of integrity, rather than judgment.

Help people if they ask, guide them if they need assurance, but do not be upset because they decide to do things you find foolish or distasteful. Remind yourself that you made mistakes along the way. Run your own life at your own pace on the path that you have chosen, but do not expect anyone else to be where you are. This is the essence of detachment.

● Examine the traditions that you practice and live in your daily life. If they serve you, and you enjoy them, then by all means honour them. But remember that an attachment to a tradition often involves creating barriers between peoples, and shutting out those who are not a part of the tradition. Be in command of your conduct rather than letting the past behaviour of others dictate your way of being. If you feel that you 'must' behave the way your ancestors dictated, then you are attached to that tradition, and you are not living an enlightened life. Be free enough inside, where you really live, to conduct the affairs of your life without attachments to how it was done before you. Certainly, celebrate the traditions that serve you and all of mankind. But if they do not serve you, or if they contribute to barriers rather than bridges to others, then have the courage to trust your own inner demands. Remember that all traditions started with some human beings deciding on them at some time. You are as valuable a human being as those who lived here before you. You too have the right to start traditions which are loving and respectful of everyone.

● Practice looking in the mirror and lovingly acknowledge the signs that indicate your form is aging. Say out loud, 'Go ahead and do anything you have to do – you are the package that holds me. I am not only this body.' It is important to understand that you are not only your body. You cannot age thoughts. You cannot age spirit. You cannot kill thoughts. You cannot kill higher consciousness. This will help you to detach yourself from your body and get on with accomplishing the mission that you put yourself here for in the first place.

To be attached to your physical appearance is to ensure a lifetime of suffering as you watch your form go through the motions that began the moment of your conception. How can you keep a hair from graying, a wrinkle from appearing, a limb from growing to its exact perfect length? The death of your form is also set in that moment of conception. But the higher-consciousness part of you, the part that thinks, the place where you do all of your living, is impervious to these rules of form. Knowing this, you can forget about having to have a body that is eternally youthful. Instead, put your own thinking energy into the divineness that is you. You can stop the worry and posturing and go past that form.

You can take good care of your form and still be

detached – detached in the sense of not identifying yourself exclusively with your packaging. The irony will again appear. Your body will be better taken care of when you concentrate less on it, and more on being an awakened person.

• Set some time aside each day specifically to practice not making other people wrong. Instead of attacking when you find yourself in disagreement, try saying something like 'Tell me more – that's a point of view I've never considered before.' Your detachment from the need to be right will defuse suffering and antagonisms and help you to create a more peaceful inner life. You already know that most people are not going to have the same opinion. By detaching yourself from the need to disagree, you open up the lines of communication, end your frustration at the people who disagree with you, and find yourself more in balance. It can be done without much of a struggle. Simply open yourself up by offering others your comments and thoughts, rather than jumping down their throats with your opinions and your attachment to proving them wrong.

• Read the following without any attachment to making me wrong. Ready? 'Money will come to you in sufficient amount to take care of your needs only when you stop needing more of it. The more you give away without any expectations, the more you will receive back.' I know this is a radical notion, but it has worked for me. When I gave up my attachment to money, stopped putting a price tag on everything I encountered, and continued doing what I loved doing, I found money arriving in my life in unbelievably large amounts.

Stop yourself from thinking about money a few moments at a time. Think instead of the exquisitely beautiful things in life that no amount of money could buy. Detach yourself from the need to acquire and hoard money. Give it away freely in whatever measure you find appropriate. Take the price tag off your life and all that you see and do. Enjoy things simply for the beauty they offer, rather than for the bargains they provide.

• Remind yourself that the best way to win is to not need to. Your best performances are accomplished when you are relaxed and free inside. Take this kind of pressure off your children and other loved ones, as well. Allow them to do and enjoy, rather than evaluating them on the basis of who they defeat. You can detach yourself from this insidious need and find yourself a much happier person each day.

• Get into the networking habit. Send out to others as gifts what you would like to share. Do this without any expectations that they have to thank you. The more you link yourself to others in a networking fashion, the more they too will pass on the message. The more you give to others all that you find valuable, the more you contribute to harmony in the world. Your sense of purpose will intensify as well as your satisfaction.

The voiceless people of our world, those who are not a part of any huge bureaucracy, have a powerful tool in networking. Connecting yourself to one other person who will spread the word to another is a monumentally effective way to make a difference in the world. When you give something away, anything at all, the recipient is somehow charged with the energy of your giving act, and he or she wants to do the same. While the communications channels appear to be invisible, the impact is nevertheless empowering. Give it a try the next time you are inclined to want to go with your old bureaucratic training. Rather than seeing another person as an impediment to your own aspirations, see him as an ally. Give him what you were trying to accumulate for yourself. Detach yourself from the need to accumulate influence and power, and see that individual as someone who is his own centre of power, who will pass it along to another and so on in an infinite network of powerful influence.

This, then, is detachment – perhaps the most misunderstood universal principle in our culture. Try looking at it from a metaphorical point of view.

Imagine yourself listening to a symphony and telling yourself that it is impossible to enjoy any of the musical notes until you have heard all of them. As the symphony nears completion, you realize that this music is not a completed picture that you can own. It is one note and then another flowing through your senses. Each note flows and you experience it in its relationship to the other notes and instruments, throughout the symphony. This is the principle of detachment in action as it operates in your daily life. You can never get the entire thing into a neat package that you own. Never! You can only let it flow through you, enjoying it in the moment, and then experiencing the next. No ownership, no control – only enjoying without any attachment to a belief that it should be otherwise.

Music is an energy that flows through you with each and every note, one at a time. You cannot wait until all of the notes are completed before you enjoy it. The energy of the music flows outward and through you, and the moment you have an attachment to it in any way, you lose it. One note at a time, in this 'onesong' that is our universe. No attachment to any of it, only the endless flowing of it all. Every attachment keeps you from enjoying the flow that life is.

It is a lot like trying to grab that handful of water. Remember that the tighter you squeeze, the less chance there is of having water to experience. But when you relax, allowing your hand simply to enter the water, the water is there for you to enjoy as long as you wish. Release attachments, in favour of allowing it all to flow, just as the music flows one note at a time out from the instruments through you, and just as the water flows always available for you to enjoy, as long as you remain detached.

6

Synchronicity

The universe is complete and perfect. There can be no mistakes. Nothing is random. The entire 'onesong' is exquisitely synchronized.

To understand synchronicity and to implement it, we are required to suspend some of our old ideas, to give up our notion of coincidence, of mistakes, our belief that people are imperfect. The principle that every single event and every single person is connected seems almost too much to accept. Most of us would rather hang on to the 'principle of randomness' and 'error.' We seldom consider that everything within our perfectly operating universe may also be operating perfectly. It appears easier to believe that unexplainable coincidences occur for no reason.

The term 'synchronicity' was first used by Carl Jung. He spent his life attempting to unravel the mysterious threads that seem to wind together in a pattern that is impossible for us, in form, to decipher. He described synchronicity as 'the simultaneous occurrence of two meaningfully but not causally connected events.' He hypothesized that a collaboration exists between people and events that seems somehow to involve fate, and is always operating in the universe.

The basics of belief in synchronicity are that every single life has a purpose and a deeper meaning that we are generally aware of. Behind all form is an intelligence that is exquisitely perfect, and that works in a synchronized fashion. Everything happens for a purpose, and the puzzle pieces of life fit together perfectly. When you trust and know these thoughts, you will daily recognize evidence for your belief in synchronicity. I am convinced that this phenomenon is omnipresent in my life and that there are no accidents of any kind.

Carl Jung went on to say:

At the very moment when we are struggling to sustain a sense of personal autonomy we are also caught up in vital forces that are much larger than ourselves so that while we may be the protagonists of our own lives, we are the extras or spear carriers in some larger drama . . .'

Or, as we have explored, there is only one dream, God's dream, and we are all characters in it, similar to the characters that we create for our individual dreams.

Synchronicity in all our lives

For the past several years I have asked my lecture audiences, 'how many of you have had the experience of thinking about someone and then receiving a letter or phone call from that person the same day he or she appeared in your thoughts?' And 'Have any of you run into someone you had not thought of in years, just after his or her name happened to come up in conversation?' Every hand in the audience usually goes up. Synchronicity, or the connection between seemingly random events and thoughts, seems to be a universal human experience. It happens to all of us quite regularly, and it tends to repeat itself in a series of appealingly unexplainable happenings. The fact is that the more we loosen up and allow ourselves to flow in the energy system of the universe, the more we experience this phenomenon. Ultimately we cease being surprised by these happenstances and recognize them as part of the mysterious perfection of our existence.

I would bet that you have had the experience of absolutely knowing who was calling on the phone before you answered it. I am sure that you have had what has been labeled a *déjà vu* experience, wherein you knew that you had been in that very moment and lived that exact situation previously. I would also wager that you have found yourself doing something that you had never done before and were unable to explain why you were doing it until later when you could look back and clearly see the reason. Let me give you an example of one such situation in my life.

Some years ago my publisher offered me a sizable advance for a nonfiction book that would be a follow-up to *Your Erroneous Zones* and *Pulling Your Own Strings*. I thought about the possible content of my new book for months, and frankly I was stuck as to what avenue to pursue. One day I was sitting by the ocean thinking about what to write when I felt a strong urge to get up, get dressed, and get into my car. It was totally uncharacteristic of me to want to leave the tranquility of the beach at that time of the day to get in my car and drive unnecessarily. Yet I drove, without thinking about where I was headed, and after thirty minutes or so I found myself parking at the Pompano Fashion Mall. I was baffled by my behaviour. I generally avoid shopping malls and would never consider spending a beautiful sunny afternoon at one.

I walked directly to the bookstore and immediately went to the section on psychology. One book was sticking out from the others, about to fall from the crowded shelf. I pulled that book out, glanced through it, and went to the checkout counter and purchased it. I drove home, walked back to my beach spot, and read the book from cover to cover.

And I knew precisely what I had to write about. I outlined the book which later became *The Sky's the Limit* in a matter of a few hours. My subject was self-actualization, or what I called no-limit living. I felt a clear sense of being able to make this area of human psychology more understandable and available to the average person. I knew that what I must write about was how to become a person who lives life at the very highest levels, and how to cultivate a sense of purpose and meaning. It was clear to me after that strange experience of being propelled to read a new book.

The book that practically fell into my hands was Abraham H. Maslow's *The Farther Reaches of Human Nature*. His earlier writings had been a powerful influence on me, but this book was the impetus for my writing *The Sky's the Limit*. When I was stuck, a seemingly coincidental force guided me exactly where I needed to go. And so I dedicated *The Sky's the Limit* to Dr. Maslow. I feel a special kind of mission to carry on his work and make his ideas on mankind's potential greatness available to more people.

I am sure you can recall similar kinds of eerie happenings in your life, where you did something totally out of character, and suddenly saw, very clearly, why. How can we even begin to explain such things? How did the card get inside the seat-belt buckle that led me to my father's grave? How can a thought suddenly connect you to someone or something that seems so unconnected? The word 'connectedness' is vital to understanding the principle of synchronicity. In some mysterious, undefinable way, everything seems to be connected, even though we cannot see the connections. In some strange way, the right person or the right series of events crops up just in time to help us over the threshold of some troubling problem. Once we understand that everything is connected in some way, even though we cannot see the connectors, this universal principle of synchronicity becomes more believable, and ultimately more available to us.

There is a rhythm to the universe. When we are able to get quiet enough, we experience how we are a part of that perfect rhythm. I keep coming back to the concept of perfection, because for many, there is such a strong belief in imperfection. I believe our world cannot be anything other than perfect. The precise amount of energy required to heat and sustain our planet comes from the sun, without burning up its own energy source. The earth rotates perfectly on its axis without being in danger of falling off. The entire universe has an intelligence supporting it, which I call God, and you can call anything that you like. The salmon swimming upstream back to their spawning site is mysteriously perfect. The swallows show up on the same day century after century. The spider knows how to build his web without going to web school. The instincts for making the entire onesong work perfectly are built in by an intelligence which permeates all form. And we know very little about how any of it works. Yet it is all connected in some way, from generation to generation, throughout all species, and into infinity. If we can begin to grasp this process of connectedness even in a tiny way, we will also begin to understand ever so slightly the principle of synchronicity, to start to believe in this phenomenal intelligence that supports all life so perfectly.

In order to see that there are connectors in the universe that we cannot always see with our eyes and hold in our hands, let me take you on a brief excursion of 'connectedness.'

The easiest connectors to believe in

Obviously, the easiest things for us to believe in are those that we can see. Hence the notion 'I'll believe it when I see it' permeates our linear, form-only culture. If you see a child pulling a toy with a long string, you have very little difficulty in seeing and believing in the connection between that moving toy and the child's actions. There is the string – I see the connection! When something is connected, and we can see, hear, touch, taste, or smell that connection, we have no difficulty in believing in its connectedness. Thus, when we put gasoline in a car, and start the engine and begin to burn the fuel, we see the connection between our actions and our ability to move about via an automobile. We are not in a state of confusion or disbelief about how automobiles move from one point to another. So the easiest connectors that make things hang together are those that

you see with your own eyes, those that allow you to say
to yourself, 'I see how that works, and I believe it.'

More difficult connections: form to hidden form

When you turn on the light from a wall switch, you cannot see the connection between that switch and the room
suddenly alive with light, but you know that a connection
exists, know the connectors are hidden inside the walls.
We do not have to see the connectors, we simply have
to believe that they are present, even though they are
hidden, and we then have a knowing about how this
process works. This category of 'hidden connectors' is a
bit more difficult to comprehend, but not terribly so, since
we place tremendous faith in the fact that the connectors
are still in form. Even though they are out of view, we can
find them if we really want to.

Even more difficult connections: form to invisible form

You are sitting in your living room watching a television
programme. Rather than getting up to change the channel,
you take in your hand the remote control, which is in no
way connected to the television set. You press one of its
buttons, and the channel changes. The television set is
responding to some sort of invisible signal. How does this
work? You cannot see any connectors. You cannot smell
or hear anything. You can even place a piece of paper in
front of the remote control and the connection still exists.
What is going on here?

This category of connectors is something that all of
us have grown accustomed to. We buy our children toy
automobiles which run by remote control. A left turn for
the toy car twenty feet away is accomplished by pressing
a left-turn button. Something travels through the air and
instructs the car to turn left. No wires, no strings, no visible
connections, and yet we believe in these connectors, even

though most of us know almost nothing about how they work. We believe that invisible signals fly through the air because that is what we are told, yet we have never seen those signals. So now we are becoming more aware that a connection between any two objects does not require form, as we perceive it with our senses, to be present. We believe in and live with, connections that defy our senses. We believe in them, and they work. After a few years of living with these kinds of connectors, we even begin to take them for granted, despite the fact that they are a complete mystery to us.

Invisible connections: human form to human form

The next time someone is talking to you across a room and you are listening, stop and ask yourself, 'How is this happening? That person is ten feet away, moving his mouth, there is nothing but air between us, and yet I instantaneously hear and process everything that he is saying. How can this be?' When you stop to consider this everyday, ordinary occurrence, it becomes mind-bending. Invisible things called sound waves travel between a mouth and an ear, and you are able to process it all with your brain. Where are the connectors? I see his mouth moving. Is he sending them out of his mouth? I do not try to make my ears pick up these invisible signals, yet they appear to do just that. We unquestioningly believe in a whole classification of connections between people that our rational mind simply cannot fathom.

We know that these invisible waves connect us from one person to another, or even from an object such as a radio, or a door slamming, to a person. We do not bother to make an attempt to figure it all out. We simply accept a principle called 'sound' as something that exists, something that is part and parcel of our humanity. We never say, 'It simply cannot be. If I cannot see it and touch it, then it must not exist.' Our belief in this principle allows us to function as human beings. There are invisible connectors between people, and you participate in them every day.

Our own connections: our thought to our form

You are dancing with your partner, effortlessly gliding across the dance floor. Your feet are doing exactly what they are supposed to do. There is some kind of mysterious connection that exists between your thoughts and the neuromuscular activity of your feet. Why do your feet move perfectly in response to a thought which tells them to move? What is the connection? How can this be?

Every single time you move the limbs and appendages of your form, they are responding to a thought. But a thought is invisible and formless, and that formlessness is somehow commanding those actions. You cannot see the connection. You cannot explain it. But nevertheless, the fact that you scratch your nose, or walk to the kitchen, or move your head, or move toward a fly ball hit from a baseball bat and put your gloved hand up to catch it, or make any other of the myriad movements that you engage in every day, gives evidence that invisible connectors exist which allow you to move about effortlessly in your everyday life.

Mental energy directs muscular energy. Mental energy is thought. Therefore thought is some kind of a connection between a desire and a physical outcome. You believe very strongly in this connection even though you cannot explain it. You accept this automatic stimulus-response connection as a way of life. You believe in it. You function within it. You never question whether such a connection exists, for millions of daily movements give you absolute proof that there is a connection between the formless and the world of form. Keep this in mind as we move into the final areas where those connections exist.

Incomprehensible connections: human thought to another human form

My wife is sitting in one part of the house and our baby is in another part of the house, out of hearing range. My wife suddenly says to me, 'The baby is crying – will you go check on him?' Sure enough, he is crying; yet it was impossible for her to have heard the sound. Every mother who reads these words will nod her head in agreement, knowing that an invisible connection does exist between her thoughts and the actions of her baby.

We have now gone beyond the comprehensible. There can be a connection between the thought of one person and the actions of another, without the benefit of any of the five senses. We all know that such an invisible connection can exist. My wife will be ten miles away from the baby and say to me, 'We have to go home now – the baby is ready to eat.' I say, 'How can you know that he is hungry? Do you just know his schedule that well?' She responds, 'My milk just came in, and it always comes in when it is time for him to eat.' What is this connection between her body and that of an infant ten miles away? Her body knows precisely when to produce the milk based upon the thought of hunger in her infant, and it works perfectly every time. The connection is invisible, but it is definitely there for us to observe.

If such an invisible connection can exist between a baby and mother, can it be tapped and utilized between *any* two humans? Can we refine this relationship between our thoughts and the world of someone else's form?

While I was giving a speech recently, in Sacramento, California, a father in the audience was holding his baby, who started crying. The father became nervous and upset about disturbing the rest of the audience and started walking out, obviously still trying to hear my presentation. I suggested that he relax about his own discomfort and communicate that serenity to his infant.

He smiled at me from the audience, relieved that I was not going to judge him for having his baby there, and he noticeably relaxed. The baby stopped fussing and for the next three hours never made a peep. There was an invisible connection between his thoughts and the baby's behaviour – a connection which defies description.

Your own connections: thought to thought

We do not even know what one thought is, and yet we all know and believe that a thought exists and that a connection also exists between any one thought and another thought. For example, I sit here writing, thinking about what I am going to write. That thought leads me to another thought that I should probably say it this way or that way. Then I have another thought that allows my fingers to type out what those previously connected thoughts led me to.

We can sit quietly and have any thought, since we are the source of thoughts. Then we can have another thought based upon that first thought, and perhaps even ten more thoughts, until we then decide to put them into the world of form, or just to forget them.

It is not the thought process that I am addressing. It is the existence of *connections* between thoughts. Connections most assuredly exist between two formless things called thoughts within you, the being that you are in this moment. If you can accept that these connectors exist, you are ready for the next level. If you are not ready, then I want to hear from you! Tell me how can there not be connections between thoughts, when one thought leads to another?

Synchronicity: human thought to other human thought

This is what I have been leading up to. Of course, the connectors are hidden, just as they have been in all of the categories except for the first one. Yet you believe in the existence of all the other connections. So now, try to open up your heart and let in the fact that maybe, just maybe, this invisible connection also exists in our universe, and that once you start to believe in it, you will see it surfacing everywhere. The evidence, while hidden to your senses, will show up and overwhelm you if you believe it. Let's see how they show up in your life and mine.

The Formless connections between human beings

Imagine a container the size of a grapefruit, with a lid for the top. Now try to make an educated guess about how many pennies you could store in this container. You might come up with a guess in the neighbourhood of three hundred pennies. If I were to ask you, 'How many thoughts could you store in this container with the lid tightly sealed to avoid spillover?' you would probably answer, 'How can you store thoughts in a container? Thoughts are formless and dimensionless. You cannot store something without physical specifications or boundaries in a container.'

Now ask yourself, 'What is memory?' Eventually you have to conclude that memory is nothing more than thoughts. So where are those dimensionless thoughts stored, in order for us to recall them as we do? Many people truly believe that memory is stored in the brain, yet the brain is a container about the size of a grapefruit. It is form. Can you store thoughts, which are formless, in a container which is form? Of course not. So what is memory and where is it if it is not stored in the brain? Hang on and we will speculate about this.

Now let me ask you another question that I often hear: 'Where do we go when we die?' Most people try to come up with some kind of place that fits into their 'form only' orientation. But I believe that most of what we are is outside the rules of form. And so my response to the question is another: 'Where do all of those characters that were there with you in your dream go when you awaken?'

206

Form has a place; you can store it. Nonform (thought) does not require a place, since it is dimensionless. Thought is infinite and so is impossible for us to comprehend from a position of form only. Experiencing our universal spirituality requires entering another dimension of being, where beginnings, endings, and storage places are unnecessary.

Many religions speak of God creating heaven and earth in the beginning. When asked, 'When did God begin?' they respond, 'God always was.' That answer is acceptable to most of us, and we cease speculating on beginnings and endings. What is it that you think of when you think of this infiniteness that most people call God? That is the formless, no-beginning-and-no-end, always existing dimension that I speak of throughout this book? It matters not what you call it. What matters is to let in the notion of the dimension in which you reside for the two-thirds of your life that you are awake. Thought, to me, is a part of that transcendent dimension.

There are many labels for that formless dimension: spirituality, higher consciousness, inner wisdom, enlightenment, altered states of consciousness, and so on. I call it thought, because we are all part of it, and it is a part of all of us. Here in the universally recognized human activity of thought is a place to begin to comprehend the formless dimension.

In some Eastern traditions, this higher dimension is called the Tao, which translates to 'the unfolding.' It has been said that 'the Tao that is described is not the Tao.' This is because form, in words, whether spoken or written, *describes* the experience. What we *experience* with our senses is quite a different thing. The description differs from the experience in the dimension of thought. But in order to write about it one uses words to make it as available as is possible. Otherwise, this book would be a series of blank pages. Now if we were as enlightened as we might like to be, that would suffice! You would put the book down after careful study and say, 'Profound indeed!' But we are not there yet, at least I am not. So, as a writer, I find myself writing about that which cannot be described, here in this territory of synchronicity, the dimension of thought.

If memory (thoughts) cannot be stored in our brain, then we have to be open to the possibility that they are outside the brain in some way. The mysterious happenings that seem so inexplicable may somehow come under the heading of thoughts meeting thoughts. If there are invisible connections between thoughts and form, then why not between thoughts and thoughts as well? And if thoughts do indeed meet with other thoughts, and we are the source of thoughts, then it seems possible that we create synchronistic situations.

Consider thought as something that we create all the time. We are the source of this creative process through our connection to the divine and the infinite. With this awareness we can dismiss 'coincidence' and believe in the divine intelligence operating in our universe. Of course, once you believe it, you will truly see it working every day. Synchronicity is not a passive speculative principle. It is here, it works, and you are a part of it. Believe it or not. See it or not.

What are these connectors made of?

When we examine the connectors between form and form, we can clearly delineate precisely what makes up these bonds. But once we move to the area of formlessness, we must stop relying on our senses and use intuition to tell us how connections link thoughts to form, and thoughts to thoughts. Three possibilities for what constitutes thought are (1) energy that resonates in the universe; (2) invisible waves, vibrating so fast that we cannot perceive or measure them; (3) part of morphogenetic magnetic-like fields that surround members of a species.

But in spite of a great deal of speculation and research and many books devoted to analyzing these subjects, there is still no agreement on what constitutes thought and how thoughts are transmitted. And so I suggest that we shift from analysis to synthesis. Analysis is a form of intellectual violence wherein we break up an object of study, look for patterns, try to put it into a scientific mode, and come up with a formula. Synthesis is a way of bringing everything together, by starting from what is obvious. Thoughts are formless. They exist in our universe. We participate in this process. We do not need a formula to tell us that there is a connection between thought and everything that we do. We know that we cannot store thoughts in a container. Thoughts are in some way a part of the invisible world that exists, though hidden from us.

Reshad Feild, writing in his thought-provoking novel *The Invisible Way*, presented this brief dialogue:

'I understand what you are saying, John,' Nur replied. 'There was a time when I could see that other world. Each idea was a shape that could be understood, rather than seen with the eyes.'

Reshad Feild's words suggest a world that we have been impervious to because of our experience of living almost exclusively in form: the world of ideas, of thought; this amorphous formless stuff called thought, which both originates with a person and simultaneously is that person. Thought is out there *and* in there at the same time. It is everywhere. Energy? Perhaps. A resonance? Perhaps. A chain link of morphogenetic fields? Perhaps. Invisible? Definitely! Something from which we can never escape? Definitely! Just try not thinking for even a few moments and you will see that thought is something that you are inextricably tied in to.

Once you accept that thought could possibly exist outside of you, then you are on your way to understanding synchronicity. The hookup between seemingly unconnected events is really the hookup of thoughts, the essence of our universe, this vibrating energy that we cannot see or define. Similarly, the hookup between your thoughts and those of someone else is easier to consider with the idea that thought is energy flowing unimpeded in the universe, not just in one individual. Those seeming coincidences seem elegantly appropriate when we are tuned in to the dimension of thought. The answer for me to the question 'What are these connectors made of?' is simply: 'They are thoughts.'

Thoughts contemplated as energy are hooking up not out of coincidence, but because we are both the source of thought and a part of universal thought. The ability to be thought and create thought gives us the ability to make virtually any connection to thought that we choose. As we awaken to this probability, coincidences no longer are surprising. Before long we come to expect them. And then, trans-form-ation, as we are able to create them at will. Acknowledgment of synchronicity in our lives nurtures our divine connection to the invisible, formless world. It allows us to begin the awakening process and to see that we can use our ability to think and be thought, to reshape and redirect our entire lives.

The awakening process

Stage one: your beginnings on the path. Remember when your heart was broken and you felt you would never get over the trauma? Your mind probably seemed to be working against you because of your endlessly painful thoughts of how miserable you were right then and how awful the future seemed. Perhaps it was a romantic crisis, a divorce, a financial disaster, an illness or accident of some kind. You were unable to view it with hindsight.

The experience of a crisis immobilizes us for a long period of time. Our mind is focused on the disaster aspects of the situation, and we are unable to function effectively.

We are unable to sleep or eat, and do not know how we are going to get past the terrible set of circumstances. We use our minds to focus on what is wrong, how painful it is, and how terrible it is going to be in the future. Advice from friends and relatives seems unrelated to our problem and usually results in anger and frustration. We cannot see any way out of our misery.

This is a typical response for all of us who are traveling our life paths in the belief that the external signposts are all there is to our reality. We cannot imagine that there is a valuable lesson in the trauma. We reject any suggestions that someday we will recall this experience as a necessary step in our development. We simply want to wallow in our hurt, believing that someone or something outside of us is creating this pain, and wishing that those externals would change.

I acknowledge having been in this place for a part of my life. I can recall being immobilized over romantic and family crises, and being so sad and weepy that I functioned ineffectively. My mind seemed to be stuck in place on a particular problem and I was unable to go more than a few minutes without having those thoughts in my head. I felt possessed by the problem, and could not imagine why this was happening to me, nor could I visualize anything positive ever resulting from these difficulties.

All of us at this point on our personal journey of awakening are possessed by our traumas. We truly believe that the events are making us unhappy, and have not yet learned that we are stranded in the misery by the way that we are processing the events.

J. Krishnamurti, in *Commentaries on Living*, writes of a man who is reacting to the loss of his wife:

'I use to paint, but now I can't touch the brushes, or look at the things I have done. For the last six months I also have seemed to be dead ... The other day I picked up the brushes, and they were strangers to me. Before, I didn't even know I held a brush in my hand; but now it has weight, it is cumbersome. I have often walked to the river, wanting never to come back; but I always did. I couldn't see people, as her face was always there. I sleep, dream and eat with her, but I know it can never be the same again ... I have tried to forget, but do what I will, it can never be the same again. I used to listen to the birds, but now I want to destroy everything. I can't go on like this, I haven't seen any of our friends since then, and without her they mean nothing to me. What am I to do?'

The widower describes dramatically how his mind is stuck in suffering. All of us have experienced or will experience similar painful emotions. We are unable to consider that there may be a gift in the unfolding drama that is our life in the moment.

Stage two: the middle ground. As we become more awakened, we use our power to create our world through thought in a much more transcendent way. Looking back, we almost always see the benefit to us. The divorce that we thought we would never get over now seems to be the best thing that ever happened. Youthful crises which felt life-threatening at the time now seem a natural part of our development. The bout with alcohol addiction that was ruining a life is now viewed as the most important thing ever experienced – it taught how much strength was really deep down inside, even though days of drunkenness seemed to destroy all that was important at the time. The bankruptcy is seen as the necessary catalyst that caused the shift to a more rewarding way of life. The severe illness is recognized as the message to reexamine priorities and slow down. Hindsight provides new eyes to see the opportunity in what was happening at earlier stages of life.

Stage two is the middle ground of enlightenment because it is the place where we no longer need hindsight to see the opportunity. As we approach this stage we are becoming aware of the benefit right now, as it is happening. We stop focusing on thoughts of what is missing and stop catastrophizing about the future. Instead we shift to 'What is in this for me right now? How can I turn this into an opportunity without having to go through years of suffering before I see how necessary this all is? This is an important step in the enlightenment process, and helps us to see how synchronized the onesong really is. Certainly we still experience the pain and suffering, but we simultaneously know that there is something magnificent in this as well. We are able to be gentle and accepting with ourselves, and to honour and love even the part that is creating this crisis. We probably will not cognitively understand why this pain is occurring right now, but we will have an underlying knowingness and belief in the value of it.

I heard Ram Dass describe his feelings during the death of his beloved stepmother. He wondered why she was required to suffer so, in the advanced stages of melanoma. He knew in his heart that suffering was a part of the journey, and that it always led to something grander, but this, this horrible pain, this beautiful woman whom he loved so dearly – why? As she passed through the final stages before her death, he noticed that she was becoming more peaceful, and he saw a look of exquisite serenity and joy overtake her, and she seemed to enter a new realm, a blissful state, as she left her form. The suffering was over, since pain is experienced by the senses in form. She was free, and Ram Dass, watching this scene unfold, said to himself, 'Yes, and even this too leads to a higher state.' He saw that the suffering was leading to something grander for her, and he did not need to wait several years to realize it. As she left, he was at peace with her departure, for he knew that death is a reward, not a punishment. He had that peace within himself too, knowing that the suffering had within it a blessing.

Stage two, then, involves being in the present moment with everything that we are experiencing, rather than having to spend long periods of time suffering before we realize the blessing inherent in the struggle. I became aware that I was past Stage One on October 15, 1982, in the city of Athens, Greece. I had decided to run the original Greek Marathon, and after a training program, had made the trip to Greece. The distance of twenty-six plus miles was not threatening to me, since I had already completed four marathons. But I had no idea what I was going to encounter when fifteen hundred of us lined up at the starting line in Marathon, a tiny fishing village twenty-six and a fraction miles from the finish line at the Olympic Stadium in Athens.

The race was delayed by about an hour because of some technical snafus. It was 10:20 A.M. when we finally began, and the temperature was eighty-eight degrees, heading upward into the hottest part of the day. The terrain was a gradual uphill run for almost seventeen of the twenty-six miles. After fifteen miles I knew I was in serious trouble. The heat and uphill running were beginning to take their toll. Runners were dropping out. Some were on the side of the road, vomiting, and many, victims of heat exhaustion, were being placed in Red Cross ambulances.

I could feel myself getting queasy, and for the first time in my running career, I stopped in the middle of a race and had to lie down and give in to nausea and vomiting. I would stay on the ground, drink a quart or so of water, and then get back up and run a few more miles, and then be back on the ground. By the twenty-one-mile mark I was at a point of physical exhaustion that I had never experienced before. I was shaking and vomiting green bile, but unable to fathom that I had flown all the way to Greece to accomplish something that I had dreamed about for years and was not able to finish the race.

I simply could not let that thought into my consciousness. I contemplated what it would be like to fly back to the United States and then look back at this moment and see what benefit there was in it for me. I could not get that picture as I lay on the street five miles outside the city of Athens, with people coming to my aid, telling me to get into the ambulance for the ride back to the Olympic Stadium. So I stayed in the moment, and asked myself what blessing or opportunity there was in this. I put my suffering aside and genuinely asked myself if I really wanted to go back home without having completed what I had set out to do. Could I somehow reach down inside myself and find the will (through thought) to run for five more miles?

Something came over me at that moment that I can only describe as a miracle. I felt that I was lying there in the heat and vomit to see if I had the inner courage to do what seemed impossible at that moment. Five more miles at that moment seemed like five hundred. Yet I saw with my thoughts that I could use that situation as a blessing and truly grow as a human being by transcending my physical condition. My physical insides literally changed. I went from weakness to strength in a moment, the moment when I gave myself permission to see the opportunity to discover how much strength I could draw on. I righted myself, told the ambulance attendants to help someone else, and I proceeded toward the finish line five miles ahead.

As I entered Athens, I realized that my troubles were not over. The streets had not been blocked off, and so we were required to run down the highway on the lane markers with cars driving alongside us, and policemen trying to keep the automobiles away from the runners. The fumes were the worst I had ever experienced in my life. Cars were changing lanes right in front of runners, the drivers ignoring the pleadings of the policemen attempting to direct traffic. It was growing hotter by the moment. Yet, with each new obstacle, my resolve seemed to intensify, and my legs stopped cramping and quivering. I was getting stronger, not weaker.

I finished that race. I finished despite having spent almost thirty minutes on the ground. I finished in the top third overall, which was my highest finish ever, even though it was my slowest time. But the time was insignificant. So too were the cheers and the medals we received. I had learned something very valuable about myself, and I did not have to wait several years to know what the blessing was in the suffering.

This short verse from raymond ng's *reflections from the soul* sums up my thoughts nicely:

> Out of mud the lovely lotus blossoms,
> Out of trials something higher vies

When we can seize that higher something in the moment, we are advancing along the path toward that third and ultimate stage wherein pure synchronicity lies, and where we take a much more active role in co-creating our world.

Stage three: pure synchronicity. If Stage one of enlightenment is to notice with the benefit of hindsight that every obstacle is an opportunity, and Stage Two is to catch ourselves as the obstacle appears, noticing the blessing as it is happening, you are probably wondering, 'What else is there?' The answer is difficult to comprehend for those who cannot see anything beyond their form. For the third and highest stage of enlightenment gives us the choice of thought at its purest. If offers the possibility of thought experienced without intermediary, material, so-called causes. It is synchronicity in context with the notion that we are thought, and that thoughts reside both within and outside us.

In this stage of enlightenment we are able to see the obstacles on the horizon as simply 'events' which we have a choice about. At this stage we do not need to create or become caught up in the obstacles to have the learning experience. The negative-sounding 'obstacle' is replaced by the more neutral term 'event.' I believe that today, at this point of my development, I do not need to get so sick running a marathon to experience my Self in thought as I did in the Greek Marathon. I can be with that strength or essence or Self in thought if I so choose. I can know that aspect of myself without having to go through an obstacle or event. And, yes, in this third stage, the lotus blossom can bloom in thought without needing the mud to create it.

The divine part of ourselves which I have labeled thought and God is a force in the universe which we are capable of tuning in to if we believe in it and if we are willing. In the purest stage of synchronicity we have a choice about experiencing thought in form or in pure thought. We get an intuitive sense that to act or continue acting in a certain way is creating a forthcoming event. Inner intuition tells us that we are heading toward this situation and we sense we have a choice about whether or not we need to go down this road again. In pure synchronicity we are able to bypass the experience in form by having the thought without the need to play it out in form. It is literally getting out in front of it rather than learning from it through hindsight or in the present moment. When we permit thought its synchronized flow, its passage as part of the perfection, without resistance or denial, it flows through naturally without need to manifest externally.

Recently my wife and I were considering purchasing a new home which was under construction. We liked everything about it and planned to sign a contract. Then both of us had an intuitive feeling that there were difficulties down the road if we made such a commitment. We have come to trust those inner signals, and so we decided, simply on the basis of our intuition, not to enter into an agreement with the builder. At previous times in our life together we have made some decisions that turned out to be costly. Here we were at least at Stage two, knowing that we had lessons to learn. The blessing in those obstacles turned out to be that we learned to trust our inner signals and avoid unpleasant outcomes in the future.

That third stage of enlightenment, in which my wife and I are able to get out in front of ourselves and have choice about an impending event, occurs regularly when we are in disagreement. We can both see such events coming, and we are willing to look ahead and live out, in our thoughts, the consequences of acting in certain ways. A great deal of suffering is eliminated by contacting the obstacle in thought only and then removing the need to translate it into form.

Utilizing thought to write the script for ourselves in form is a marvelous stage to get to in life. Here, in partnership with our inner selves, we can write the script for our outer selves in the most loving way imaginable. We can live in that graceful dimension of formless thought almost exclusively, programming for the form all that it needs to experience in its self-actualizing process. At the same time, having learned some lessons through traumas, we do not need to keep repeating them.

In Stage one we find the Krishnamurti dialogue with the man who was experiencing painful suffering over the loss of his wife. Let us look now at the next segment of that conversation:

There must be suffering as long as there is no understanding of the ways of the self; and the ways of the self are to be discovered only in the action of relationship.

'But my relationship has come to an end.'

There is no end to relationship. There may be the end of a particular relationship; but relationship can never end. To be is to be related, and nothing can live in isolation. Though we try to isolate ourselves through a particular relationship, such isolation will inevitably breed sorrow. Sorrow is the process of isolation.

'Can life ever be what it has been?'

Can the joy of yesterday ever be repeated today? The desire for repetition arises only when there is no joy today; when today is empty, we look to the past or to the future.

We have the power to use our minds to make the present joyful, with our ability to use thought. Loss of a particular

218

relationship is unbearable when there is no relationship to Self. This is the magic of synchronicity. The traumas and obstacles are truly the events to enable us to understand, to know the Self.

Thoughts meet thoughts, and you decide whether to transfer them into form or not. As you more and more tune in to the exquisite force that is your mind, trusting in yourself as the source of thoughts, the mystery slowly but surely begins to fade and it makes more and more sense to you. Events that seemed so impossible to figure out now become nothing more than thoughts meeting thoughts in a universe that is all vibrating thought. Where you once said, 'Wow, I simply can't believe the remarkable string of coincidences that led up to this,' you start saying, 'I trust it all.'

Let me share with you more of how this has worked for me.

Miracles?

I have experienced many synchronistic events that seem to be miracles to those who cannot comprehend how it all fits together. For me, they are simply the result of believing in the universal intelligence that supports all form and allowing it to work in perfect harmony. So when someone says to me, 'Come on Wayne, be more realistic,' my instant response is: 'I am realistic – I expect miracles.' I genuinely do.

When I began to see thought and form as one, and to see that I am somehow divinely connected to all thought, I saw that thought was something that I could use. This became increasingly clear as I began to meditate and seemingly leave my body for extended periods of time. I experienced the world of thought unencumbered by form. At this point, I started to experience the tremendous power inherent in our thinking capacity. Soon I knew that thoughts were something more than mysterious amorphous items in our heads. I realized that thought is the very stuff of the universe. It is energy, as is everything else in our universe. It has unique vibrating characteristics, as does other energy, but is unavailable to me through my five senses. That sixth sense became a new awareness for me.

Let me give you an example. Several months ago I received a letter from a church in Monterey, California, asking me to speak to its congregation. I photocopied the letter and gave it to my secretary, telling her to call for the details. The following day she told me, 'I called them and there was no answer. In fact, I called several times.' I was surprised that a church would not answer, and so I uncharacteristically decided to call.

A pleasant-sounding female voice said, 'Hello, Wayne. Why are you calling me personally? I talked with your secretary only yesterday.' Now I was more than confused. In the course of our conversation she related that she worked in the church bookstore. She said they would love to have me speak at a future seminar. I told her that 'coincidentally' I was going to be in Monterey on Monday (two days later) and that I would be speaking at the Hyatt Regency, and then spending five days in isolation, writing an article that was overdue. I informed her that *no one* knew that I would be staying in Monterey, but that I would contact her during the week. I emphasized that I did not want any media coverage, since I would be there strictly for writing and researching.

I immediately called my secretary and asked her why she had told me that no one had answered at this church, when in fact she had talked to someone there just yesterday. She then realized that she had mistaken that church for one she had called in Southern California.

I arrived in Monterey on Monday, gave my speech, and was settling into my writing on Tuesday afternoon when I received a telephone call from a woman who had a radio show that aired from 3:00 to 4:00 in the afternoon on weekdays before the baseball broadcasts. It was now 2:15

P.M. and she wanted me to be her guest in less than one hour.

I asked her how she could possibly have known that I was in Monterey. She told me that I had sent her, as part of a large mailing, some nine months earlier, a complimentary copy of *Gifts from Eykis*, and she had been carrying it when she visited the church bookstore earlier in the day. She said, 'While I was having my purchases rung up, the cashier noticed my book and mentioned that you were here in town at the Hyatt Regency for the week to complete some writing and research. My heart started racing at the idea of having you as a surprise guest on my radio show. Would you consider letting me pick you up to do the show at three o'clock?'

I debated with myself for several minutes, trying to come up with some excuse to avoid this interruption. I knew that if I agreed to her request, my afternoon of writing would be over. First I said, 'I can't believe how short notice this is.' Then, 'I deliberately told no one other than one lady at a church bookstore, and here you are calling me.' Finally I just gave in and said, 'Okay, pick me up in front of the hotel in twenty minutes.'

I did the show on this very small radio station. On the way back to the hotel, I suddenly blurted out, 'Where is that church bookstore? I would really love to stop in and say hello to that cashier.' We were within a few blocks of the store. As I walked in, the cashier said, 'I knew you would come into the store. The show went beautifully. Would you please autograph a few copies of *Gifts from Eykis* that we have in stock? We have had several phone calls.'

While I stood in a corner of the bookstore autographing their stock, a huge man, at least six feet ten, entered the store with tears streaming down his face and asked the cashier, 'Where can I get a copy of *Gifts from Eykis*? I must read it.'

She replied, 'The author is right over there. Why don't you go over and say hello?'

He came over to me and hugged me intensely. He was crying almost uncontrollably, and related this story to me.

'I've been deeply depressed for months, and this morning I had decided that I was going to end my life today. I made all the necessary arrangements, and then I took my radio to the park to listen to my last baseball game.

'As I tuned in to the station I heard you beginning to talk, and I listened as I've never listened before. I heard you talking about living life to the fullest and always choosing life. I heard you mention Eykis and the miracles that she brings to us all, and I decided that I would read this book that you seemed so in love with, and that I was going to begin to choose to think about all that I have to be grateful for. I want to thank you for saving my life.'

I walked out to the car, filled with the awe that I always feel in such moments. So many events had to have taken place in order to set in motion what had just happened. My secretary had to have made a mistake. I had to make a phone call myself. I had to reach the one person who would inform a stranger whom I'd sent a book to, some nine months previously, that I was in Monterey. I had to do a show I did not want to do. I had to decide to go to a bookstore on the spur of the moment. Another stranger had to decide to listen to his last ballgame and tune me in on that radio station at precisely that moment.

What is this all about? A huge series of coincidences? Or a universe that is working perfectly and giving us the opportunity to make choices within a perfectly formed, already completed universe? It brought home Jung's paradoxical comment that we are at once the protagonists in our own lives and the extras in a larger drama.

I choose to believe that series of events like these are part of this universal principle called synchronicity. A collaboration with fate, in which each of us makes choices within a larger context in which it is all perfect. No principle of science currently available to man can explain such happenings. Yet there is not a person reading this right now who cannot relate a similar 'mysterious' story. It happens all the time. This is truly thought meeting thought and being played out in form. All of my hemming and hawing about whether to do the radio show can be seen from hindsight as meaningless. It was already done, and the evidence is that it occurred. A free will within a completed universe. Of course it is a huge paradox, but what isn't when you start considering such things?

Several years ago I was driving home when suddenly the skies opened and it was raining harder than I had ever seen in my entire life. I could barely see out of the car windows. As I drove, I saw a woman standing next to her stalled car, hitchhiking in the drenching rain. I obeyed a very strong impulse to stop and give her a ride. As she got into the car, she explained that her car has stalled in the rain, and she needed a ride to a telephone so that she could call for assistance. I decided to drive her home instead.

As we introduced ourselves, Shirley exclaimed in stunned surprise that she had been told by two friends that she should contact me about some personal matters in her life. As a matter of fact, she had been told that day that she would meet me soon. I dropped her off at her apartment, gave her a copy of *Gifts from Eykis*, and encouraged her to contact my wife about some concerns that she had told me she had about childbearing. My wife is an expert in this area, and I felt that they would become friends.

Several weeks later, Shirley came to our home with a video-tape which was to become the impetus for my exploration into some of the metaphysical principles which are a part of my life today. All because of a 'chance' meeting in a rainstorm.

Shirley had several long talks with my wife about the value of using her creative powers to visualize herself giving birth to a baby. She affirmed her ability to create such a situation, though she was unmarried and uninvolved, and thirty-eight years old. Two years later, the following letter arrived from Shirley.

Dear Marcie and Wayne

Remember me? The wet hitchhiker, befriended by a blue auto whose driver's tapes echoed the theme of my health clinic?

Shirley Lorenzini – here I am, almost two years in Los Angeles. Marcie, you will beam at hearing that I am blissfully married. My husband just had his vasectomy reversed, and parenthood is looming. Life is wonderful. I'm enclosing a little snapshot of us one hour after the wedding festivities. Thus the relaxed look. Joe is everything I had on my list. Thanks for your belief and encouragement that he would show up.

Wayne, I love seeing you in my Nightingale-Conant literature and I quote you often in my health discussions. Just last week I told the story of your stopping on Federal Highway to rescue me from three miles of torrential hiking. That incident was providential. I think of it so often to remind myself of the miraculous nature of life. Did I create that incident out of just having listened to your tapes and needing to meet you? Did God know that I needed a morale booster?

And then, Marcie, you appear, so genuinely loving and listening. Listening to all my dreams and fantasies. Assuring me that I'll be a happy wife and mother.

You two are really angels.

So on your next magical appearance in California, please call.

Hugs to all of you,
Shirley

So many truly wonderful things have come about as a direct result of my following an impulse to give a woman a ride. Shirley became a catalyst for me, and we became catalysts for her on her journey. My life took a sharp turn, and some of the material that she felt compelled to bring to me altered my own spiritual journey in a way that I could not have predicted. Moreover, Shirley became a great friend to us, and we helped her to believe in her own power of co-creation and visualization, truly helped her to beat all of the odds, including having a vasectomy reversed, and becoming a mother to a beautiful little soul who was absolutely destined to be with Shirley and Joe.

How can we possibly know what seemingly insignificant event is waiting to change the course of our life? And what role do we play in it all? Synchronicity is the basis for allowing these forces to meet and work for us in our life, but we must say 'Yes' to life. One 'No' response anywhere along the path stops the flow of energy. This is why I believe so strongly in the notion of positiveness. Every single positive response in life allows the next one to flow, not as a cause and effect, but as a continuation of the energy that is in each of us and in everything else in the universe. You, with your own mind as the source of thought, which is the source of energy, which is really the source of life, can make all the difference in the world. A 'No' response to that intuitive knowingness within you, stops it all, and you stay stagnant. But one positive 'Yes,' one internal acknowledgment that you choose to go with that flow of energy, and it continues in its own perfectly miraculous way.

As human beings we are the very source of thought, that eternal connection to the divine intelligence that is in and in front of and behind all form. Our willingness to say yes, to be positive, unafraid to take the next step, to go with our internal intuition (thoughts), gives us the power to co-create with that divine intelligence that is our universal essence. We *can* make choices in a completed universe, and our willingness to say yes to life allows it to flow.

The stories of my experience in Monterey and our 'chance' encounter with Shirley are but two in a list that could go on for a hundred more pages. They are simply a part of the tapestry of my life today. I see them because I believe, and the more I know this within, the more evidence I have for it every day.

A few months ago I was reading a fascinating novel called *Winter's Tale* by Mark Helprin. Toward the end of the book, the author included a short chapter that was completely separate from the story he was telling. I must have read this chapter, 'Nothing is Random,' fifty times, and I still had great difficulty in accepting it as I read it. Today, I know it is true for me, and it is how I now see this entire onesong. With the permission of the author and the publisher, I reproduce it here.

Nothing is random, nor will anything ever be, whether a long string of perfectly blue days that begin and end in golden dimness, the most seemingly chaotic political acts, the rise of a great city, the crystalline structure of a gem that has never seen the light, the distributions of fortune, what time the milkman gets up, the position of the electron, or the occurrence of one astonishingly frigid winter after another. Even electrons, supposedly the paragons of unpredictability, are tame and obsequious little creatures that rush around at the speed of light, going precisely where they are supposed to go. They make faint whistling sounds that when apprehended in varying combinations are as pleasant as the wind flying through a forest, and they do exactly as they are told. Of this, one can be certain.

And yet there is a wonderful anarchy, in that the milkman chooses when to arise, the rat picks the tunnel into which he will dive when the subway comes rushing down the track from Borough Hall, and the snowflake will fall as it will. How can this be? If nothing is random, and everything is predetermined, how can there be free will? The answer to that is simple. Nothing is predetermined; it is determined, or was determined, or will be determined. No matter, it all happened at once, in less than an instant, and time was invented because we cannot comprehend in one glance the enormous and detailed canvas that we have been given – so we track it, in linear fashion, piece by piece. Time, however can be easily overcome; not by chasing the light, but by standing back far enough to see it all at once. The universe is still and complete. Everything that ever was, is; everything that ever will be, is – and so on, in all possible combinations. Though in perceiving it we imagine that it is in motion, and unfinished, it is quite finished and quite astonishingly beautiful. In the end, or rather, as things really are, any event, no matter how small, is intimately and sensibly tied to all others. All rivers run full to the sea; those who are apart are brought together; the lost ones are redeemed; the dead come back to life; the perfectly blue days that have begun and ended in golden dimness continue, immobile and accessible; and, when all is perceived in such a way as to obviate time, justice becomes apparent not as something that will be, but as something that is.

How radically different this point of view may be from that which you likely have assumed over a lifetime. How could everything be synchronized when it appears to the naked eye that everything is happening in a random fashion? If you want to begin to see how this all might be possible, I suggest that you initiate a fascinating study of quantum reality by reading Gary Zukav's *The Dancing Wu Li Masters* and Fritjof Capra's *The Tao of Physics*. Both of these books give an overview of the new physics and how 'hard scientific evidence' fits in with the metaphysics I have been postulating: Here is a brief taste of *The Dancing Wu Li Masters:*

The astounding discovery awaiting newcomers to physics is that the evidence gathered in the development of quantum mechanics indicates that subatomic 'particles' constantly appear to be making decisions! More than that, the decisions they seem to make are based on decisions made elsewhere. Subatomic particles seem to know instantaneously what decisions are made elsewhere, and elsewhere can be as far away as another galaxy ... the philosophical implications of quantum mechanics is that all of the things in our universe (including us) that appear to exist independently are actually parts of one all-encompassing organic pattern, and that no parts of that pattern are ever really separate from it or from each other.

To me, this simply is the scientific world beginning to catch up with all that spiritual masters have been relating for centuries. Subatomic particles are so small that they defy our rational understanding. They (you included) are the very essence of the universe, and they do not behave in ways that Newton and other early scientists formulated. They do not need time as a variable between one point and another. They are instantaneously both particles at the very same time. As *The Dancing Wu Li Masters* points out:

A particle over here can communicate with a particle over there (by shouting at it, sending it a TV picture, waving, etc.), but that takes time even if only milliseconds. If the two particles are in different galaxies it could take centuries. For a particle here to know what is going on over there while it is happening, it must be over there. But if it is over there, it cannot be here. If it is both places at once, then it is no longer a particle. This means that particles are related with other particles in a systematic and intimate way that coincides with our definition of organic.

Yikes! Subatomic particles that are two places at the same time, defying everything that we have come to believe about the nature of our existence and that of the universe. After we read about the new discoveries in physics and the new questions being asked, it is evident that our old views are no longer valid. Just because we cannot see how it is all connected does not mean that is is not.

All that we think we know about how life hangs together is really some kind of illusion that we have perpetrated on ourselves because of our limited vision. What appear to be inanimate objects such as stones turn out not only to be alive in the same way that we are, but also in many infinitesimal ways to be affected by stimuli just as humans are. The distinction between animate and inanimate simply cannot be made when you enter the world of quantum mechanics and try to determine how those apparent sub-atomic particles, of which you and everything else in our universe is composed, are all tied together. The point is that physics and metaphysics show there is a pattern to the universe that goes beyond our capacity to grasp it with our brains. Just the fact that we observe something with our thoughts affects what we are examining, even though we may think we are at a distance. That is how inextricably it all hangs together.

In this tiny little excursion into the world of the new physics, we find those apparent subatomic particles are so small that one of them in an empty fourteen-story building representing one atom would be the size of a grain of salt. And don't forget that a peek into our most powerful microscope reveals millions upon millions of fourteen-story buildings, in the tiniest object we can observe. Armed with this, can you begin to believe in the concept of synchronicity? How can you not? The essence of our universe from the perspective of the tiniest particles at the subatomic level outward to the endlessness of the void seem composed of a systematic, synchronized pattern that we too are very much a part of. We are each a subatomic particle, both here and someplace else at the very same time, all connected in the inspiring pattern of it all, behaving as unique beings and yet at the very same moment connected to all other beings, just like those subatomic particles within an atom, within a molecule, within a cell, within a being, within a universe. It is synchronized and perfect, and so are we. There are no accidents. The study of quantum physics reveals that the tiniest particles all work with some mysterious perfection individually, and in concert with all other particles anyplace in the universe at the exact same moment. No time lapse needed.

It does not seem difficult then to see that we are subject to the same system – that we are part of the seemingly impossible synchronized dance, and that while we appear to be making many decisions in the running of our daily life, at the same time, *and I mean the exact same time*, we are also part of the largest picture of all, which is already complete and perfect. Accidents and random occurrences are simply out of the question.

Everything that has happened had to happen; everything that must happen cannot be stopped

Think back to those examples I gave regarding Shirley Lorenzini and the man in the Monterey bookstore. Every single event of my life before then was necessary in order for me to be driving along Federal Highway at that moment, or to walk into the bookstore when I did. Had anything been different, I would have been different, and something else would have had to take place. But you know that nothing else could have taken place except that which did. So whether I believe that I could have altered it or not, the fact is that it came out exactly as it did, and nothing can change that.

The belief that we have a choice as things are happening is enough of a reason to make it true for me. I see both contexts very clearly now, and one does not preclude the other. As paradoxical as it may sound, 'We are all doomed to make choices.' Just as those subatomic particles can literally be in two places at the same time, instantaneously connected in different places, so too can I. It is simply in the way of things. I know that I am always making choices, and that each choice leads me to the next, and that as long as I am not interfering with the flow of the energy that is the universe, I am going in the appropriate direction. I know that when I say yes to life, trust my intuition (which I cannot define), and keep moving in a direction of harmony and love for myself and others, everything is balanced and perfect. I also know that I have the power to interfere with the harmony by acting in discordant and aggressive ways. My ability to think aligns me in the universe much as the subatomic particles are aligned, even though everything that we observe with our senses tells us that it is all random. I know that a closer, more thoughtful view reveals that nothing is random, including myself and all of my choices.

You can use this alarming realization to benefit your life

each day. Once you know that everything that you encounter, everything that you think and feel, everything that you do, is all part of the synchronicity of this universe, and at the precise same instant that you are directing it as well, you will have removed the shackles from your life. You will begin to see that all of your life steps are synchronized. You can stand in back of yourself, in your mind, and see where your form is heading. You can be detached from any need to interfere in an aggressive way with anyone, and be more receptive to all that is surrounding you, as well as all that you are surrounding. You can stop the endless analysis of everything and instead flow more peacefully, knowing that the divine intelligence that supports your form is working perfectly, and that it always will. How could it not? How could anything so immense, so balanced, so perfect, not be trusted to continue that way for you into infinity?

Trust in this. Know that it all hangs together in perfect harmony. Know that you too are a part of that perfection, and that your every act, thought, intuition, and placement anyplace is also part of that perfection. Once you accept this synchronization of the universe, the seemingly impossible coincidences are met with a nod and an inner knowing, rather than an incredulous shock wave of disbelief about a series of happenstances.

But before you can begin to get this principle working at all times, you need to let go of some old beliefs. Here are a few of the reasons you may find it difficult to start applying the principle of synchronicity in your life. Examine them carefully to test your willingness for allowing these 'miracles' into your life.

Why you may find it difficult to embrace synchronicity

• We have been taught not to believe something until we see it with our own eyes. Since we cannot see synchronicity or experience it directly with our own senses, we become skeptical of it. Our Western culture teaches that all of the mysterious connections are really only random happenstance, and it is easier to believe in these coincidences than in something which eludes our senses.

• We believe very strongly in our separation from the rest of humanity, as well as in our individuality. We see synchronicity as a conflict with our need to be our own unique individual, separated out from the rest of humanity. If everything is synchronized and perfect, then somehow fate is playing a very large role in our lives. If it is all in the hands of fate, then we do not have the ability to make individual decisions and exercise a free will. Many people find it exceedingly difficult to embrace both the concept of free will and that of a larger intelligence in the universe that is total and complete. If we believe that one principle precludes the other, we will find the universal principle of synchronicity difficult to embrace.

• Form rather than thought is the guiding principle of our lives. If we identify solely with our form and are unable to imagine a dimension of being beyond our form, we will have tremendous difficulty with the entire business of synchronicity. The world of formlessness may make us uncomfortable, since it all seems to centre on our faith, and very little else. For those who work in the business world where facts and profits are the true bottom line, skepticism about universal synchronicity is not only understandable but expected. (Although the evidence for synchronicity is become more and more clear each day, even to the most hardened linear scientists of our academic and business communities.)

• We may find this universal principle of synchronicity in conflict with our traditional religious upbringing. If we have been trained to believe that God watches over everything, keeping track of our sins, and is ready to punish those who have disobeyed the rules of our particular church, then a belief in a universal intelligence which is a part of us will be troublesome. Furthermore, the idea that all is perfectly synchronized may not fit in with beliefs that man is imperfect and that he must spend a lifetime suffering to atone for his imperfection. When we know we are in a perfect universe, and that God is not only outside but also very much a divine part of us, and that it all hangs together perfectly, there is very little need to be dictated to by anyone who has an interest in keeping us and our lives controlled. If our traditional religious practices teach something else, then we are bound to find ourselves in conflict over synchronization.

● Finally, it is difficult to begin to comprehend the enormousness of this universe, and how it could all be perfectly synchronized. Trying to imagine the behaviour of subatomic particles so tiny that there are trillions of them in the tiniest speck imaginable, and then seeing that they all behave in ways which indicate that they are each making decisions, and that those decisions are made based upon decisions made elsewhere, can be quite beyond our capacities. Then to imagine that each of us as a human being is nothing more than an energy system, made up of these infinite subatomic particles, and that if they are capable of such 'magic' by behaving based upon decisions made elsewhere, then why not us as well, is similarly difficult. And that is only a look inward to the smallest imaginable, and we stop looking further inward because of the limitations of our measuring devices. It is conceivable, I suppose, that a subatomic particle has zillions of sub-subatomic particles, and inward to infinity. Then to look outward, through the telescope, knowing that the universe is endless, which makes us sub-sub-sub-subatomic particles in a context of forever, and then trying to imagine us behaving just like those particles, is all quite overwhelming indeed.

Yet is *is* all possible, rather quite probable, rather definite, if you give yourself permission to get this fabulous perspective. Your resistance may come from the need to stay with what is familiar to you and leave all this speculating to others!

Some ideas for putting synchronicity to work

● Tell yourself you do not have to give up being the protagonist in your own life drama. You do not have to give up a belief in your ability to make choices and possess a free will. All you need do is accept the paradox that we live in both form and formlessness simultaneously at all times, and the rules for each dimension are quite opposite, even though they are operating at the same time for us. Once you know that you have a free will within a perfect universe, you can stop the stressful thinking that occupies so much of life.

As you start to become stressed out about one thing or another, gently remind yourself that it is all perfect, that you could not have changed one iota of it, and that there is a marvelous lesson to learn in whatever transpires. This attitude of knowing that everything happens as it is supposed to, that there are no accidents, and that we are precisely where we are supposed to be, doing what we are supposed to do, takes a tremendous amount of pressure off, and it eliminates our need to be judgmental.

Just try standing back in your mind and imagining how stupendous a thing it is to be a part of this living pattern of perfection. See it all as a magnificent tapestry playing out before and through everyone, and stop second-guessing any of it. This will not lull you into complacency. Rather it will vitalize you with the energy of someone who is at once participating in this enormous drama as an extra in God's dream, while simultaneously creating whatever you choose within that dream. Your awe will allow you to flow with it, rather than to judge or question any of it.

*

• Take responsibility for your role within the larger drama at *all* times. Do not view that apparent accident as being in the wrong place at the wrong time. See it as something that you can learn from and something that you created. When you know that you create your own reality within a perfectly synchronized universe, and you refuse to blame anyone or anything for your experiences, and when you know that what you put out there into the world is what is flowing back to you in a perfect energy pattern, then you will see a shift in your 'luck.' You will not endlessly encounter the same negative happenings when you are willing to absorb the lessons inherent in the happening. And once you are willing to learn from your 'misfortune,' you will not need to keep repeating it. When you receive that traffic ticket and you know in your heart that this is a message for you to slow down and drive more cautiously, you will have learned the lesson. If you simply gripe about it endlessly, you may have to participate in something more drastic. That is, you will continue to drive carelessly until you create that accident, or lose your driving privileges, or whatever. By knowing within that there can be no accidents, that even the tiniest subatomic particles are working on purpose, and so are you, you can genuinely turn your life around.

Try it! Give it a few months' tryout. If you would like to see something different, even if it is only a change in your 'luck', try believing something new, and I can assure you that you will start manifesting in your life what you believe. I know this to be true for me, and I am absolutely certain that you can make it true for yourself.

• Stop worrying! What do you have to worry about in this perfectly synchronized universe? It makes no sense to worry about those things over which you believe you have no control. And it makes no sense to worry about the things over which you have control, because if you have control over them, there is no reason to worry. Moral of the story: there is nothing to worry about. It is all handled for you already. So just flow with it, rather than fighting anything.

● Quiet your mind to experience the perfect rhythm of the universe. When you go within and allow yourself the freedom to be at peace without judgment, simply meditating and experiencing the oneness of it all, you soon start to connect to that energy that I have been alluding to throughout this book. That quiet mind state, if practiced enough, will convince you of the perfection of it all.

I have created what others would call miracles in moments of quiet meditation. I have gone into the incredible light that is part of my meditation, and felt myself become pure thought, though still conscious of having a body. When I return to this form it is as if I am recharged with an incredible energy. I know what the dimension beyond form is like, because I am able to experience it at will, and I urge you to put aside your resistance to this notion and just give it a try. If you are patient with yourself and are willing to stay with it, I assure you of positive results. It is not an accident that the most enlightened spiritual people who have ever walked among us all practice some sort of daily excursion into trans-formation, or meditation. Surely you can see that you too are divine enough to partake of this magnificent practice, if you are willing to stop identifying yourself exclusively as form for a few minutes each day.

● Review the three stages of enlightenment and ask yourself in which you currently reside. If you are in Stage one, and still having to wait for time to elapse before you see the lesson in your traumas, then work at being there with the problem and trying to glean something positive from it while it is happening. This means suspending for a few moments your anger and frustration at the situation, and shifting to a different attitude: 'All right, I created this mess for myself somehow, even though I don't quite understand how. What can I learn from it now?' This exercise takes you off what is missing or what is wrong, and puts you back on purpose.

If you are in Stage two, and you are looking for the lesson in it as it is unfolding, then see if you can play the entire thing out in your mind, actually seeing the consequences in thought, and then working at eliminating the need to play them out in form, where suffering is bound to take place. Simply stop the trauma in its tracks with your powerful mind, and then follow your instincts as to how to let it go, since you have already seen what the results are going to be if you continue, and you know within your heart that you do not need to go there anymore.

● If you are in Stage three, and you are able to bypass those traumas, or at least minimize them by actually getting out in front of them in your mind, then by all means help those around you to do the same. Share your gift with others, and let them see the beauty of someone who is trans-formed.

● Work to rid yourself of the idea that invisible connectors are not real. I have shown you many such connectors that you use every day of your life. Once you know that thoughts can connect form as well as thoughts, and that everything without exception in our universe is energy vibrating, then you will be able to grasp how everything is synchronized and perfect. With this internal insight, you can begin to work at creating synchronistic events and happenings for yourself. You can use the great power of your mind to focus on your healing, to strengthen your relationships to others, and to bring a sense of balance and harmony within. It is all accomplished by focusing on what you want to create, and the belief that you can co-create, along with the intelligence that supports your form, whatever you want for yourself without restrictions. But first you must know that your ability to be thought is the vehicle for bringing about this transformative process in your life. Through thought and thought alone you accomplish the miracles that may so far be eluding you.

• Practice trusting your intuition or 'that feeling' inside yourself. That very intuitive process is your higher consciousness in action, and if you ignore it, you are reverting to responding out of habit and to what you have been told for a lifetime. If you feel it within, and know that is the way to go, remember, this is the same process as if you wait it out, analyze it to death, and then go with the most logical choice.

An intuitive inner feeling is a thought. It is divine. It is you and you are it. Trust it – it is your basic human/divine early-alert system working. If you are afraid of it, or you want to hear from someone else first, then you are actually inhibiting that system from functioning, and you are teaching yourself to ignore it. Before long, out of disuse and mistrust, that early-alert system of thought or intuition will stop kicking in, and you will be responding to life according to the wishes and demands of others.

While you are playing a tennis match, you do not stop to think through and analyze each response. You allow your form to respond simultaneously with your thoughts. The more you allow this, the more it works effectively for you. Respond automatically with your intuition, trusting the synchronicity of this perfect universe to flow through you.

• Remember that 'analysis' is a violent intellectual act, one which breaks up thought and carves up the universe. When you have to break something up and look ever more closely at each component part, you are literally using your mind to break up wholes. It is an act of violence in that it keeps you from seeing the whole, and it keeps you focused on the breaking-up process. You are doing yourself a large disservice metaphysically by carving up yourself, your relationships, your very life activities, and trying to find the hidden meaning in each individual piece of behaviour.

● Remember that 'synthesis' is the opposite of 'analysis.' You can shift from analyzing to synthesizing and at the same time shift from intellectual violence to intellectual harmony. To synthesize means to bring it all together, to see how it fits with the whole. You can see your behaviour and that of everyone else in terms of how it relates to your entire universe. You can look for ways to bring yourself into a more centred whole, and concomitantly, bring yourself into harmony with all of those who make up the Human Being. It is almost second nature in our Western culture to analyze, to think only of ourselves and forget about others, and even to break ourselves up into more and more parts – into our personality, emotions, thoughts, form, athleticism, cultural heritage, and so on. To transcend this intellectual violence which inhibits us from seeing the perfect synchronized whole, we can shift to the process of synthesizing, seeing ourselves as connected to all and a connector as well. We can stop thinking of how everything affects only ourselves. Instead, we can shift the perspective to serving others.

I look for how we all fit together in virtually everything that I read, see, and do. I refuse to see myself as anyone's enemy, regardless of what the current crop of politicians may say. I think globally in all of my intellectual pursuits. I know that a world which spends $25 million a minute on weapons and allows forty children on our planet to die of starvation every minute is one which spends too much intellectual energy on carving up the planet and focusing on how different we all are. I know that I can resist my temptation to believe that anyone anywhere on our planet is separate and distinct from me. Every time I see other human beings, of any colour or persuasion, regardless of where they come from, I know I share something with them: my everyday experience of humanness. They know what it is like to be human, to be hungry, to love children, to digest food, to feel stomach cramps, to think. We all share that with each other. The more we think in synthesizing rather than exclusively analytical ways, the more likely we are to bring it all together. And the more likely we will be to stop the terminal emphasis on what separates us.

Remember each day as you look out at your world and see millions upon millions of flowers opening up that God does it all without using any force. It is all done with synthesized perfection.

And speaking of flowers, I've recently been told a story about a bouquet that turned out to be far more special than its donors knew.

A New Jersey couple had a big greenhouse attached to their home, and they kept if filled with flowers – including nasturtiums, rarely grown in a greenhouse.

One snowy January evening the husband and wife went off to a rehearsal of an amateur orchestra in a nearby town where they had once lived. They decided to take a large bouquet of nasturtiums to give away at the rehearsal, for they felt that the sunny colours – orange, yellow, red – would warm up that cold night.

As they got to the town, the husband turned off onto a byway by the river. The snow was falling, the area was deserted, but a little old lady was walking all alone. They recognized her as the mother of their former next-door neighbour and stopped to ask whether they could give her a ride. She seemed confused but finally told them where she was going, and they drove her there. As they left her, they offered her the bouquet of flowers.

Three days later, they received a note from her, thanking them for the ride and the flowers and telling them what their gesture had meant to her. She had been a practical nurse her whole working life, but had realized that day that she was too old and infirm to continue her work. She didn't want to be a burden to her family, and so she had made up her mind to throw herself in the river – unless God gave her a sign that he didn't want her to. That bouquet had literally saved her life.

How many 'chances' were involved in this one incident? If that couple had not decided to take flowers to a rehearsal, if the husband had not taken a byroad, if they had not arrived at the river just as the old woman was approaching it, if she had not recognized their gift as a sign, she would have lost the last several years of her life, and her family would have been deprived of their happiness in caring for her.

Let me end this chapter with one final story. It happened to me in February 1959, when I was nineteen years of age.

On a particularly cold evening I was hitchhiking home to Michigan from Patuxent River Naval Air Station in Lexington Park, Maryland. My oldest brother would be visiting too, and I would be seeing him for the first time in two years. I had reached an isolated rest stop somewhere in the middle of the Pennsylvania Turnpike. The temperature hovered around minus twenty-five degrees, and the wind was blowing so hard that I could stand hitching at the edge of the entrance ramp for only ten minutes or so at a time. It was about 3:00 in the morning, and I was walking out to do another stint of hitching when I passed another sailor returning to warm himself in the gas station. It was too dark to see anything but the outline of his uniform, but since we were both in uniform we briefly exchanged words.

'Be careful out there, buddy,' the freezing sailor said to me. 'It's so cold that you can only stay out there a few minutes.'

'Thanks,' I said, "I appreciate it.'

That was it. I went to see if I could snare a ride, and the sailor returned to the comfort of the rest area. After fifteen minutes of standing there with no 'luck,' I had to return to the rest area. As I walked into the warm room,

I saw the sailor with whom I had just talked in the dark. It was my oldest brother, Jim, who was hitching home from Norfolk, Virginia, to be with his family and to see me.

How many variables had to be precise to bring us together in the middle of nowhere, talking to each other in the dark, stranded in a freezing windstorm? I don't pretend to know the answer, but I do know that there are no accidents in a perfectly synchronized universe. You will see it only when you believe it.

Forgiveness

To forgive . . . you must have blamed

Achieving an awakened life is virtually impossible until we put the universal principle of forgiveness to work in our daily lives. I include a chapter on forgiveness because I know that an inability to forgive truly is the cause of many many people's suffering. In working with thousands of individuals over the years I have come to the conclusion that an absence of forgiveness is tantamount to staying imprisoned in an unawakened life. It is as important to learn and practice as are all of the other principles.

We cannot become awakened and truly live an enlightened life as long as we believe that we are restricted to form. As we have seen, enlightenment and abundance go hand in hand. For an awakened life, we must transcend our bodies, must learn to be detached, and to tune ourselves more finely to the synchronicity of the universe. But if we have not learned forgiveness, we may master all of the other principles and still remain prisoners. To genuinely feel forgiveness is to understand and apply all that you have read in this book. Forgiveness is the ultimate test for the person who is willing and able to live the enlightened life.

In the introduction to this book I included a story about visiting my father's grave in 1974. That story is a story of forgiveness. And that act was, without question, the catalyst for moving me into a new life of abundance and love. It was the most freeing and loving thing I had ever done. Once I rid myself of the hatred and anger that I had been storing inside myself for this man whom I did not even know, I had inner space to be receptive to an entirely new way of living and perceiving my world. That new worldview, devoid of judgment and hatred, became the turning point in my life.

If you want to walk the path of higher consciousness, then you must take a hard look at your own willingness to forgive. Most of us simply are not very good at it. Most of us hang on to our judgments and hatreds. Most of us are very good at blaming others for the shortcomings of our own lives. Forgiveness – I mean true 100 percent forgiveness – involves a dramatic shift. Here we go again; back to the very stuff of the universe, and the very stuff of our existence. Thought! Not to forgive is not to understand how the universe works and how you fit into it.

The universe does not forgive because it does not blame

Life is a series of events which we have created and attracted to ourselves. The universe is also a series of events, all of which occur independently of our opinions about them. It all just is, and it is perfect. The stars are all in their proper places. Each snowflake that falls lands exactly where it is supposed to. The temperature each day is just what it is supposed to be – in fact, even the assignment of a number on a thermometer is a kind of judgment about it when you think about it. The storms, the floods, the droughts, the position of the rivers and mountains, the orbit of the planets – all of it just is. The universe with all of its perfection is presented to us. There is nothing to forgive, because there is nothing to judge and no one to blame.

When we know we create all that we need for our existence, then we are in a position to know that we created all the hatred and anger we have toward others. We even have created the others in our life for the purpose of having someone to blame.

Our need to forgive is a monumental misperception. The belief that others should not have treated us the way that they did is, of course, the ultimate absurdity.

The universe is always working just the way it is supposed to, and so is everything in it, even the things that we have judged to be wrong, improper, cruel, and painful for us and others. Our desire to improve those things is also a part of the perfect universe. How can others not have treated us the way they did? Instead of being angry at the way we were treated, regardless of how horrible we have assessed it to be, we need to learn to view that treatment from another perspective. They did what they knew how to do, given the conditions of their lives. The rest of the stuff that we carry around with us is ours. We own it all. If it is hatred and judgment, then that is what we have elected to carry around with us and that is what we will have to give away to others.

You have literally given control of your life to those whom you have judged to have wronged you. Learning to forgive involves learning to correct the misperceptions that you have created with your own thoughts. Once you have your thoughts clear, you will assume total responsibility for yourself, including how you are treated, and you will get yourself to the point where forgiveness is no longer something that you must practice. You will have corrected all of your misperceptions and eliminated the three sources of your discontent which create the need to forgive in the first place.

Understanding these 'thought distortions' will lead to practicing forgiveness and ultimately to freedom from ever having to forgive.

Ridding yourself of blame, revenge, judgment

I believe that my arriving at this place in my life has to do with having rid myself for the most part of these three big destructive practices. As long as I had a trace of them in my life, the forgiveness principle got entangled with them, and I was unable to live naturally and unimpeded. Now that I live without them, forgiveness simply never comes up for me, except as something that I share with others who are suffering so much because of their desire to hang on to those ways of thinking. As long as we continue to think in these ways, we have to work at forgiveness. When we transcend this kind of thought, forgiveness is no longer an issue.

Blame

If we are unable to forgive those we perceive as having wronged us at some time in the past, we need to look at the decision to blame them for our unhappiness. Blame runs rampant in our culture, and very likely it runs just as out of control in your life. The lawsuit explosion is testimony to the unwillingness of most people to take responsibility for their own lives. Instead, they sue as many people as possible, disregarding personal negligence, and ultimately making someone else pay for a misfortune. Advertisements offering legal assistance proclaim, 'It's not your fault, regardless of the circumstances. You should think about suing for damages now.' This mind-set of assigning responsibility to others for our life circumstances and misfortunes is the product of an attitude of blame. The more you have exercised it in your life, the more likely you will find forgiveness difficult to practice.

You must be completely honest with yourself if you are ever to rid yourself entirely of blame. The way to begin is to take total responsibility for everything that you are in your life right now. That's right. Say to yourself, 'I am the sum total of my choices up until this moment.' Your enculturation may make this a difficult precept for you to accept. You may want to say, 'I couldn't help it,' or 'It was someone else's fault,' or 'I was in the wrong place at the wrong time,' or 'I was dealt a dirty deal,' or 'Family circumstances created my misery,' or whatever other excuse you have developed to absolve yourself of responsibility.

Discard all of that and look at your life from a different

perspective. Everything that happened to you is a lesson you can be grateful for. Everyone who came into your life was a teacher, regardless of how much you choose to hate and blame him or her. There truly are no accidents. This universe is working perfectly, including all the subatomic particles that make up you, and those you blame. It is all just as it is supposed to be. Nothing more, nothing less! All of those situations, including when you were a small child, contain immensely valuable lessons for you to absorb and benefit from, lessons which are blocked by feelings of hate and blame.

Assess how much you resist this principle of taking total responsibility for your life and believing that there truly are no accidents in this perfect universe. Follow this logic. Someone has harmed you in some way in your past. You feel hurt and angry, and that anger ultimately turns to hatred. This is *your* hatred. You carry it around with you wherever you go. You own it. It is you and you are it. The hatred is all thought, and is with you wherever you go. You have given someone permission not only to hurt you once, but to continue controlling your inner life. The hatred infects your life while the other person is still on his or her path doing exactly what he or she knows how to do, independent of your current miserable state. The absurdity of blame is that it gives other people control over us at the moment of their dastardly deed, and continues to give them control over how we interact with others. We become prisoners without hope of achieving a higher sense of awakening and happiness for ourselves.

This is how blame works in us, and why it is a futile and destructive activity. As long as we blame others for the way we feel today, we will have to wait for them to change before we can grow out of our current immobilized state. Forgiveness is a tool to use to transcend the negative effects of blame. Once we have forgiven another, we no longer need to blame him. When we have forgiveness for all, there will be no one left to blame for anything. Ironically, then we also will have no need to forgive anymore, and that is the real lesson of this chapter.

Forgiveness means changing your misperceptions. When we forgive another for anything that he or she may have done to us, we are really saying, 'I no longer give you the power to control who I am, how I think, and how I'll behave in the future. I take responsibility for all of that now.' Thus, we really have nothing to forgive, since we create our own reality by how we choose to process the behaviour of others. We processed it in a way that hurt us when we chose blame. We might have chosen not to have hatred within ourselves and simply let it go. Once we change our perceptions of life's hurts and pains and see that we create all that we need for this dream, including the scoundrels, we no longer need to blame anyone for anything. This is the most freeing stage to reach that you can imagine.

Being totally free from blame and taking complete responsibility for life requires a great deal of discipline. It is a discipline of self-love rather than self-contempt. When we love ourselves, we refuse to allow others to manage our emotions from afar. Forgiveness is our means to that end. When we choose this option, it eventually becomes an automatic reaction toward those who treat us contemptuously, and then, of course, forgiveness is no longer required. Forgiveness is an act of self-love, rather than some altruistic saintly behaviour. It gives us control over our inner life and thoughts. Knowing that nothing is random, and that all of life is purposeful, even people who seem so destructively different from us, allows us to accept those 'accidents' and those 'scoundrels' as events with some meaning for us. I can assure you that once you no longer need the lessons in your life that unpleasant events offer you, you will no longer have these events. If forgiveness is something you need to practice, you will continue to attract opportunities to practice it. If your reaction is anger and hatred and defiance, then 'those kinds of people' and 'weird unlucky breaks' will continue to be in your life. I rarely run into these things in my life anymore. I look for the good in everyone, and I take responsibility for all that comes my way, and I mean all of it! Consequently, I see what I believe, over and over again. You too are seeing what you believe, and if you are blaming and full of hate, that is what you believe, and, of course, that is what you see as well.

Revenge

We live in a world which endorses anger and revenge. It is a world whose people are almost always at war in one way or another. War is our extreme tool for handling disagreement. War is waged between nations by those within the nations who are not at peace with themselves. Wars are waged even as an attempt to solve human problems -- 'wars' on poverty, drugs, illiteracy, and hunger. We pray to those who endorse forgiveness, we claim to love and respect great spiritual masters and their teachings, but when it comes to enacting forgiveness, we opt for revenge and war. Gunfire in Bethlehem on Christmas Day and in Jerusalem on Easter Sunday are sad reminders that forgiveness often is something that we pay lip service to, while crucifying designated enemies.

Revenge is the acting out of the thoughts of blame. Blame is in the mind, and revenge is acted out in form. The acting-out part immobilizes those who choose revenge as a life-style, and violates the most sacred sacrament available to us: 'Thou shalt not kill.' Yet kill we do, in numbers too large to comprehend, and we are building weapons so massive in their destructive ability that entire cities can be rendered into ashes along with all of their inhabitants. While this is all part of the perfect way of things that is so paradoxical, so too is the desire to end it that peace-loving people feel within their hearts. So as this violence continues and intensifies, we all must ask ourselves, 'What is the lesson that we as a total body of humanity are struggling to learn in this situation?" The existence of ourselves and future generations depends on our finding that answer.

Every day we hear of people who have been wronged somehow – injured, killed, maimed, raped, and robbed – and of the desire to exact revenge on the perpetrators. Families of victims are filled with anger and motivated by revenge. Hate flourishes along with demands for punishment similar to the pain inflicted on their loved ones. Yet, even when that penalty is carried out, the victimized continue to feel pain, suffering, and hatred. They poison their souls with debilitating anger, and cannot continue their lives free of this unwanted pain. They are victimized not only by the criminal, but by their need to exact their revenge.

I remember a case that Earl Nightingale told me about. It really impressed upon me the importance of forgiveness. A woman lost her only daughter to a violent criminal act. For the next eighteen years the woman was consumed by the desire for revenge, which remained unfulfilled, she believed, only because the death penalty had subsequently been banned in the state where the murderer had received his death sentence. For eighteen years, the mother was unable to function in a satisfying way, the way she once wanted to. Throughout the years she sought help for her unhappiness from a variety of sources. It was ultimately the act of forgiveness that freed her. When she visited and forgave her daughter's murderer, still on death row eighteen years later, she described it as a spiritual experience of love for herself, her daughter, and the murderer.

Blaming others for the conditions of your life fuels anger. There are many everyday folks and professionals who endorse anger as a healthy response to the world. To the degree that anger is one of many feelings (thoughts) that we, as human beings, are capable of, I concur. It would seem as unlikely for us never to have anger as for the sky never to have clouds. The problem occurs when we hang on to it deliberately or helplessly, and find that we have blame, revenge, and judgment which we are unable or unwilling to let go of. I do not approve of hitting children to teach them not to hit others, or believe that the *expression* of anger is always therapeutic. Nor do I believe in blaming others for my emotional state.

I recommend being gentle with yourself and loving yourself regardless of how others respond in the universe. Try not being attached to any belief that others should not be what they are, and instead understand that they are on their own path, and that your opinion about them has nothing to do with how they behave. Fill yourself with love even toward those who would do you harm, which is what all spiritual leaders have said, and see if you still have anger and revenge. This is difficult only if you are attached to having the world be other than the way it is. If you can accept even that which you want not to be and send love where you previously sent hatred, you will not need to have angry thoughts anymore. You will not need to 'get even.' Instead, you will find yourself unable to hang on to anger, or to immobilize yourself with those thoughts.

When you teach yourself to be the thoughts that are harmonious, rather than those that are discordant and divisive, you will find anger an option you no longer elect. Once you stop the blaming and take responsibility for all of your inner world, the anger dissipates as well. When you finally send away anger completely, you will no longer have your life distorted by the need for revenge. You will not opt to turn control of your life over to those who you perceive have wronged you. You will find a sense of peace through your act of forgiveness, and you will remain on the path of enlightenment. If enough individuals integrate forgiveness consciousness into their lives, perhaps we will one day make this our policy toward other nations as well.

Young people are dying today to avenge their ancestors. They are fighting in the Holy Land, where Jesus walked preaching forgiveness. They wage war interminably. What does it prove? Where does it lead? To peace? Never! The vanquished respond with vengeance and increase the human toll in battles over ancient enmities. It can all begin to change with you, if you learn the universal principle of forgiveness, learn to transcend hatred as a response to hatred, and to give away peace in its place. It is not weak to forgive, it is a gallant and brave act.

Fighting weakens everyone who participates. Everything that you are against weakens you in some way. As Paul beseeched us in Romans 12:21, 'Be not overcome of evil, but overcome evil with good.' You simply need to forgive, and never let yourself behave in ways which you despise yourself. An ancient Chinese proverb tells us, 'The one who pursues revenge should dig two graves.'

Judgment

Blame you can eliminate. Revenge you can send out of your life. But the best you can do with judgment is to reduce the amount of it in your daily life. Judgment means to view the world as *you* are, rather than as *it* is. It is impossible to avoid judgment completely, because virtually every thought has some judgment in it. To tell yourself that this is a beautiful day is a judgment. To send someone love is a judgment. To evaluate anyone or anything is a judgment. Thus, you can only avoid judgment when you avoid thinking altogether, and that would be absurd.

But you can significantly reduce the amount of negative judging that you do, and this is a kind of forgiveness that will help to improve the quality of your life dramatically. The first thing to remember about judgments is that they do not alter anything or anyone in the universe. Just because you dislike someone or react negatively toward some behaviour does not change the person or behaviour you are judging. I remind you again to keep in mind that when you judge another, you do not define that person, you define *yourself*. Your judgments only say something about you. They describe *your* likes and dislikes. They do not define the person being judged. That person is defined by his or her own thoughts and actions. Once you recognize this, you begin replacing your inclination to judge with acceptance, and this is forgiveness in action.

When you accept others, you no longer experience the hurt that goes with judging them. When someone acts in a way you find disagreeable, understand that your hurt, anger, fear, or any strong emotion is how you have chosen to process that person's behaviour. If you are unable or unwilling to notice that emotion and subsequently let go of it, then it is your self that is in need of attention. That person's behaviour has collided with something unfinished or unacknowledged in your life. Distress at the person's behaviour is your way of avoiding something inside of you. A fine distinction, perhaps, but a very significant one.

Your thoughts about how others are behaving are yours. You own them. You carry around the results of those thoughts. If you do not judge those around you but instead accept them for precisely where they are on their own path, eliminating your need to be upset by them, you have put forgiveness into practice. Forgiveness is really just correcting our own misperceptions. You really have nothing to forgive, other than yourself for having judged or blamed in the first place.

All three of these qualities, blame, revenge, and judgment, are deeply ingrained thinking habits. They develop in a culture which prizes itself on blaming everyone else for everything that happens, and suing endlessly to invoke 'justice.' They result from having thoughts of revenge drummed into your head when you were a child, and justifying it all as 'only proper,' patriotic, or just. Yet all of this behaviour is extremely self-defeating and irresponsible, to say nothing of unenlightened. And it is very stupid – to use a judgment!

Whenever you find yourself caught in this style of behaviour, remind yourself that you are the ultimate victim here. You are allowing your entire life to be controlled by the behaviour of others, and no matter how much you may justify it, you are still a slave to the whims of others when you act this way. As Maslow reminded us, 'There is no such thing as a well-adjusted slave.' Such behaviour also keeps you in an unawakened state. You cannot get to a sense of purpose and live a life of harmony and balance while simultaneously allowing someone else to dictate your thoughts and actions. You cannot let your purpose find you, live a spiritual and loving existence, and at the same time blame and judge others, or be motivated out of revenge. Enlightenment demands that you take responsibility for your life. Responsibility means literally to *respond* with *ability*. Obviously, this is impossible when you are disabled by hatred, blame, and revenge.

Take a look at the lives of many who are most admired in history. Those who were fixed on revenge led us into war after war, killing indiscriminately, destroying everything in their path, all in the name of blame and anger. How can anyone make a positive contribution and tune in to the force of love when he is preoccupied with vengeance? Impossible.

Listen to the words of those you admire, and rather than put a label on yourself such as Christian, Jew, Moslem, Buddhist, or whatever, instead make a commitment to being Christlike, Godlike, Buddhalike, and Muhammadlike. We, and all of the world, will be much better off for that commitment, and we will begin living forgiveness every day, rather than only talking about it in church, and then heading back to our daily lives to help build more weapons, sue our neighbours, and judge those who are not in geographic proximity to us.

Forgiveness

One of the most poignantly memorable covers of a national magazine appeared several years back. It was a picture of

Pope John Paul II, sitting in a dungeon with the man who attempted to assassinate him. That portrait of forgiveness left a lasting impression on me. People whom we consider holy, or spiritual, or role models of decency always are able to forgive without qualification or doubt. They do not cloud their consciousness with thoughts of anger, hatred, and revenge toward those who have attempted to wrong or harm them. Rather, they provide us with a model of forgiveness that we can use in our daily lives. Perhaps the picture of Christ forgiving those who are in the process of torturing and killing him is the most powerful utterance of this spiritual master. 'Father, forgive them, for they know not what they do.' This is the very essence of Christianity, and yet very few are able to live up to these words.

It is important for each of us to consider the meaning of those words 'they know not what they do.' People who are inflicting harm on others really and truly do not know what they are doing to others. They are always acting out of their own anger, hatred, blame, or revenge. What they direct at others says nothing about the others. However, it says something very powerful about them. This is what you must learn about forgiveness. Those people who have behaved toward you in any way which you find disagreeable or hurtful really and truly do not know what they have done to you. 'Why?' you might reasonably ask. Because they are unable to see that we are all connected. They are living out of their separateness. They see themselves as separate from everyone else. They are like that cancer cell in the body that has no reference to the whole. Because they are composed of disharmony, they act out on their adjacent fellow humans in the same way that the cancer cell gobbles up the adjacent cell, ultimately killing the body and itself in the process. You would not blame a cancer cell for being a cancer cell, would you? Obviously, you would expect it to do precisely what it has to do, given its makeup. This is true of those who are behaving in ways which you dislike. They cannot know what they are doing to others, because they feel no reference to others. They are sending out their disharmony toward you because that is what they have to give away. Hating them for their behaviour is akin to hating moss for growing on a tree and destroying the appearance of the tree. The moss only knows how to be moss, and regardless of your opinion about how it should not be behaving in such mosslike ways, it will still continue doing all that it knows how to do. Victimizers too are acting out on the basis of all that they know, and the only way you can help them to stop behaving in such ways is to help them to convert their disharmony into self-acceptance and self-love, so that eventually that will be all they have to give away.

This in no way implies that victimizers should not be held totally accountable for their actions. But it is you I am talking to here, not the abuser.

Compassion for others is impossible when you are filled with a belief that you are separate and distinct from other human beings. Once you know, truly know in your heart, that you are connected to all others, even those who behave in evil ways, you then have reference to the entire being called Human Being. With this new awareness comes the ability to forgive as a guiding principle in life. They know that those who send out hatred are only acting out from where they are and how they have been thinking up until this moment. The enlightened person is sure enough of his own divineness that he does not judge himself in any negative manner because of the actions of others. Indeed, forgiveness is man's highest achievement, because it shows true enlightenment in action. It illustrates that one is in harmony with the very stuff of the universe, that is, with the energy of love. It is the ability to give this love away in the most difficult of circumstances.

Our role models remind us that the people who choose harm's way for others *know not what they do*. For it is as true of anything I know about human beings that we cannot give away what we do not have, and we only give away what we do have. If we give away hatred or harm in any way, it is because that is what we have. It is impossible for someone who has only love within to give away hatred. This is why your ability to forgive will come automatically when you truly become awakened. Mark Twain said it so beautifully, when he wrote: 'Forgiveness is the fragrance the violet sheds on the heel that has crushed it.' A grand image indeed, and one to keep in mind as you work on this universal principle of forgiveness.

My own voyage of forgiveness

As I stood at my father's grave back in 1974, I was not aware of the changes and challenges that lay ahead of me, but I knew that I was participating in some very powerful drama. As I talked to my father, with tears streaming down my face, I sensed something changing for me, and by the time I left Mississippi, I knew that I was a new man. I knew somehow, in some inexplicable way, I had been sent to that gravesite for a reason. Forgiveness, that is, correcting my misperceptions about why I was carrying around all of that hatred for so many years, freed me to do the things that were waiting for me. I created a life of excitement, abundance in every sense of the word, and love that I had previously known nothing about.

I set about writing, speaking, making tapes, and doing a great deal of media publicity over the years. I was making regular appearances on national television, speaking to large groups and earning more money than I had imagined for myself. Then one day I received something in the mail that was to put my newfound ecstacy to a real test. A registered letter arrived from an attorney, informing me that I was going to be sued. Though I felt the lawsuit was without merit, I was in shock. No one had ever threatened me with a lawsuit, and I did not even know an attorney.

After thousands of dollars and almost two years spent in legal battles, I realized I had slipped back into old vengeful ways. The anger that I felt filled me with a rage that was destroying me. I was not eating properly. I lost a great deal of weight. I felt terrible all the time, and still the anger mounted in me. I felt like the ultimate victim. Not one day would go by without me thinking angrily, 'Why is this happening? Why won't it go away?'

Then one evening, after giving a speech to a large group of people and relating the story of how I had forgiven my father at his grave, and of all the mysterious happenings that had occurred in order for me even to find his grave, a beautiful light exploded inside of me. It finally hit me that forgiveness is the key. Not hatred and anger, but forgiveness. In that moment it was all over for me as far as that unjust lawsuit was concerned. That night I had the first restful night's sleep in a long time. I thought about the people who were suing me, and I sent them all forgiveness. The next morning I completed my act of forgiveness totally. I was no longer going to participate in this absurdity. I let go of thoughts about any problems that might come my way, and instead I focused all of my thinking on the people involved. My heart opened up to them and I stopped the angry thoughts. That morning I sent them flowers and a selection of books to read. I notified my attorney that I was through paying legal bills for this thing and that he should simply stand by and not respond to anything else concerning this case. My thoughts which previously were full of anger were converted to love almost instantly. I knew in my heart that I could handle any contingency that might arise from this case, and that it was all going to be fine.

Three days later, I received a notice from the group's spokesperson that they were dropping the case, and apologizing for any problems they had caused. They had signed a release. It was all over!

While I had spent thousands of dollars, and lived a nightmare for two years, I had finally learned the lesson of forgiveness that I had been introduced to back in Biloxi. I had to re-create a miserable existence again in order to have the message really clear this time, and all that I spent, and all that I went through were all done for a powerful reason. To teach me the lesson of love over hatred. To get it firmly entrenched this time. That the only response to hatred is love; everything else will bring you down again. I do not regret one penny that I spent on the experience. The moment I switched from anger to forgiveness it was all over for me. I was free in that one simple swift instant, and the rest simply had to be played out in form.

After that brush with the legal system had disappeared from my life, I made a pledge to myself that I would put forgiveness completely into practice. I contacted every single person in my life toward whom I had any hostile or even mildly annoyed feelings. I decided to clear them all out with forgiveness. I wanted to be absolutely certain that if I died in the next moment, not one single person on this planet would have any leftover animosity toward me that I had not tried to rectify, even though it was obvious to me that 'none of it could have possibly been my fault.' (Don't we all feel that way?) There were several people who had borrowed money from me and obviously were not going to pay me back. I had not talked to them in years, and the fact that they had not repaid the debts had damaged our relationships. I sent each of those people autographed copies of my books, some tapes that I had produced, and some flowers, with a note saying that I was wishing them well, sending them love, and trusting that they were happy and joyful. I did not mention the debt. In my heart I had let it go by deciding that it was okay for them not to repay me. It was over, and I had not only forgiven, but I had sent them expressions of love instead of annoyance and bitterness.

In every other area of my life, I made an internal commitment to forgive, regardless of how minor the events were. It only took a few hours and it was all behind me. No enemies left at all. No one to direct any hatred toward on the entire planet. No family members to blame for anything that had taken place years and years earlier. No former colleagues or bosses with whom I had disagreements. I was now on a forgiveness bandwagon, and it was working dramatically.

My relationship to all of those people was clean, and I was not only sending love, but receiving it as well! Several of the debts came in, and though some have never been repaid, it is fine. I love them all, and now, today, as I write this book, I cannot think of a single person on this planet that I have any leftover bad feelings with.

Moreover, I now know that I truly have no one to forgive, and I never did. I simply had to correct my misperception that others were causing me to be miserable, that they were the cause of my discontent. Paradoxically, through the act of forgiveness, I have come to the place where forgiveness never comes up for me. I have learned to accept others exactly as they are, and never pretend that I love something I don't. But I also know I no longer need the immobilizing emotional reactions that used to accompany my encounters with people who were behaving in ways which I disliked. Consequently, acceptance has allowed me to see them for what they are and where they are, and to remind me of the same thing in myself. Any hostile or negative reaction in me, as a result of the behavior of others, really just lets me know where I am, or am not, and no longer requires any forgiveness. I have come to the point of not needing to forgive, by forgiving. One more paradox.

Putting forgiveness into action

It is obvious to me, and I am sure to you as well, that we all resist forgiveness when we prefer to use blame. We seek out revenge when we live in a world which practices it in every corner of the globe. We find forgiveness a plausible principle when we read our holy books, yet extremely difficult to live by, because it violates that need to get even and to 'right the score.' We also fail to look realistically at what an inability to forgive does to the person who is carrying around the anger and hatred. The first time we read about someone performing an absolutely horrendous act of violence on someone else, our innate reaction is: 'I hope they kill the bastard!' When someone wrongs us in some way we tend to forget these important words on forgiveness and say to ourselves, 'I'll get even,' or 'I hope he gets his.'

The entire business of putting forgiveness into action on a daily basis involves accepting the other six universal principles in your life. The forgiveness part will come automatically when you go through the gate – when you befriend your own personal transformation and honour the intelligence that is behind your form and all form. When you use your power of thought to be at harmony rather than fighting the flow of energy that is our universe. When you stop carving up your world and live in oneness with all human beings, knowing that we are all connected by that divine intelligence, all of us, even those who do not think and behave as you would prefer. When you know in your heart that what you think about expands and you stay focused on what you love and what you are grateful for. When you release yourself from all attachments and let yourself live fully. When you have the knowledge that everything is synchronized and working perfectly in this onesong.

When you start living this way and thinking this way and allow others to do the same, then forgiveness will come automatically. You will have no hatred or disharmony left inside to give away. The forgiveness will come as naturally and automatically as Nureyev performs a leaping pirouette after thousands of hours of practice, or as Isaiah Thomas twists and turns for a driving lay-up. No one can tell these two geniuses how to perform their seeming miracles. They do it from intuition after practice, practice, practice. Forgiveness is very much like that. After practicing the lessons of higher consciousness, you will find forgiveness the easiest of all the universal principles to put into your daily life. It will happen automatically. If it is not happening automatically now, then you have more practice to do on the other areas of your life.

Do not bemoan your inability to truly forgive. Simply work at living the principles of higher harmonious consciousness, and before long you will find it happening without any effort. When you see others practicing the acts of blame, anger, and vengeance, forgive them and be open to supporting them in changing their choices to hurt themselves and others. You will start devoting yourself to helping others to eliminate their vengeful, unforgiving thoughts, and then you will know that it has happened for you as well. It will be as if you were on automatic pilot, reacting with your thoughts the same way you react automatically, without consciously thinking, when you do something that you have practiced many many times. But until that automatic act of forgiveness clicks in, here are ways to speed up that process.

Giving is the key to forgiving

This is one of the greatest lessons I have ever learned in my life. If you can master this one without any cynicism, you will find forgiveness is a way of life for you. Giving is the answer to 'Why am I here?' Since you cannot own anything, and all of your attachments prevent abundance from arriving in your life, then all that you can do is give, of yourself, and of all of those things that keep circulating back into your life. Most of us are so into hoarding all that we can get for ourselves and our families that we forget the need to keep it in motion. In our rush to acquire, we find ourselves creating angry relationships, even with strangers, as we set up defenses in anticipation of their taking something away from us.

Keep in mind that it is impossible to create any bitterness or hatred toward others when your primary objective is to be a giving human being. Forgiveness comes almost automatically when you detach yourself from the need to get something and instead focus on reaching out to others. The irony is that the less you are obsessed with getting and the more willing you are to give, the more you seem to get.

What you think about expands. Thus, if your thoughts are on getting all that you can and beating the other guy who you believe is trying to do you in, then you are constantly thinking about, worrying about, and planning on the notion of deception. Your thoughts are focused on the dishonesty of the other guy and the callousness of the world. That is what will expand in your life, because that is what you are thinking about. Consequently, you will find yourself getting more and more fearful about being cheated, insuring yourself against the possibility, hiring attorneys to protect you, and loading yourself up with adversaries. You literally put yourself in an adversarial relationship with almost everyone that you meet. And sure enough, you find this sort of thing continuing to expand.

Now take a look at the opposite approach to your life. Your thoughts (you) now shift to a new perspective. You are not thinking about your own quotas, your own acquisitions, your financial picture, at all. You are instead giving away what you have inside. That is, harmony and acceptance. Since you are not looking to gain anything from anyone, you have nothing to fear. Suppose someone enters your life who might be determined to cheat you, and that person encounters in you someone who truly cares about him as a human being. The likelihood of the cheating behaviour will be dramatically lessened when there is no expectation of it. Looking for harmony and cooperation and giving it to others will most likely result in your receiving the same kind of treatment. You will not attract enemies, because you are not putting yourself into an adversarial position with anyone, regardless of what anyone sends you. Giving becomes the key to creating relationships in which forgiveness is unnecessary. This truly works! Bear with me before allowing any of your enculturated skepticism to creep in here.

Of course, I am aware that there are people who behave dishonestly in the world. I know that horrible criminal acts occur regularly. I know that many people believe that we should keep building more and more prisons and put all of 'those kinds of people' away for good. But building more prisons to put away more and more people simply is not working. We have doubled and quadrupled the number of prisons in the past decade, and they are still overcrowded. The answer will come when we discover why we have so many people who want to take from others, and work at correcting that approach to life. Raising our own consciousness is the only way that we can begin such a journey. I have found that the quickest way to disarm anyone who is focused exclusively on what he can take from me is to let him know, with kindness, that I do not live that way.

I recently purchased an automobile and found after the closing that the dealer had added a charge of almost two hundred dollars into the contract, over and above the price that we had agreed upon. I did not discover this until I had returned home and looked over the final papers more carefully. For me, this was a perfect opportunity to practice all that I have been writing about in this book. Years ago, I probably would have been angry, felt cheated, and had an unpleasant exchange with the car dealer. Not this time. I simply called, and expressed my opinion to the salesman about what had happened, and explained that I did not feel that he acted from integrity in the closing. I also talked to the owner, and I again expressed how I felt about it, without any anger or bitterness. We had a pleasant exchange, and the dealer apologized, but felt that he could not refund the money since we had signed the papers and after all a 'deal is a deal.' I told him that I did not respect this particular business practice, and I then let it go. I did not need to forgive him, since I was not owning any anger about the situation. I vowed I would look more carefully at contracts before closing in the future. That was the end of it. Until the following letter arrived some ten days later.

Dear Wayne

After giving our conversation on the phone further thought, I have decided to refund the $188.50 that is in question. I feel that it was a misunderstanding and not an attempt to mislead. However, our customers' positive feeling toward us is very important and I hope that this refund will be evidence of that.

If I can be any other assistance, please let me know.

Thank you.

I donated the money that I received to the End World Hunger cause, and five days later I received a cheque for $988.50 from Argentina, for royalties on something that I had written fifteen years ago. I gave six hundred dollars of that money to help out some relatives, and six days later I received a check for $6,269.50 from Mexico, also totally unexpected, for something I had done many years ago. For me, speaking from my heart, I truly know there is truth in the maxim 'What goes around, comes around.'

You know that there are certain principles working within you to keep you alive and functioning, such as salivation, digestion, elimination, and the like. Know also that the principles of abundance, synchronicity, detachment, and oneness are operative in the universe. All you have to do is tune in to them and let them work through you exactly as do the principles that maintain your physical perfection. When you are in harmony yourself, you want to give that internal bliss away, and that is the focus of your life. Since you are energy, and everything else in the universe is also energy, all you want to do is keep it flowing. No blockages, only flow. When you send it out, it will keep coming back. Remember to give for the sake of giving, and to keep it circulating as it flows back, and you will soon see it working in your life.

If you doubt this principle it will not work in your life. Your doubt is the blockage. But everyone that I know who has truly put it to the test finds that it works beautifully. For me, I am beyond believing. I simple know it to be true. Thus I seldom encounter those who might cheat me. When I do, I act from love rather than anger, with the realization that they cannot experience what I am talking about while they are fixated on getting rather than giving. The quality of their lives is affected by their thoughts of scarcity and trying to get from others, and they believe they will never have enough. I believe I will always have enough, no matter my circumstances. Consequently, I can give, and it keeps coming back almost magically. I keep it all circulating, since I do not want to be attached to any of it. People simply do not steal from me.

This realization about giving hit me strongly a few years ago when I began giving away large numbers of my book *Gifts from Eykis*. The more I gave, the better I felt and the more abundance kept coming back into my life. I realized that giving and receiving were the exact same thing. No difference. Every gift I gave gave me something back. I found a profound shift taking place as I practiced giving.

This was not a conscious choice to be more philanthropic. I still resist when someone tells me what to give. It was an automatic response to the shifts that were taking place in my consciousness. The giving was truly enriching my life in ways that I had not anticipated. In a meditation one night, I saw that we are truly here only to give, and that love is the most important thing to be giving, regardless of the circumstances.

I still, however, have great difficulty in suspending anger when I see evidence of man's inhumanity to man. The newspaper picture of the angry young man who has just murdered two innocent people is a very tough test. I sometimes stare at that photo, which we all have seen, and ask myself, 'Am I capable of giving him love too?' I try to see that person as a tiny baby. To see his innocence and the fact that he too, regardless of his crimes, is deserving of love. This is admittedly a tough place to get to, particularly when you or a loved one has been the victim. Our judgment of him does not define him, he is already defined by his own thoughts and actions. Joel Goldsmith, writing in *Parenthesis in Eternity*, says:

Loving our neighbour as ourselves, then, is giving our neighbour that same recognition of godliness that we give ourselves, regardless of the appearance of the moment. That neighbour may be the woman taken in adultery or the thief on the cross, but we have nothing to do with that. What we have to do with is to love all our neighbours by knowing their true nature, just as we would be loved by having them know our true nature, in spite of what outward appearance may temporarily be evident.

We can begin by sending love and compassion to the part of ourselves who is struggling with pain and sorrow and anger. When we can truly be there for ourselves, we are able to be a part of that universal energy, that higher consciousness, that godliness that is in each and every one of us, and we are able to give it even to those who harm us, because it is what we have inside of ourselves. It truly is in every one of us, to be love, if we allow it.

Giving, in any capacity that you can muster, without any expectations of return for your efforts, is the biggest step that you can take to bring abundance into your life and to eliminate the need to forgive. Paradoxically, as long as you do not expect it, you will find yourself receiving more and more as well. Ultimately, you will discover that giving and receiving are one and the same.

Forgiving yourself: and why not?

When you are living the principles discussed in this book, you will find yourself being gentler to yourself. This is the act of self-forgiveness, which shows that you are living the awakened life. I have a beautiful pillow in my office that says, 'I'm allowed.' It was made by my sister-in-law many years ago. For me it is a reminder that I am allowed to live my life as I please, to make mistakes, to learn from those mistakes, and on and on. Many live their lives believing they are not allowed. Judgmental adults succeeded in convincing them that there are irrevocable rules which state what you can say or not say, which order you never to be late, not to drink or smoke, to hate the enemies assigned to you, never to masturbate, to disregard all religions except the one you were born into, to dismiss those who appear different from you, never to get divorced, and so on. At some point in your life you adopted these rules for yourself and made them a lifetime code of conduct. Yet you also found that it was impossible to live up to all of them all of the time. Consequently you filled yourself with guilt for not having lived up to the judgmental code that was imposed upon you.

This guilty feeling is something that inhibits your own awakening, and the only way to escape it is to forgive yourself for everything that you have done. Once again, the absurdity of the need to forgive surfaces. You really have nothing to forgive yourself for, and yet if you don't, you still wallow around in your own guilt. The more you learn the lessons of higher consciousness and live your life from this perspective, the less inclined you will be even to think about needing to forgive yourself.

Look at any and all beliefs that you carry around with you in terms of how well they serve you in living a life of harmony and purpose. If you behave in a way that is in violation of those supposedly irrevocable rules, you have not really done something wrong! You have merely done something. And it is done. If you are, however, plagued with remorse and guilt, then judging the action as wrong seems appropriate to prevent its recurrence. Does it? Probably not. So, instead, learn from it by deciding if it is something that you want to repeat based upon *your* values, and then move past it. It takes effort to determine if you are still operating on the controls imposed by others. The effort is well worth it if you are not taking responsibility for your own mind. You are allowed, plain and simple. You do not need to be forgiven by anyone else, only yourself, and even that is truly unnecessary once you accept yourself completely. You will know when you have mastered the art of self-forgiveness. When you are no longer judgmental toward others, you will have forgiven yourself and be on your path of enlightenment.

Releasing judgment of another is actually releasing judgment of yourself. Your need to put others into categories defines you, not them. When you stop doing this, you have forgiven yourself for whatever aspect of yourself you see in them. The more at ease you are with the behaviour of others, even if you would not act that way yourself, the more you are at ease with yourself. The more you continue to react with intellectually violent responses to the conduct of others, the more you know that you have work to do on self-forgiveness.

Say to yourself, 'I'm allowed.' Not because I tell you you are, or because your parents are no longer in charge of you, or because some authority figure granted you permission, but simply because you are lovingly there for yourself. No guilt, no anger, no self-flagellation over things that you consider mistakes. A simple understanding that you do not fail in life, you only produce results, and you have the right to learn and grow from any results that you produce. The word 'failure' is itself a judgment, and if you label yourself a failure in any context, you are judging rather than accepting yourself. Self-acceptance will turn into self-love, and when you are filled with self-love, that is what you will have to give away.

Consequently, the willingness to forgive yourself is the necessary step to being in harmony with all of the universal principles. It gives you permission to be whatever you choose. And it gives you the right to self-determination. Everything that you have done is over, regardless of your opinion about it. It simply is. Try to simply *be*. The past is over, and everything you did got you to the point that you are at right at this moment. Everything had to happen exactly as it did, without any exceptions in order for you to be here, reading these words in the exact location in which you find yourself right now. You needed to do it all, and all you have to do, to really learn this lesson of forgiveness, is to allow that thought in and lovingly forgive yourself. Receive the lesson from it and be in harmony with yourself and everyone that you encounter. The more peaceful you are with that idea, and the more willing you are to be gentle with yourself, even if you slip, the more you will find forgiveness your way of life. Which means the more you will find acceptance, which is the absence of the need to forgive, as your way of life.

You will notice so many others violate the values and beliefs that you hold. Refuse to judge them. Reach out to help when asked, and know that where you are on your path, you can choose to be unaffected by their conduct. The more you know that you are thinking and acting in harmony with what the universe can be, the less you will be inclined to judge others. And you will have stopped judging yourself as well, and that is a glorious aspect of this process. You are treating yourself the way you truly want to be treated, as the divine being that you are. You have the intelligence that supports all form running through you at all times. You are important enough to know that, and divine enough to give it away.

Surrendering: the ultimate act

I am bringing this book, this wonderful labour of love for me, to a close with a final concept that I call surrendering. This in no way implies giving control of your life over to another person, organization, or set of ideas. By surrendering I simply mean trusting in the forces and principles that are always at work in this perfect universe, just as you surrender every day to the principles that make you a working, loving unit, without questioning, fighting, demanding, or even asking to fully understand them all. And just as you surrender also to the greater principles that govern the universe and all of the living beings contained within it.

The act of forgiveness is easier when you surrender. When you know that all of us are on our own paths, doing exactly what we know to do at the moment, given the conditions of our lives, then you can let go of any malice toward others for acting out their own destiny. You also know that you brought every person and his or her behaviour into your life in some way, and for some reason. With surrender, you sense that there is a powerful lesson for you as a result of that person's being in your life, even if he or she visited havoc and pain on you. Forgiveness comes with surrendering to the perfection of it all. Surrendering replaces questioning why some things are so painful and difficult to grasp.

Surrendering goes beyond forgiveness, and can easily carry the burden not only of this particular chapter but of the entire book as well. Inherent in the business of surrendering is the notion of trust. With surrender you trust the perfection and beauty of it all, and at the same time know the paradox that all of the suffering that seems to go on all over our planet is a part of that perfection, as is your own strong desire to end it.

Death is not a punishment, but a transition. The only thing that dies is form, while thought is eternal energy.

You are that thought, and can never die. Surrender completely and stop fighting anything and everything. When you have this trust you will wonder why you did not surrender long ago, because of the peace and serenity that you will feel.

One way to move in to surrendering is to make a personal commitment to forgive every single person that you have ever had any conflict with. Send each one a gift and a note wishing him or her well, and when you are tempted to haul out those old thoughts of bitterness and anguish, remind yourself that that relationship has healed with the balm of forgiveness. It is as if you knew you were going to die tomorrow, and you knew also that you could not make the transition if you left any people behind you that you hated. Imagine heaven requiring love for everyone, no exceptions, and you having the capacity to make that happen. In many ways, heaven on earth does require exactly that – love that is not conditional, that is free from demands, that allows the loved one the right to be anything that he or she chooses without losing your love. This is the kind of surrendering that I am talking about, a kind of trust that everything is in perfect working order in the universe, including yourself.

As I approached the writing of this work, I surrendered. I accepted that the principles that I was writing about are true and omnipresent in the universe. I trusted that completely, as I do right now. As I proceeded to write, I allowed myself to flow throughout this entire project, no strain, no worry, no fear that I would not be able to complete my undertaking. I surrendered to the idea that this book would be written and that I had nothing to fight or struggle about in the production of this work. I would sit down and simply outline the ideas that I have had as a result of my own life experiences, my research and reading, my listening to great spiritual masters.

Everything that I needed seemed to come in at just the right time. While working on a particular chapter, I would receive a tape in the mail from someone who had heard me speak, telling me that this would clarify some of the points. It always did. On other occasions, someone would send me a book in the mail, telling me that I simply had to read it. That book would be the one that I needed on that particular day. Many many times when I wanted a special quote to use, I would reach into the massive pile of books and pamphlets on my huge glass table, and my hand would bring out a book. While I sat at the typewriter, I would open that particular book to a page, and there it would be – perfect. Just what I wanted to embellish the point I was making. Never before have I had this experience of effortless perfection for such an extended period of time. I surrendered to it in my writing, and allowed it to flow unimpeded through me to you. No worry, no stress, no fighting any of it, simply knowing that it is all working perfectly.

I am not advocating an absence of planning or caring. In fact, you will find yourself caring and preparing even more than ever before. What I am describing is the process of knowing that everything is going to work out because you are at harmony within. You only have love and serenity to give away. In the process of going about your life's work, have that inner knowledge that it is all going to be as it should be.

This is what surrendering is about. Inner knowingness. Inner contentment that overtakes you when you trust the force of the universe to be in harmony with yourself. Knowing that abundance is your birthright and that it all flows to and through you when you are no longer challenging anything. It is like having a guardian angel or a loving observer as a part of your consciousness, a companion that you are always having compassionate silent conversations with, a consciousness behind your form. That part is always perfect. There is no struggle or suffering in that part of you. That is your transcendent dimension of thought.

A sensitive Norwegian poet, Rolf Jacobsen, wrote a beautiful poem titled, 'Guardian Angel.' It deserves to be read slowly and lovingly.

I am the bird that knocks at your window in the
    morning
and your companion, whom you cannot know,
the blossoms that light up for the blind.

I am the glacier's crest above the forests, the
    dazzling one
and the brass voices from the cathedral towers.
The thought that suddenly comes over you at
    mid-day
and fills you with a singular happiness.

I am the one you have loved long ago.
I walked alongside you by day and look intently at
    you
and put my mouth on your heart
but you don't know it.

I am your third arm and your second
    shadow, the white one,
whom you don't have the heart for
and who cannot ever forget you.

We all have our own connections to that invisible part of us. There is much more to life than simply living out our days as form, and then disappearing into an abyss of infinite nothingness. Our thoughts are a magic part of us, and they can carry us to places that have no boundaries and no limitations. In that dimensionless world of thought everything is possible.

It demands nothing of you, this awakened life, only that you fill yourself with the life energy that makes the dynamic work, and that you celebrate the invisible part of you as well

as the visible. Let these ideas in and simply see where they
lead you. As you do:

Remember, you do not have to struggle . . .
You do not have to fight . . .
You do not have to win . . .
You only have to Know.

NAMASTE
I celebrate the place in you
    where we are all one.

*It is all very well to copy what you see, but it is better to draw what
you see in your mind . . . Then your memory and your imagination
are freed from the tyranny imposed by nature.*   Edgar Degas

Index

Abdollahi, Mariam, 92-4
abundance, 7-8, 117-152,
    160, 187, 243, 262, 273
  freedom and, 129-30
  ideas for achievement of,
    148-52
  openness to, 57
  paradox of, 126, 154
  resistance to, 141-2,
    156-8
  tuning in to, 124, 127-9
  visualization of, 51-3, 57
  as watchword of universe,
    118-9
acausality, 60, 65, 78-9
Adams, John Quincy, 5
affirmations, 123, 151
aggression, 96, 98, 99, 114,
    230
Allen, Steve, 43, 49
"alone" and "all one", 116
analysis;
  synthesis vs., 209, 239, 240
  as violence, 209, 238-9
anger, 67, 68, 69, 81, 82,
    111, 113, 150, 169, 236
  blame as cause of, 250
  forgiveness and, 244, 248,
    250, 251, 254, 255,
    258, 263, 267
astral world, 54, 66, 77, 107,
    125

attachment, 79, 171, 251
  to being right, 169,
    178-80, 193
  defined, 155
  emotional, 165
  enjoyment vs., 162
  to food, 182
  to form, 177-8, 192
  to ideas, 178, 179-80
  as impediment, 155, 157,
    159, 195, 262
  to judgmental habits, 168
  to money, 180-82, 193
  most common types of,
    172-84
  to other people, 173-4
  to other people's opinions,
    165
  parental, 170-71, 174,
    187-8, 194
  to past, 175-7, 191-2
  to perfection, 166
  to stuff, 162, 172-3, 190-1
  suffering and, 172, 173,
    175, 176, 178, 179, 191,
    192
  in thought, 155
  in winning, 182-3, 189,
    194
authenticity, 137, 150
autonomy, 114, 197
awakening:

from dreams, 61, 63, 65,
70-1, 81-2, 108, 125,
155, 206
see also enlightenment

Be Here Now (Ram Dass),
16
Bhagavad Gita, 15, 172
Bible:
eternity in, 78
transformation in, 20
blame, 73, 110, 235, 243,
244, 245, 253-4, 255,
261
anger caused by, 250
how to rid oneself of,
245-9
revenge vs., 249-50
blessings:
in obstacles, 223
in suffering, 213, 216
Branch, Bobbe, 120-2
broccoli metaphor, 39-40
Buddha, 27, 101, 254
bureaucracy, 184-5, 194
business world, 102-3, 114,
184-6, 232
networking in, 186

cancer, 96, 98, 100, 114, 255
Capra, Fritjof, 89, 227
Carson, Johnny, 50
Castaneda, Carlos, 165, 167
cause and effect, rules of, 61,
65, 78-9, 225
centering, 181
children, 204-5
conditioning of, 177
detachment from, 170-1,
174, 187-8, 194
love of, 170, 187-8

coincidence, 196, 208, 210,
219, 231, 232
collective consciousness,
88-91
physics and, 89
Commentaries on Living
(Krishnamurti), 211
competition, 182, 183,
189-90
conformity, 177
connectedness, 199, 200-210
connectors, 200-210
of form, 200-205, 237
formless, 206-8
hidden, 201
incomprehensible, 204-5
invisible, 201-3, 206,
208-9, 237
stimulus response, 203
of thoughts, 203-10, 219,
225, 236
conscience, 90
consciousness:
collective, 88-91
after death, 79
dreaming, 61, 63, 70, 107,
155-6
higher, 61-2, 63, 98, 106,
107, 155, 157, 180,
192, 207, 238, 244,
262, 267, 268
scarcity, *see* scarcity
consciousness
of soul, 178
three levels of, 61-2, 106
waking, 61, 63, 64, 65, 66,
106
courage, 90, 176, 215
creation of one's own life,
80-1, 119, 244
crises, 210-11

critical mass, 88-9, 90
crystals, 90

Dancing Wu Li Masters, The
(Zukav), 89, 227
death, 79, 192, 206
"die while you are alive",
63-4, 69, 70
dream consciousness
compared to, 63, 107,
155
fear of, 21, 23-4, 63, 66,
71, 107
of loved one, grieving for,
211, 213, 218-9
as reward, 213
as transformation, 107
as transition of form, 66,
107, 271
see also immortality
Degas, Edgar, 275
déjà vu, 197
Descartes, René, 94
deserving, 128, 148, 150
detachment, 79, 153-195,
243, 263
from children, 170-1, 174,
187-8, 194
defined, 155-6
from external opinions, 166
implementation of,
188-195
love and, 167-8, 173-4, 179,
187-8, 191
from outcome, 166, 190
from ownership, 168, 190,
191
paradoxes of, 154, 155,
166, 169, 175, 178,
180, 183, 185, 190
resistance to, 154, 186-8

suffering eliminated by,
171-2, 175, 176
determination, 55
disease (dis-ease), 95, 97, 98,
99, 112
Divine Romance, The
(Yogananda), 101, 177
dreams, 51, 59-71
awakening from, 61, 63,
65, 70-1, 81-2, 108,
125, 155, 206
beginnings and endings
missing from, 60, 65-6,
79
cause and effect
unconnected in, 61,
65, 78-9
consciousness in, 61, 63,
70, 71, 107, 155-6
creation of all needs in, 60,
67-8, 70, 80-1, 105-6
as formless world, 59, 61,
63, 71, 107, 125, 206
of God, 107, 108, 197,
234
obstacles as opportunities
in, 60, 66-7, 79
oneness and, 105-8
as out-of-body experience,
59-61
physical reactions to, 61,
70-1, 79
seven rules applying in,
61-2, 64-71, 77-81
singleness of, 106-8, 197
spiritual masters in, 62
time in, 61, 65, 78, 79
waking dreamer of, 61, 63,
64, 65, 66-7, 68, 69,
77-81
wet, 61

Dyer, Jim, 242
Dyer, Marcie, 31, 32, 45, 167-8, 217, 223, 224
Dyer, Melvin Lyle, 9-13
Dyer, Wayne W:
  books by, 14, 42, 43, 50, 91, 121, 185, 198
  career of, 10, 11, 13-14, 36, 43-50, 130-6, 198, 20-1, 257-9
  childhood of, 9, 42-3, 61-2, 130-1, 160-1
  family of, 9-11, 32, 42-3, 45, 61, 87-8, 135, 241-2
  Greek Marathon run by, 214-16
  philosophy of, 22-31, 43, 48-9, 91, 214-5, 258-60
  transformation of, 9-14, 31-2, 43

Einstein, Albert, 57, 99
  on oneness, 84
  time as viewed by, 53, 65, 78
Ellis, Albert, 42
Emerson, Ralph Waldo, 42, 165, 176
endlessness, 60, 66, 79, 117, 152, 208, 253,
enemies, 239, 263
  attachment to past and, 175, 176
  reevaluation of, 113-4
energy:
  flowing of, 156, 160, 209-10, 225, 230, 235, 265
  of giving, 194
  mental, 203
  muscular, 203
  music as, 195
  thought as, 209-10
  in universe, 55, 156, 157-9, 197, 200, 208, 209-10, 230, 237, 265
enlightenment (awakening) 48, 143, 157, 177, 186, 190, 191, 207, 243-4, 253, 256, 269
  process of, 210-19, 236-7
  Stage One of, 210-12, 216, 237
  Stage Two of, 212-6, 237
  Stage Three of, 216-9, 237
  suffering as part of process of, 212, 213, 214, 216, 218, 237
eternity:
  in Bible, 78
  as concept, 66, 78
  in each moment, 79
exercise, 28-9, 38, 178

failure, 58-9, 269
faith, 232
Farther Reaches of Human Nature, The (Maslow), 199
fear, 79, 148
  of changing, 74
  of death, 21, 23-4, 63, 66, 71, 107
  of not having enough, 126
  Spinoza on, 42
  of unfamiliar, 73
Feild, Reshad, 209
Fitzgerald, F. Scott, 180

flow charts, 184-5
flowing, 161, 183, 186, 188,
    189, 190, 195, 198
  of energy, 156-7, 160,
      209-10, 225, 230,
      235, 266
  of thought, 209-10, 217
forgiveness, 13, 14, 243-275
  anger and, 244, 249, 250,
      251, 254, 255, 258,
      263, 267
  Christ as teacher of, 251,
      255
  giving as key to, 262-7
  implementation of, 260-7
  judgmental habits and,
      244, 252-3, 268
  lack of, suffering caused
      by, 243
  of oneself, 268-9
  resistance to, 247
  spiritual masters as
      teachers of, 249, 251,
      255, 256
form:
  attachment to, 177-8, 192
  changes in, 19, 22, 63
  connectors of, 201-5, 237
  death as transistion of, 66,
      107
  defined, 18
  formlessness vs., 78-9,
      155, 206, 209, 232,
      234
  God as support of, 22,
      116, 159, 225
  hidden, 201
  identification with, 72,
      177-8, 182, 232, 236
  as illusion, 107
  intelligence as support of,

      22-3, 73-4, 77, 159,
          188-9, 197, 219, 225
  invisible, 201-3
  labeling and, 112
  suffering as dependent on,
      107, 172, 192, 236
  in transformation, 18-9,
      20
  vibrations of, 55
formlessness, 74, 117, 156,
    176
  acausality of 78
  connectors in, 206-8
  in dreams, 59, 61, 63, 70,
      108, 126, 206
  form vs., 78-9, 155, 206,
      209, 232, 234
  of thought, 203, 206, 207,
      208-9, 218, 219
freedom:
  abundance and, 129-30
  defined, 130
  expansion of, 130
  in universe, 129
free will, 223, 226, 232, 234
Frost, Robert, 44-5
Fuller, Buckminster, 23

Gandhi, Mohandas, 123,
    126-7
Gibran, Kahlil, 170
Gifts from Eykis (Dyer), 42,
    121, 185, 221, 222, 266
giving, 156, 160, 175, 185-6,
    193
  energy in, 194
  as key to forgiveness,
      262-7
goals, paradoxical approach
    to, 112-3

God, 20, 34, 77, 118, 177, 217, 232-3, 240, 241, 254
  as dreamer, 106, 107-8, 197, 254
  Gandhi on, 123
  infinity and, 207
  Jung on, 22
  as oneness, 89
  as support for form, 22, 116, 159, 225
  universe supported by, 200, 208, 225
god force, 73, 158, 217
golden rule, 38
Goldsmith, Joel, 267
Gould Donna, 46, 49
Greene, Shecky, 49
"Guardian Angel" (Jacobsen), 274
guilt, 268-9
Gulliver's Travels (Swift), 95

Happiness Is the Way, 121
harmony, 104, 119, 129, 159, 188, 194, 230, 251
  inner, 98-9, 105, 114, 116, 183, 237, 265, 273
  intellectual, 239
  love and, 75, 82, 95-6, 98, 115, 256
  in universe, 157, 220
  war ended by, 90
hatred, 247-8, 250, 252, 254, 255, 256, 257, 258, 262
head-in-the-sand approach, 33
Helprin, Mark, 226-7
Herbert, Nick, 89
Holmes, Oliver Wendell, 7
Hugo, Victor, 47, 84

Hundredth Monkey, The (Keyes), 88-9
hypnosis, 37

"I'll believe it when I see it" mentality, 8, 33, 74, 200-1, 231
images:
  actions as result of, 51-3
  positive, 74-5
  practice in creation of, 74
imagination, 19, 36-7, 43, 78
immortality:
  of invisible essence of self, 79, 192
  of thought, 20, 24, 63, 66, 78, 192, 271
individualism, 114
infinity, 117, 152, 233
  God and, 207
inner peace, 169, 170, 171, 188, 193, 213, 251
  signs of, 21
intelligence:
  form supported by, 22-3, 73-4, 77, 159, 188-9, 197, 219, 225
  universe supported by, 200, 208, 220, 225
intuition, 217, 225, 230, 238
Invisible Way. The (Feild), 209

Jacobsen, Rolf, 274
James, William, 16, 27, 42, 82, 101, 105, 106
Jesus Christ, 114, 178, 254
  forgiveness taught by, 251, 255
John Paul II, Pope, 255
judgmental habits, 37-8, 48,

70, 72, 80, 110, 115, 166, 167-8, 169, 189, 234
  attachment to, 168
  forgiveness and, 244, 252-3, 268
  guilt and, 268-9
  reduction of, 252-3
Jung, Carl, 22, 196-7, 222

Keyes, Ken, 88
Kierkegaard, Søren, 36
Krishna, 101, 106
Krishnamurti, J., 211, 218

labeling, 36-7, 108-9, 112, 176
Lao-tze, 151
leadership, 102, 103-5, 114
limitations, 146-7
  transcending of, 19, 129
Lincoln, Abraham, 42, 105
Lives of a Cell, The (Thomas), 89, 97
loneliness, 154
Lorenzini, Shirley, 223-5, 230
love, 29, 69, 77, 112, 113, 115, 150, 170, 171, 189, 213, 254, 259, 266-7, 273
  of children, 170, 187-8
  defined, 95
  detachment and, 167-8, 173-4, 178, 187-8, 191
  harmony and, 75, 82, 95-6, 98, 115, 256
  of objects, 161
  of oneself, 122, 248-9, 250, 256, 269

  unconditional, 168, 173-4, 272
  as universal synthesizer, 95-6
  of work, 136-46, 150, 181
luck, 118, 235

Maslow, Abraham H., 199, 258
materialism, 153-4
meditation, 165, 181, 183, 236
  technique for, 38-9
memory, 206, 208
miracles, 13-4, 20, 23, 62, 119, 215, 236
  as synchronistic events, 219-29
Mohammed, 101, 254
money, attachment to, 180-2, 193
Moss, Richard, 85
motherhood, 204-5

negativity, 37-8, 48, 137,145 149, 252-3, 256
networking, 184-6, 194
New Science of Life, A (Sheldrake), 89
Newton, Sir Isaac, 228
New York Times, 47
ng, raymond, 216
Nightingale, Earl, 250
nocturnal emission, 61
no-limit living, 198
nuclear age, 97-8
Nureyev, Rudolph, 261
nutrition, 28, 38, 48, 78

obstacles:
  blessings in, 223

as events, 216, 219
as opportunities, 60, 66-7,
    79-80, 215
oneness, 83-116, 236
    dreams and, 105-8
    Einstein on, 84
    as God, 89
    paradoxes of, 114, 155
    resistance to principle of,
        108-11
    scientific credibility of, 90
    suggestions for applications
        of
    principle of, 111-16
    thoughts of, 98
onesong, 83-4
    see also oneness
openess, 57
ownership, 124-7, 151, 155,
    164, 167, 171, 173, 262
    detachment from, 168,
        190, 191

Palmer, Arnold, 58
Papush, Howard, 49-50
parables:
    of caged parrot, 63-4
    in *Gulliver's Travels*, 95
    of lost key, 71
paradoxes, 222, 223, 230,
    234, 249, 260, 267, 271
    of abundance, 125, 154
    as concept, 16, 114, 180
    of detachment, 155, 156,
        166, 169, 175, 178,
        180, 183, 185, 190
    "More is less" as, 162
    of oneness and detachment,
        · 151
    of oneness and
        individualism, 114

in pursuit of goals, 112-3
    of single dream, 108
    of suffering, 271
Parenthesis in Eternity
    (Goldsmith), 267
parenting, 170-1, 174, 187-8,
    194
patriotism, 114
Paul, Saint, 20, 252
peace, 145
    see also inner peace
Peace Pilgrim, 21
Peale, Norman Vincent, 42
perfection:
    attachment to, 166
    of universe, 196, 199-200,
        233, 234, 244-5, 272
perseverance, 55
"phase transistion", 89
Picasso, Pablo, 14, 15
Pine, Arthur, 47
postiveness, 225
Prophet, The (Gibran), 170
Provenzano, Marie, 162-4
Pulling Your Own Strings
    (Dyer), 198
Pyle, Joanna Spamer, 138-40,
    144

quantum mechanics, 227-9

Quantum Reality (Herbert),
    89
Ram Dass, 16, 213
randomness, 196, 197-8, 229,
    232
    Helprin on, 226-7
reactions to illusions, 61,
    68-70, 81
reflections from the soul (ng),
    216
remote control, 201

Rentz, Earlene, 160-1
resistance:
  to abundance, 141-2,
    156-8
  to detachment, 154, 186-8
  to forgiveness, 247
  to importance of thought,
    71-4
  to principle of oneness,
    108-11
  to principle of synchronicity,
    231-4
  to transformation, 32-5
responsibility:
  acceptance of, 73, 80, 188,
    246, 249, 254
  as word, 258, 254
results, production of, 58-9
revenge, 249-52, 253, 254,
  255, 260
  blame vs., 249-50
right-versus-wrong
  dichotomies, 179
Road Less Traveled, The
  (Frost), 44-5

scarcity consciousness, 7, 53,
  122, 123, 124, 127, 128,
  138-9, 141, 142, 145,
  148, 266
  origins of, 147
  transcending of, 118-9
Schweitzer, Albert, 127
self-actualization, 198
separateness, 83, 88, 101,
  108-11, 112, 255
serenity, 167, 271, 273
service, 126-7, 145, 186, 239
Shakespeare, William, 42
Sheldrake, Rupert, 88
shyness, 53

sixth sense, 220
Sky's the Limit, The (Dyer),
  199
soul, 8, 20, 22
  consciousness of, 177
  as intelligence supporting
    form, 22
Spinoza, Baruch, 42
spiritually, *see* consciousness,
  higher
spiritual masters, 63, 67, 101,
  106, 107, 116, 227
  in dreams, 62
  forgiveness taught by, 249,
    251, 255, 256
Stevenson, Robert Louis, 136
stimulus-response connection,
  203
subatomic particles, 227-9,
  233-4
suffering:
  attachment and, 172, 173,
    175, 176, 178, 179,
    191, 192
  blessing within, 213, 216
  detachment and, 171-2,
    175, 176
  in enlightenment process,
    212, 213, 214, 216,
    237
  form and, 107, 172, 192,
    236
  in ability to forgive as
    cause of, 243
  paradox of, 271
surrendering, 188, 271-5
symphony metaphor, 195
synchronicity, 196-242, 243
  Jung on, 196-7
  miracles as explained by,
    219-29

pure, 216-9
religion vs., 233
resistance to principle of, 231-4
suggestions for applications of
    principle of 234-2
as word, 196-7
synthesis, analysis vs., 209, 239, 240

Tao, 207
Tao of Physics, The (Capra), 89, 227
Teilhard de Chardin, Pierre, 95-6, 98
Teresa, Mother, 105
thankfulness, 118-9, 149
Thomas, Isaiah, 261
Thomas, Lewis, 87, 97
Thoreau, Henry David, 50, 61
thought, 23, 41-82
attachments in, 155
beginning and end of, 66, 78, 207
connectors of, 203-10, 219, 225, 236
defined, 41-2
dimension of, 19, 66, 67, 78, 107, 125, 155, 207, 218, 219, 273, 274
expansion caused by, 119-22, 124, 127, 137, 145, 263
feelings as result of, 53
flowing of, 209-10, 217
as flowing energy, 209-10
formlessness of, 203, 206, 207, 218, 219

immortality of, 20, 24, 63, 66, 68, 192, 271
indebted, 76, 119
independent, 72
nothingness, 125
of oneness, 98
pure, 15, 59, 62, 68, 105, 216, 236
rearranging of, 75-60
resistance to importance of, 71-4
self-defeating, 74
as thing, 51, 52
universal, 210, 219, 220
see also dreams;
    visualization

time:
in dreams, 61, 65, 77, 78
Einstein's views on, 53, 65, 78
as illusion, 65
nonexistence of, 53, 61, 65, 77, 78, 103, 226-7
in quantum mechanics, 229
Tonight Show, 42-3, 50-1, 55
tradition, 175-6, 191-2, 232
transformation, 8, 18-40, 125, 210, 236, 238
in Bible, 20
death as, 107
defined, 18-19, 20
form in, 18-19, 20
religious beliefs and, 34
resistance to, 32-5
suggestions for, 35-40
traumas, 210-12, 218, 219, 236
Twain, Mark, 257,
type-A behaviour, 78

uniqueness, 86, 115, 232
United Nations, 105
universe:
  abundance as watchword
      of, 117-8
  as circle, 88
  completeness of, 196, 222,
      223, 224, 226-7
  energy in, 55, 124, 156,
      157-9, 197, 200, 208,
      209-10, 229, 237, 265
  freedom in, 129
  God as support for, 200,
      208, 225
  harmony in, 157, 220
  infinity of, 117, 152, 233
  intelligence as support for,
      200, 208, 220, 225
  perfection of, 196,
      199-200, 234, 244-5,
      272
  rhythm in, 199, 236
  trusting of, 186
  as vibrating thought, 219
  as word, 83

vibrations, 55, 124, 219, 220,
    257
violence, 154, 250
  analysis as, 209, 238-9
  visualization, 51-9, 74-5,
      76, 113, 129, 166,
      223, 224
  of abundance, 51-3, 57
  four principles of, 51-9

war, 88, 98, 99, 101, 111,
    175, 180, 251, 254
  competition compared to,
      183
  ending of, 90, 145

  revenge and, 260
weapons, 99, 101, 110, 176,
    239, 249
wellness, creation of, 120
Whitman, Walt, 128
willingness, 55-7, 225
Winter's Tale (Helprin), 226-7
win/win approach, 186
worrying, 235-6
Wright, Orville and Wilbur,
    54

Yogananda, Paramahansa,
    101, 116, 177
Your Erroneous Zones (Dyer),
    14, 43, 50, 57, 198

Zen, 143, 182
Zukav, Gary, 89, 227-8

TITLES OF INTEREST
PUBLISHED BY ARROW

☐ Pulling Your Own Strings	Dr Wayne W Dyer	£5.99
☐ What Do You Really Want For Your Children?	Dr Wayne W Dyer	£5.99
☐ Women Who Love Too Much	Robin Norwood	£6.99
☐ Daily Meditations for Women Who Love Too Much	Robin Norwood	£5.99
☐ The Road Less Travelled	M Scott Peck	£5.99
☐ The Different Drum	M Scott Peck	£5.99
☐ What Return Can I Make	M Scott Peck	£5.99
☐ Love, Medicine and Miracles	Bernie Siegel	£5.99
☐ Peace, Love and Healing	Bernie Siegel	£6.99

ALL ARROW BOOKS ARE AVAILABLE THROUGH MAIL ORDER OR FROM YOUR LOCAL BOOKSHOP.

PAYMENT MAY BE MADE USING ACCESS, VISA, MASTER-CARD, DINERS CLUB, SWITCH AND AMEX, OR CHEQUE, EUROCHEQUE AND POSTAL ORDER (STERLING ONLY).

EXPIRY DATE .... SWITCH ISSUE NO. ☐☐

SIGNATURE ....

PLEASE ALLOW £2.50 FOR POST AND PACKING FOR THE FIRST BOOK AND £1.00 PER BOOK THEREAFTER.

ORDER TOTAL: £................................. (INCLUDING P&P)

ALL ORDERS TO:
ARROW BOOKS, BOOKS BY POST, TBS LIMITED, THE BOOK SERVICE, COLCHESTER ROAD, FRATING GREEN, COLCHESTER, ESSEX, CO7 7 DW, UK.

TELEPHONE: (01206) 256 000
FAX: (01206) 255 914

NAME ....

ADDRESS...

....

Please allow 28 days for delivery. Please tick box if you do not wish to receive any additional information. ☐
Prices and availability subject to change without notice.